NEW YORK, NY 10014 BJ
1725
·M67
1994

Moral Development in the Professions:
Psychology and Applied Ethics

Moral Development in the Professions: Psychology and Applied Ethics

Edited by

James R. Rest
Darcia Narváez
University of Minnesota

LEA   LAWRENCE ERLBAUM ASSOCIATES, PUBLISHERS
1994   Hillsdale, New Jersey   Hove, UK

Copyright © 1994 by Lawrence Erlbaum Associates, Inc.
All rights reserved. No part of this book may be reproduced in
any form, by photostat, microfilm, retrieval system, or any other
means, without the prior written permission of the publisher.

Lawrence Erlbaum Associates, Inc., Publishers
365 Broadway
Hillsdale, New Jersey 07642

Cover design by Jan Melchior

Library of Congress Cataloging-in-Publication Data

Moral development in the professions : psychology and applied
  ethics / James R. Rest and Darcia Narváez, editors.
      p. cm.
   Includes bibliographical references and index.
   ISBN 0-8058-1538-4 (alk. paper).—ISBN 0-8058-1539-2
(pbk. : alk. paper)
   1. Professional ethics. 2. Moral development. 3. Moral education. 4. Applied ethics. I. Rest, James R. II. Narváez,
Darcia
BJ1725.M67 1994
174—dc20   94-11072
                                                         CIP

Books published by Lawrence Erlbaum Associates are printed on
acid-free paper, and their bindings are chosen for strength and dura-
bility.

Printed in the United States of America
10 9 8 7 6 5 4 3 2 1

Contents

	Contributors	vii
	Preface	ix
1	Background: Theory and Research *James R. Rest*	1
2	College Teaching and Student Moral Development *Steven P. McNeel*	27
3	Education for Ethical Nursing Practice *Laura J. Duckett and Muriel B. Ryden*	51
4	School Teachers' Moral Reasoning *Fon-Yean Chang*	71
5	Counseling and Social Role Taking: Promoting Moral and Ego Development *Norman A. Sprinthall*	85

6	Ethical Reasoning Research in the Accounting and Auditing Professions *Lawrence A. Ponemon and David R. L. Gabhart*	101
7	Influencing the Moral Dimensions of Dental Practice *Muriel J. Bebeau*	121
8	Moral Reasoning in Medicine *Donnie J. Self and DeWitt C. Baldwin, Jr.*	147
9	Moral Reasoning in Veterinary Medicine *Donnie J. Self, Margie Olivarez, and DeWitt C. Baldwin, Jr.*	163
10	Applied Ethics and Moral Reasoning in Sport *Brenda Jo Light Bredemeier and David Lyle Light Shields*	173
11	Tracking the Moral Development of Journalists: A Look at Them and Their Work *Tom Westbrook*	189
12	Moral Judgments and Moral Action *Stephen Thoma*	199
13	Summary: What's Possible? *James R. Rest and Darcia Narváez*	213
	Author Index	225
	Subject Index	231

Contributors

DeWitt C. Baldwin, Jr., Scholar in Residence, American Medical Association, Chicago, IL 60610

Muriel J. Bebeau, Associate Professor, School of Dentistry, Education Director, Center for the Study of Ethical Development, University of Minnesota, 15137 Moos Tower, Minneapolis, MN 55455

Brenda Jo Light Bredemeier, Professor, Department of Human Biodynamics, University of California at Berkeley, 200 Hearst Gym, Berkeley, CA 94720

Fon-Yean Chang, Associate Professor, Taiwan Pingtung Teachers College, 1 Lin Sen Road, Pingtung, Taiwan , Republic of China

Laura J. Duckett, Associate Professor, University of Minnesota School of Nursing, 6-101 Unit F, Minneapolis, MN 55455

David R. L. Gabhart (Deceased), Department of Accounting, Bentley College, Waltham, MA 02154-4705

Steven P. McNeel, Professor, Department of Psychology, Bethel College, St. Paul, MN 55112

Darcia Narváez, Assistant Professor and Research Associate, Center for the Study of Ethical Development, Department of Educational Psychology, University of Minnesota, 206-F Burton Hall, 178 Pillsbury Drive, Minneapolis, MN 55455

Margie Olivarez, Research Assistant, Department of Humanities in Medicine Texas A&M University College of Medicine, College Station, TX 77843

Lawrence A. Ponemon, Director, Center for the Study of Ethics and Behavior in Accounting, Binghamton University, Binghamton, NY 13902-6000

James R. Rest, Professor, Educational Psychology, Research Director, Center for the Study of Ethical Development, University of Minnesota, 206-A Burton Hall, 178 Pillsbury Dr. SE, Minneapolis, MN 55455

Muriel B. Ryden, Long-Term Care Professor and Director, Research Center for Long-Term Care of Elders, University of Minnesota School of Nursing, 6-101 Unit F, Minneapolis, MN 55455

Donnie J. Self, Professor, Departments of Humanities in Medicine, Philosophy, and Pediatrics, Texas A&M University College of Medicine, 164 Reynolds Hall, College Station, TX 77843

David Lyle Light Shields, Peace and Conflict Studies, University of California at Berkeley, 200 Hearst Gym, Berkeley, CA 94720

Norman A. Sprinthall, Professor, Department of Counselor Education, North Carolina State University, 520 Poe Hall, Raleigh, NC 27695-7801

Stephen Thoma, Associate Professor, Department of Human Development and Family Studies, University of Alabama, 205 Child Development Center, Box 870158, Tuscaloosa, AL 35487-0158

Tom Westbrook, University Baptist Church (and University of Texas at Austin), 2200 San Antonio, Austin, TX 78705

Preface

The challenges of morality are diverse and multifaceted. One set of concerns has to do with crime and destructive behavior. The United States is the most violent nation in the industrialized world. Over 2 million people each year are beaten, knifed, shot, or assaulted. Every school day 100,000 children bring guns to school. Arrests for rape and violent crime are increasing for both young males and females. The United States has high rates of alcohol and drug abuse, and the highest teenage pregnancy rate of all the nations of the industrialized world. Many neighborhoods, schools, subways, and streets in this nation are not safe. U.S. cities—for instance, Los Angeles and Miami—seem ever on the brink of rioting.[1]

Concerns for the moral development of professionals, however, deal with different issues—not with shooting, knifing, mugging, or rioting. To be sure, there is white-collar crime. But people in the professions—by virtue of having made it through years of schooling and supervised work—usually have at least average impulse control, self-discipline and self-regulation abilities, ego strength, and social skills. Morality in the professions is not so much concerned with issues of rudimentary socialization.[2] Rather, the issues involve deciding between conflicting values, each value representing something good in itself (e.g., the accountant who is faced with disclosing financial shortcomings of a company that pays for the audit; the school teacher who must decide whether to give more attention to students with

---

[1] Extensive discussions of destructive behavior in the United States are contained in Etzioni (1993) and Lickona (1991). Although the exact numbers quoted in the statistics may vary from report to report, the magnitude of the problem is immense.

[2] Discussions of issues in fundamental socialization and the basic, primitive elements of morality are emphasized by psychologists, like Bandura (1991), and moral educators, like Lickona (1991). In contrast, discussions of the morality of professionals usually assume more advanced psychological maturity—for instance, one usually assumes toilet training among professionals.

learning difficulties or to give equal time to all students; the nurse who is asked by a patient about his condition but who obviously has not been fully informed by his doctor; the dentist who discovers shoddy, substandard dental work in a new client previously seen by a colleague).

Lyndon Johnson was fond of saying, "It's not doing what is right that's hard for a President. It's knowing what is right," according to White House advisor, Joseph Califano (1991, p. 124). Many psychologists would say just the opposite, that the crux of morality is doing what you know is right. However, there are problems in both knowing what is right and in doing what is right. Researchers concerned with crime and destruction, who study children and deviancy, are likely to emphasize the "doing" part of morality. On the other hand, researchers concerned with adults in professional life are more likely to emphasize the "defining" problem in morality.

Preparing professionals to discern the right course of action in problematic work contexts has become an immense enterprise. One estimate of the number of applied ethics courses taught annually in colleges and universities in this country is 10,000.[3]

If courses in ethics are worth curricular space and student time, then at least three assumptions must be true:

1. Some ways of deciding what is right (making ethical decisions) are more justifiable than others. Given some moral problem, we do not assume that every conceivable action or reason is as good as every other.

2. There must be some agreement among "experts" on what the more justifiable ethical positions are. Although there might not be complete agreement on one unique line of action, nevertheless, presumably fair-minded people familiar with the facts must agree that some positions are defensible but that others are less so. Defensibility cannot be completely idiosyncratic.

3. Ethics courses influence students in some positive way. The way students will live their lives as professionals is constructively influenced by ethics courses.

If any of these three assumptions is not true, then there is not much point in having applied ethics courses.

What documentation do we have on the validity of these three assumptions? Much has been written regarding the justifiability assumption (Assumption 1). The field of applied ethics today largely consists of constructing philosophical arguments. Professionals in the applied setting (nurses, accountants, dentists, teachers, etc.) and philosophers are the main contributors to discussions of Assumption 1. But what documentation is there on the other two assumptions (Assumption 2, dealing with agreement, and Assumption 3, dealing with the effectiveness of ethics courses)? Here, empirical social science has something special to contribute. The major purpose of this book is to illustrate ways in which social science—in particular, psychology—can contribute to the field of applied ethics.

---

[3] Estimates of the number of applied ethics courses come from discussions with David Smith of the Poynter Center and Brian Shrag of the Association for Practical and Professional Ethics.

Thinking about education (Assumption 3), several issues immediately come to mind: (a) What are the students like who come into ethics courses? That is, how do they interpret moral problems? What considerations do they take into account? By what logic or intuition do they arrive at judgments about what is right or best? How are the students who are beginning their professional lives likely to react to moral problems on their own, without educational intervention? (b) How do the experiences of taking classes affect these students? Is there some ascertainable and documentable way that students change? (c) What is involved in actually living out a moral life as a professional? What is the relation of classroom experience to performing morally in the outside world? What psychological processes are involved in the production of moral action?

In the chapters of this book, the authors describe what they have found concerning these questions. Drawing on the tradition of the cognitive developmental approach (associated with Lawrence Kohlberg), this research begins by using the Defining Issues Test (DIT)—a multiple-choice version of Kohlbergian assessment. Chapter 1 discusses these starting points. But the individual researchers in this volume then move in different directions. The chapters differ from each other not only in discussing different professions (nurses, accountants, counselors), but also in devising different research strategies to address different questions. Specialists in one area are usually not familiar with work in other areas. For example, nursing educators typically do not read much in the counseling literature, and dentists typically do not read much in the accounting literature. This book brings together a diversity of directions of psychological researchers in applied ethics. The new ideas described in one field may be applied to other fields. Hopefully, cross-fertilization will occur.

Some commentary is relevant regarding how key words in the book are used. Kohlberg used the term *moral reasoning* to refer to the specific variable created by his particular assessment (assigning subjects into one of six stages). We start with this research tradition, but broaden the scope to include all psychological processes involved in the regulation and production of moral behavior. *Moral development* therefore is a broader construct than moral reasoning. See the discussion of the "Four Component Model" in chapter 1 for a wider view of moral development.

There is a rich and interesting literature on the term *professional.* Barber (1963), used the term for lines of work for which there is: "a high degree of generalized and systematic knowledge; primary orientation to the community interest rather than to individual self-interest; a high degree of self-control of behavior through codes of ethics . . .; and a system of rewards . . . that is primarily a set of symbols of work achievement . . ." (p. 669).

According to this definition, nursing and journalism are "emerging professions," and sports would not be a profession at all. However, we use the term *professional* to refer to persons in a work setting with special expertise in which there is some discretion for action involving moral judgment.

The terms *morality* and *ethics* are used interchangeably in this book. Various authors have proposed distinctions, but there does not seem to be one, generally accepted distinction.

The book starts with an introduction to theory and research. Then chapters on college teachers, nurses, school teachers, counselors, accountants, dentists, doctors, veterinarians, athletes, and journalists follow. Next comes a chapter on general issues in relating judgment to behavior. Finally, there is a summary of the psychological research in professional ethics demonstrated in the chapters. The chapters are generally ordered so that points raised in earlier chapters are elaborated further in later chapters.

ACKNOWLEDGMENTS

We wish to thank the thousands of people participating as subjects, and the researchers contributing to the research literature. Thanks to Dr. Judith Amsel of Lawrence Erlbaum Associates for a quick and early response as well as continuing encouragement.

A special thanks to our Department Chair, Mark Davison, who has done so much in attending to our special needs, making work possible.

James R. Rest
Darcia Narváez

REFERENCES

Bandura, A. (1991). Social cognitive theory of moral thought and action. In W. M. Kurtines & J. L. Gewirtz (Eds.), *Handbook of moral behavior and development* (Vol. 1, pp. 45–104). Hillsdale, NJ: Lawrence Erlbaum Associates.
Barber, B. (1963). Some problems in the sociology of the professions. *Daedalus, 92,* 669–688.
Califano, J. A. (1991). *The triumph and tragedy of Lyndon Johnson.* New York: Simon & Schuster.
Etzioni, A. (1993). *The spirit of community.* New York: Crown.
Lickona, T. (1991). *Educating for character.* New York: Bantam Books.

Chapter 1

Background: Theory and Research

James R. Rest
University of Minnesota

Lawrence Kohlberg is the starting point for this research. Much has been written about Kohlberg's work, and Kohlberg himself was a prolific writer.[1] Yet many recent interpretations are amazingly distorted and ignorant of the research. Consequently, this chapter presents a brief restatement of the cognitive-developmental approach begun by Kohlberg in the mid-1950s. It provides an updated version of research findings. It describes an expanded view of morality that acknowledges the limitations of moral judgment research as well as its contributions. This chapter is background for the theory and research of the following chapters. Readers already familiar with Kohlberg's cognitive-developmental approach, Defining Issues Test, the research base in moral judgment, and the Four Component Model, may wish to skip this chapter and go directly to the next chapters.

Empirical evidence does not seem to have much to do with the popularity of psychological theories of morality. Indicators of popularity—citations in journals, coverage in introductory texts, number of presentations at conventions, availability of funds for grants—seem to be governed mostly by external social/political/ideological enthusiasms. The popularity of Lawrence Kohlberg's ideas about morality began to rise with the student protests of the late 1960s, with opposition to the Vietnam War, and with the Civil Rights Movement. In Kohlberg, many people saw a kindred spirit and scientific defense of their own views on morality at the time.

---

[1]Kohlberg's major works are the three-volume series, *The Philosophy of Moral Development* (1981), *The Psychology of Moral Development* (1984), and Power, Higgins, and Kohlberg, *Lawrence Kohlberg's Approach to Moral Education* (1989); also his two-volume scoring manual (Colby & Kohlberg, 1987); and the research monograph on the 20-year longitudinal study (Colby, Kohlberg, Gibbs, & Liebermann, 1983). There are many collections of critiques and exchanges, but the most comprehensive one is edited by Modgil and Modgil (1986).

Kohlberg's popularity peaked in the 1970s. In 1974, a scathing review of Kohlberg's theory appeared that seriously challenged the robustness of its evidential base (Kurtines & Grief, 1974). The critique was well-taken. Like it or not, one had to admit that theorizing had greatly outstripped the evidence. But this discussion of evidence did not much affect Kohlberg's popularity. Instead, the crucial factor was that public attention shifted from justice controversies to other concerns. And after the theoretical struggle between behavioral and cognitive approaches to American psychology had become resolved in favor of cognition (Kohlberg was one of the early advocates for cognition), cognition became the target of new challenges. Ironically, as the evidence for the Kohlbergian approach accumulated and strengthened, the popularity of the approach waned. In the 1980s, the rise of a particular brand of feminist ideology—denying similarities of men and women, and extolling differences—coincided with Gilligan's (1982) challenge of Kohlberg. Nowadays it is common to hear the pronouncement that Gilligan completely disproved Kohlberg. But after 10 years, there is pitifully little empirical evidence for Gilligan's theory. The Gilligan phenomenon underscores the view that popularity has little to do with evidence. Accordingly, there is reason to restate the theory and research.

THE SOCIALIZATION VIEW OF MORAL DEVELOPMENT AND THE COGNITIVE DEVELOPMENTAL APPROACH

Jean Piaget made a brief foray into morality research in the 1930s. Attention to moral thinking did not catch on in a big way in this country until Kohlberg's work in the 1950s and 1960s. Behaviorism still dominated psychology in the 1950s, and it is difficult for us today to appreciate what this meant then. In the 1950s, the study of all cognition was suspect, much more the study of *moral* cognition. The dominant view of moral development at the time was the socialization view. Accordingly, moral development was a matter of learning the norms of one's culture, of accepting them and internalizing them, and of behaving in conformity to them. Thus, if the norms of one's culture say it is right to make noise while eating soup, then it is morally right to slurp while eating soup. If one's culture has norms against extramarital sex, then sex is wrong outside marriage. If the social norms say to segregate the luncheon counters by race, then it is morally right to segregate them. In the 1950s, to be "adjusted" was psychology's highest word of praise.

Kohlberg turned the socialization view upside down. Instead of starting with the assumption that *society* determines what is morally right and wrong, Kohlberg said it is the *individual* who determines right and wrong. The individual interprets situations, derives psychological and moral meaning from social events, and makes moral judgments. Sometimes, Kohlberg argued, conformity to social norms is morally wrong (e.g., in the case of Sheriff Bull Conor, protector of segregation laws; or Aldolf Eichmann, dutiful administrator of the Nazi concentration camps) and other times nonconformity is morally right (e.g., Martin Luther King defying legal authorities). In the late 1950s, this talk was quite different from the mainstream psychology or predominant American ideology of that time. Further, Kohlberg said that psychology should study how it is that individuals arrive at moral judgments—moral judgment being the most interesting process of moral development. Thus, Kohlberg's emphasis on moral judgment drew attention away from the favorite constructs of the socialization view (such as identification with authority figures, guilt, delay of gratification, and perseverance under hardship).

Kohlberg enthusiastically embraced Piaget's general approach. Piaget in the 1950s was quite new to American psychologists, and the *cognitive revolution* in psychology had not yet taken place. Kohlberg deliberately and self-consciously undertook to extend the Piagetian line of theory and research into the study of morality in the following ways:

1. Like Piaget, Kohlberg focused on cognition—the thinking process and the representations by which people construct reality and meaning.

2. Like Piaget, Kohlberg assumed that there would be stages in the organization of moral judgment. The primary task of the psychologist was to describe stages of moral judgment development and to devise a method for assessing a person's stage. (The underlying metaphor of stages is the *staircase*—that the stages are like steps on the staircase and that people advance developmentally by going up the staircase one step at a time, without skipping any steps, and always in the same order.[2])

3. Like Piaget, Kohlberg collected data by posing problems to subjects, asking subjects to solve the problem, then probing into how the subjects went about solving it. Kohlberg devised a series of moral dilemmas to give to subjects, asking for their justifications. The challenge to the moral psychologist —according to Kohlberg— was to understand how intuitions of fairness arise.

4. Like Piaget, Kohlberg favored studies that presented the moral dilemmas to children of different ages, looking for age differences in their basic problem-solving strategies. Kohlberg was interested in explaining how the problem-solving strategies of very young children differed from those of older children or adults (how 8-year-olds as a group are different from 18-year-olds, and how both are different from 48-year-olds).

Later, Kohlberg would use longitudinal data (administering the test to the same subjects several times repeatedly at 3-year intervals) to document that people do change in moral judgment and that they change in the ways postulated by theory.

---

[2]Kohlberg adopted the *staircase* metaphor vociferously. In fact, Kohlberg may be the staunchest advocate of a "hard" stage model. At one point he state, "A single case of longitudinal inversion of the sequence disproves the stage theory.. . . A stage sequence disregarded by a single child is no sequence" (Kohlberg, 1973, p. 182). Other psychologists have argued for a less stringent stage model (see Rest, 1979, chap. 3).

A well-known moral dilemma that Kohlberg used is the Heinz dilemma. The basic story about Heinz (in case you have somehow escaped hearing about this dilemma) is that Heinz's wife is dying of cancer and needs a drug that an enterprising druggist has invented. The druggist demands such a high price that Heinz cannot raise the money. Heinz's dilemma, then, is whether or not to steal the drug to save his dying wife. This well-worn story has worked surprisingly well in engaging a vast array of subjects and in producing quite different and illuminating responses. Table 1.1 displays three types of responses.

Kohlberg would approach these responses by asking, "How are these three responses different? What basic problem-solving strategies underlie these three responses?"

Response A presents a rather uncomplicated approach to moral problems. One solves moral problems by identifying what the actor wants and what instrumentally it takes to achieve the actor's interests; answer these questions and the moral problem is solved! Only the actor's interests are explicitly mentioned.

Response B takes into account the relationship of Heinz with his wife—the bonds of affection create some special responsibilities. In addition to Heinz's interests, those of his wife are included in consideration. Further, response B is concerned that Heinz's actions be motivated by good intentions.

We might say that Response C is taking a societywide perspective into account. This is not an incident involving only Heinz, his wife, and the druggist. This specific act is seen within the context of maintaining order within the whole society. Law is the key in making moral decisions.

THE SIX STAGES

Responses to dilemmas such as appear in Table 1.1 provided the kind of data on which Kohlberg built his theory. His theory makes two very bold claims: (a) that the basic problem-solving strategies used by people the world over can be boiled down to just a few—six; (b) that the six problem-solving strategies—his six stages—comprise a developmental sequence such that all people start out using Stage 1 reasons, then move to Stage 2, then Stage 3, and so on. Kohlberg adopted the same rationale as Piaget for claiming that stages are sequenced as they are:

TABLE 1.1
Three Sample Responses to the Heinz Dilemma

A:	It really depends on how much Heinz likes his wife and how much risk there is in taking the drug. If he can get the drug in no other way and if he really likes his wife, he'll have to steal it.
B:	I think that a husband would care so much for his wife that he couldn't just sit around and let her die. He wouldn't be stealing for his own profit, he'd be doing it to help someone he loves.
C:	Regardless of his personal feelings, Heinz has to realize that the druggist is protected by the law. Since no one is above the law, Heinz shouldn't steal it. If we allowed Heinz to steal, then all society would be in danger of anarchy.

1. THEORY AND RESEARCH

TABLE 1.2
Six Stages in the Concept of Cooperation

Stage 1	The morality of obedience: Do what you're told.
Stage 2	The morality of instrumental egoism and simple exchange: Let's make a deal.
Stage 3	The morality of interpersonal concordance: Be considerate, nice, and kind: you'll make friends.
Stage 4	The morality of law and duty to the social order: Everyone in society is obligated to and protected by the law.
Stage 5	The morality of consensus-building procedures: You are obligated by the arrangements that are agreed to by due process procedures.
Stage 6	The morality of nonarbitrary social cooperation: Morality is defined by how rational and impartial people would ideally organize cooperation.

namely, that *simple* stages precede complex ones in a logical sequence. According to this, at first the most salient aspects of a situation and the most easily understood concepts—those that are simplest—become problem-solving strategies. Then as new considerations are seen as relevant and as new complexities and subtleties are appreciated, people change their moral problem-solving strategies. Each new stage is an elaboration of the previous one —which is what fixes the sequence of the stages.

As an analogy, consider two levels of mathematical thinking: One person can do long division, and the other person can only add numbers into simple sums. The ability to add must come before the ability to do long division, because long division presupposes the ability to add. Adding logically precedes doing long division, and long division presupposes addition, because long division is an ensemble of operations that includes addition. In the same way Piaget and Kohlberg want to claim that their stages represent a sequence of logically more complex mental organizations.

So what are the six stages? Short tables describing Kohlberg's six stages have appeared in many places. Such short descriptions seem to lend themselves to inventive interpretations (like Gilligan's 1982 interpretation that Kohlberg's stages depict progressive *separation* of the individual from other people). Adding to this confusion, over the years Kohlberg made many revisions and shifts in describing his stages.

I think that the best short description of the six stages is to view them in terms of six conceptions of how to organize cooperation. Accordingly, the key conception that develops over time is people's understanding of how it is possible to organize cooperation. Table 1.2 presents the six stages briefly, keying on the central concept of organizing cooperation.

At Stage 1, the young person is most impressed with the power of others. The child's caretakers make demands and the child quickly realizes that disobedience brings punishment. The first notion of getting along with people then is that you do what you are told to do. At Stage 1, being "good" is being obedient to the demands of superior others.

At Stage 2, the child realizes that all people have their own interests—the child included. This realization undermines Stage 1's sense of obligation to be obedient to another person ("Why should I be bossed around by other people -- especially if their interests are different from mine?"). At Stage 2, "doing good" comes to mean "doing what is instrumentally satisfying to me," not doing what another person demands. Although Stage 2 sees everyone as self-centered, it still has a conception of how people can cooperate. People can make short-term deals with each other, exchanging favor for favor. Cooperation becomes the simple exchange of favors; fairness is coming through with your side of the bargain.

The child at Stage 3 realizes that people do not only deal with each other in terms of temporarily arranged exchanges. There is more to human interaction than a series of one-shot deals. People also establish long-term, enduring relationships that involve loyalty, gratitude, and mutual caring for each other. In such relationships, people do not keep count of specific favors (who owes whom what favor). Rather there is general commitment and loyalty to the relationship. Thus, the central notion of cooperation at Stage 3 is to sustain these positive, enduring relationships with people. The Stage 3 conception presupposes reciprocal role taking—the ability to imaginatively construct what another's perspective would be (to role-take the other person's point of view). Stage 3 also involves the realization that the other person is trying to role-take your own point of view. Therefore with role taking going on both ways, there is a mutuality of concern and a coordination of interests. Stage 3 morality then is the morality of making and sustaining friendships, of being cooperative by being loyal and considerate and caring.

The child at Stage 4 sees a shortcoming of Stage 3, which only provides a basis for cooperating with friends and allies. It does not provide guidelines for cooperating with strangers, competitors, and enemies. Stage 4 sees the problem of morality as having to establish some scheme of cooperation for society in general, not merely for cooperating with your friends and loved ones. Stage 4's solution to this problem is through the concept of law. Society can be organized by formal, public, categorical laws and through formal role systems defined by secondary institutions. The law is public, knowable to everyone in a society, and categorically applies to everyone—everyone is under the law. By having laws (or formal role systems in secondary institutions, such as businesses and universities) we can then count on others (even strangers) to know the law and to behave in socially prescribed ways. In other words, law creates a cooperative order on a societywide basis. At the higher stages (Stage 5 and Stage 6) a person also appreciates that there must be some basis for establishing a societywide network of cooperation. But at Stages 5 and 6, the person realizes that societies can be governed by diverse systems of law. For instance, we can have an orderly and law-abiding society of slaves—like the ancient Egyptians—in which 2% of the population have a comfortable life and the other 98% of society must toil to make it comfortable for the privileged 2%. The hallmark of Stages 5 and 6 is their orientation to principles that shape whatever laws and role systems a society might have. Principles are visions of ideal cooperative societies. The principles therefore determine, regulate, and criticize the laws and role systems of a cooperative society. (Stages 5 and 6 are therefore called *principled* morality.) Whereas at Stage 4 the morally right is whatever the law says, at Stages 5 and 6 what is morally right is that which best furthers the principle.

The distinctions between Stage 5 and Stage 6 have been much discussed; however Kohlberg was still working on the definition of Stage 6 at the time of his death. From the practical point of view of doing research, we note that Kohlberg in his scoring guide (Colby & Kohlberg, 1987) does not score Stage 6. Kohlberg thought that Stage 6 occurred so rarely that interjudge reliability is actually improved by not scoring anybody Stage 6, and therefore the scoring manuals do not contain directions for scoring it. In research with the DIT (described later), Stage 5 and Stage 6 items have behaved so similarly that we have combined Stages 5 and 6 into a *principled* score. Therefore these stages are not distinguished in data analysis for pragmatic reasons.

For theoretical discussions of Stages 5 and 6, see Kohlberg (1984, 1986). The philosopher Puka (1991) made a good argument that Kohlberg was needlessly partisan in the philosophical debate between deontologists and teleologists. Kohlberg hoped to be the one to settle the dispute among philosophers once and for all. He characterized utilitarian philosophies as Stage 5 and deontologists as Stage 6. Kohlberg borrowed especially from the philosophers, Rawls (1971) and Habermas (1979), thus making him vulnerable to criticisms of being narrowly focused on *justice*, being rationalistic, individualistic, and partisan to Western liberalism. However, the broad characterization of development in moral judgment need not take such a partisan stance, or be so specific. Research with the DIT is more moderate in defining Stage 5 and Stage 6 (Rest, 1979, chap. 2). Accordingly, Stage 5 is characterized as a *political* approach to defining morality. Stage 5 appeals to political mechanisms (elections, polls, votes by representatives, due process) for making decisions that are intended to reach group consensus ("What is right is whatever is decided by due process."). In contrast, Stage 6 represents visions of an ideal society that balance the burdens and benefits of cooperative living, and optimize each person's stake and welfare in that social order. This is not done by Stage 5's *political* process. The essential distinction here is between *procedural justice* of Stage 5 and *substantive justice* of Stage 6. Philosophers have proposed different visions of how to organize the ideal society, formulating somewhat different cardinal principles (justice, utilitarianism, beneficence, respect for persons, autonomy, etc.). The trick is not just to have ideals. It is to have ideals that can win the support of other people as good ways for organizing society (supposing reasonable people). (Kohlberg, 1984, talked about this, variously, in terms of Rawls', 1971, *veil of ignorance*, Habermas', 1979, *ideal discourse*, and moral musical chairs.) And so there are various ways of being scored Stage 6 on the DIT. Most modern moral philosophies (with the exception of Nietzsche's and similar approaches) would be scored Stage 6 on the DIT. In fact, because moral philosophers as a group have the highest scores on the DIT, a person's DIT score is sometimes interpreted as "the degree to which the person thinks about moral problems like a moral philosopher."

Having taken this quick tour through the stages, I hasten to make three points: (a) The stages are ways for organizing cooperation among individuals, not ways for an individual to become progressively separated from others; (b) The conceptions of cooperation underlying the stages are *default schemas*—that is, they are the spontaneous and natural way that people make sense of social situations (unless the default is overridden by some other organizing idea); and (c) A stage analysis of a person's moral reasoning is a limited analysis.

Regarding the first point (that the stages concern cooperation, not separation), it is important to note that the stages are defined so that as we move upward through the sequence, the scope of human interaction is widened, more things are considered, and the higher stages deal with more complex social problems than the lower stages. For instance, the issues raised at the Nuremberg Trials (of German soldiers who dutifully obeyed their Nazi leaders) are not comprehensible at Stage 4 or lower. The stages are described as conceptions of how it is possible for people to organize cooperation for establishing rights and duties, and for creating networks of interrelationships. The stages do not depict the progressive separation and isolation of individuals from each other (as Gilligan said), but rather how each individual can become interconnected with other individuals.

Regarding the second point (that the stages are *default schema*), note that stages are underlying conceptions that are tacitly held. They are intuitive notions that work behind the scenes of cognition, and therefore may not be explicitly articulated as creeds or verbalized belief systems. The psychologist infers that a subject has some underlying conception by asking questions about why the subject thinks a particular solution is best, getting at underlying assumptions. To the subject, his or her solution may seem to make sense and in no need of special argument; the solution just makes sense. It is striking that people have such different ways for conceptualizing the problem.

How does an underlying conception of cooperation lead to a moral judgment of right or wrong action in a particular situation? As the stages are described here, you may have some intuitions about this process. We assume that the conceptions of cooperation are *deep* structures (that they are among the individual's fundamental categories for interpreting the social world). Now imagine that a person faces some moral dilemma (such as Heinz and the drug). The story material contains a multitude of stimuli and events. Conceptions of cooperation help the person sift among the many details to identify the most important aspects. They provide a way to link the relationships of the parties to each other and an integrating strategy for deciding which are the most important considerations that lead to advocating some course of action as morally right. Conceptions of cooperation help a person manage all the bits and pieces of dilemma information, and help guide what an individual ought to do (in order to sustain a particular kind of cooperation). The stages are default schema —they are schema for naturally making sense of situations; they are "default" in that they are engaged unless overridden by other ideology.

Regarding the third point (that a stage analysis is limited), it is limited in two ways: (a) a stage analysis is an analysis at a very fundamental level of conceptualization, and (b) any analysis of moral judgment does not take into account other component psychological processes (about which more is said in "The Four Component Model").

When we have arrived at a stage analysis of a person's response (e.g., this is a Stage 3 response, this is a Stage 2 response, etc.), we have represented only part of what goes on in the mind of a person thinking about a moral issue. Stages are coarse-grained characterizations of a person's thinking. Stage analysis does not give a fine-grained inventory of all of a person's thinking in deciding what action is morally right in a moral dilemma. Remember that Kohlberg's initial interest was to portray the major markers in *life-span* development. The interest was in depicting how 8-year-olds are different from 18-year-olds and from 48-year-olds. The interest was not in depicting how the thinking of a 24-year-old changes over a 6-week ethics course. If a moral stage analysis represents a very broad characterization of cognition, it remains for more fine-grained analyses to depict the intermediate level of concepts. Concepts such as *informed consent, paternalistic deception,* and *privileged confidentiality* are intermediate-level concepts that are often the contents of applied ethics courses. Intermediate-level concepts need to be assessed also, which a stage analysis does not do. There is even a more concrete level of conceptualization (i.e., different from a stage analysis, and from *intermediate-level concepts*) that is usually found in the codes of ethics of professional organizations. Codes usually consist of descriptions of specific kinds of situations followed by a prescribed course of action. Codes are high on specificity, low on connected rationale.

In summary, we have three levels of conceptualization of moral judgment: stage analysis, intermediate–level discussion of principles, and the very practical, concrete level of codes of ethics. A stage analysis therefore represents only the most fundamental level.

Chang (this volume) discusses the development of a test of moral reasoning for teachers that is oriented toward a more intermediate level of conceptualization and is more specific to the teaching profession. The chapter by Westbrook (this volume) also characterizes moral reasoning—at a level more specific to journalism.

Another kind of limitation of a stage analysis is that other psychological component processes are involved in the psychology of morality. We describe other psychological processes involved besides the process studied by Kohlberg (see "The Four Component Model", this chapter). There is not just *moral judgment* going on in a person's thinking, there are three other processes going on. A stage analysis does not tell us, for instance, how sensitive the subject is in initially detecting that there is a moral dilemma in the first place (see "Moral Sensitivity"). Bebeau's chapter discusses how moral sensitivity is distinct from moral judgment; she describes an ongoing research program to measure moral sensitivity in the field of dentistry. The chapter by McNeel discusses development of an ethical sensitivity test for college students. A moral judgment score does not contain information about moral sensitivity, moral motivation, or moral character—other components involved in the psychology of morality (see "The Four Component Model," which follows).

THE RESEARCH PROGRAM[3]

Many disciplines have interesting and provocative things to say about human nature and the human condition. The hallmark of social science is not only to propose ideas, but also to have ways for systematically putting those ideas to empirical test. The research discussed in this chapter is intended to clarify the meaning of the theory, to build a case for the validity of the instruments and the constructs, to provide new information about how moral judgment develops, and to clarify the role that moral judgment plays in general moral development. It is not a complete review of the thousands of studies that have now been performed using the Kohlbergian approach. Nevertheless, the sampling of research questions and findings will indicate that the theory is not just floating out some speculations about human nature (which may or may not resonate with ideologies of the day), but has solid empirical anchoring and testing. The research review is organized around seven points:

1. *Instrumentation.* How can moral judgment be measured? That is, how can we get scores for all the subjects in a sample that represent their moral thinking (not just picking and choosing a few limited quotes from selected subjects that happen to fit our notions)? How do we know that our assessment procedure generates *reliable* scores (i.e., that independent judges agree, that what a subject says in one response is consistent with what the subject says in other responses, and that there is some stability of scores from day to day, and week to week)?

2. *Age/education trends.* If we talk about a developmental pathway, what is the evidence that moral judgment does in fact change over the years and that it changes in the way described by the theory (from stage to stage)? What are the conditions under which moral judgment naturally develops?

3. *Developmental hierarchy.* What is the evidence that higher stages are better or more advanced than lower stages?

4. *Cross-cultural studies and universality.* What do studies performed on subjects in other cultures reveal about the universality (or ethnocentrism) of the six-stage theory?

5. *Educational interventions.* Is it possible to stimulate development in moral judgment by deliberate educational programs? What works with whom?

6. *Correlations and distinctiveness.* Do scores from tests of moral judgment correlate positively with other measures that are theoretically similar (*convergent* validity), not correlate with measures that are theoretically dissimilar (*divergent* validity), and show *distinctive* information not redundant with other psychological tests?

7. *Links to behavior.* What evidence is there to show that scores from our moral judgment instruments relate to real-life behavior? How is moral judgment part of a causal network in the ways that people actually live their lives?

---

[3]Note that book-length reviews of the literature are found in Kohlberg (1984) and Rest (1979, 1983, & 1986). Because this section on "The Research Program" is a brief overview, detailed documentation and citations are to be found in the references just cited.

Instrumentation

The first job of the research psychologist in developing empirical validation of a theory is to devise methods for measuring the constructs. If people are said to have some characteristic, then how are we to know which people have which characteristic and to what extent? The psychologist needs to specify some method of systematic collection of information, of converting that information into data categories used for analysis, of drawing inferences from that data, and of claiming that the procedure thus employed is reliable and valid.[4]

The Moral Judgment Interview. Kohlberg's method of assessment was straightforward, given his starting point. Accordingly, in a semistructured interview, he asked subjects to talk about several hypothetical moral dilemmas (such as Heinz and the drug), particularly attending to their rationales for saying why some line of action was more morally justified than another.

Colby and Kohlberg (1987) described the current scoring system in an 800+-page manual. What the subject said is transcribed. Then the subject's responses are compared to examples and criteria in a scoring guide. The scoring guide lists arguments at the various stages, and the scorer's job is to match a subject's utterances with the criteria in the scoring guide. Over the course of a complete interview, typically about 50 matches are found between the subject's responses and the manual's examples. Using summary rules, each subject receives an overall stage score.

The Defining Issues Test. Some years after Kohlberg had described stage characteristics (derived from interview data), the DIT was devised at the University of Minnesota (Rest, 1979). Instead of analyzing individual interview responses by a trained rater, the Moral Judgment Interview procedure, the DIT is a multiple-choice test that can be group-administered and computer-scored. In the DIT, a subject is first presented with a moral dilemma (some of the same moral dilemmas in the MJI are used in the DIT, such as the Heinz dilemma). However, the subject's task is not to produce reasons for a particular line of action (e.g., to argue why Heinz should steal or not steal the drug). The task is to evaluate (among 12 items given to the subject) those items that raise the most important considerations for deciding

---

[4]In recent years, Gilligan (1982) challenged Kohlberg's theory as being sexist and invalid for women the world over. Although in subsequent publications and talks, Gilligan has changed her position several times, the 1982 book is one of the most cited and has become the rallying point for the anti-Kohlberg view. In the 1982 book she said that women have their own, distinct path of moral development, the Care orientation (Care). Gilligan said the stages of Care are not inferior to men's moral development, but different. As evidence, Gilligan cited a handful of selected excerpts from women's interviews. From such data it is not known how representative these are of women in general, or even of the entire interviews of just these women. Because she did not interview men on the same issues as she did the women, statements about differences between men and women are gratuitous. (Walker, 1991, who did test both men and women, reported that men's responses on abortion dilemmas are similar to women's.)   *(Footnote continues on next page)*

the case. Table 1.3 shows the 12 DIT items that follow the Heinz dilemma. The subject is asked to rate the relative importance of each item on a 5-point scale (from *great importance* to *no importance*), and then to rank which of the 12 items is the most important, the second most important, and so on. The assumption is that people define the most important issue of a dilemma in different ways, and that the selection of items indicates a person's developmental level.

The items are written as fragments of a way of thinking about the dilemma (e.g., Item 1 is a Stage 4 concern, Item 2 is a Stage 3 concern, Item 3 is a Stage 2 concern, etc.). If subjects understand a particular stage of thinking, then we assume that they will recognize the DIT items written at that stage—otherwise the item appears to subjects as a meaningless jumble of words. We further assume that just because subjects understand an item, they will not necessarily rate the item highly, or rank the item as "Most Important." Subjects will find some items simplistic, childish, immature. Such items may be understood, but the subject will not like them or select them as important.

In early research we found that different groups of subjects liked different items. Junior high school subjects[5] liked Item 3 ("Is Heinz willing to risk getting shot as a burglar?"), whereas senior high school and college students liked this item less, and graduate students did not like at all. On the other hand, the graduate students liked Item 8 ("What values are going to be the basis for governing how people act toward each other?")—reminiscent of our earlier discussion of *Principled* moral thinking. To the junior high students this item seemed to them just a bunch of words.

The main problem in empirically testing the 1982 claims of Gilligan is that no method for assessing stages of the Care orientation has been proposed. More than a decade has passed since Gilligan claimed that women follow a different path of moral development than men, but there is still no cross-sectional or longitudinal evidence that this is the case. Without a measure of developmental stages of Care, no studies can be done to test whether the later stages of Care are more advanced, or whether verbal expressions using care language predict to any behavior. Neither can studies be done to examine the correlates of Care, or what conditions facilitate its development.

Although there is research that gives the percent of "Care" language to "Justice" language for a subject on a given dilemma, this kind of analysis does not provide evidence for claiming there is a distinct *path of development* of the Care orientation—that people follow one stage of the Care orientation with another stage. It is not clear that analyzing utterances into "Care" and "Justice" is anything more than attending to a style of verbal expressiveness.

Care sometimes seems to refer to sensitivity to the needs and interests of another person. Other times, Care seems to mean valuing human relationships ahead of every other value. Other times, Care seems to mean deriving moral right by making the highest duty to be nice always to your friends. Other times, Care seems to mean actually following through behaviorally on intended commitments. In discussions of Care, one meaning slides to the next. The problem in saying that Care means all these things together is that there is research to indicate that these are different components of morality that do not cohere or behave in similar ways. (See discussion of Care responses by Bebeau & Brabeck, 1989.)

[5]Junior high school subjects were the youngest/least experienced group used for comparisons because this is the youngest group that can safely meet the reading levels required for the DIT. It is presumed that much development takes place before junior high school, but the DIT requires reading skills of at least a junior high school level.

TABLE 1.3
DIT Items for Heinz Story

1. Whether a community's laws are going to be upheld.
2. Isn't it only natural for a loving husband to care so much for his wife that he'd steal?
3. Is Heinz willing to risk getting shot as a burglar or going to jail for the chance that stealing the drug might help?
4. Whether Heinz is a professional wrestler, or has considerable influence with professional wrestlers.
5. Whether Heinz is stealing for himself or doing this solely to help someone else.
6. Whether the druggist's rights to his invention have to be respected.
7. Whether the essence of living is more encompassing than the termination of dying, socially and individually.
8. What values are going to be the basis for governing how people act toward each other?
9. Whether the druggist is going to be allowed to hide behind a worthless law that only protects the rich anyhow.
10. Whether the law in this case is getting in the way of the most basic claim of any member of society.
11. Whether the druggist deserves to be robbed for being so greedy and cruel.
12. Would stealing in such a case bring about more total good for the whole society or not?

Subjects therefore differ in the way they rate and rank the items. A developmental score is based on ratings and rankings to 72 items over six stories.

The most frequently used score from the DIT is the P-score (i.e., the Principled Score), based on the relative importance that a subject gives to items representing Stages 5 and 6, principled moral thinking. The P score is a number that ranges from 0 to 95. A high number indicates high moral judgment development. The test–retest correlations of the DIT (over a period of several weeks) averages in the .80s, and the internal reliability of the DIT also averages in the .80s (Cronbach's Alpha). See Rest (1979, 1986) for details on reliability.

The DIT has been used extensively since the 1970s. Currently, the number of studies using the DIT totals well over 1,000; the total of subjects taking the DIT numbers in the hundreds of thousands; the DIT has been used in over 40 countries; and the published literature on the test is extensive, with about 150 new studies each year.[6]

Age/Education Trends

One of the first kinds of studies done with any developmental measure is to look for differences in groups of subjects at different age/educational levels. A measure claiming to be *developmental* implies that people change, and that they change in ways predicted by the theory—the higher the age, the higher the stage.

---

[6]More information about using the DIT is available from the Center for the Study of Ethical Development / University of Minnesota / 178 Pillsbury Drive / Minneapolis, MN 55455.

Table 1.4 reports group average scores on the DIT. Junior high school subjects generally average in the 20s, the senior high school subjects generally average in the 30s, the college students average in the 40s, the graduate students (who are not specializing in majors emphasizing moral thinking) average in the 50s, and those graduate students who do specialize in moral thinking average in the 60s. In the chapters that follow, averages for nurses, accountants, dentists, counselors, teachers, doctors, veterinarians, and journalists are given.

Table 1.5 shows DIT scores grouped by both education and gender. At every educational level, females score slightly higher than males, completely opposite to Gilligan's (1982) claim. However, these gender differences are slight—gender accounts for only 0.5% of the variance in DIT scores, whereas education is 250 times more powerful (Thoma, 1986). Also, in systematic reviews of the MJI, gender is a trivial variable (Walker, 1991).

Recently, the Kohlberg group (Colby et al., 1983) published a 20-year, all-male, longitudinal study. A longitudinal study tests and retests the same subjects at intervals (Kohlberg used 3-year intervals), thus using the same subjects as their

TABLE 1.4
Different Groups on the DIT P Score

P-Score	Group
65.2	Moral philosophy and political science graduate students
59.8	Liberal protestant seminarians
52.2	Law students
50.2	Medical students
49.2	Practicing physicians
47.6	Dental students
46.3	Staff nurses
42.8	Graduate students in business
42.3	College students in general
41.6	Navy enlisted men
40.0	Adults in general
31.8	Senior high school students
23.5	Prison inmates
21.9	Junior high school students
18.9	Institutionalized delinquents

TABLE 1.5
Average DIT P Score Grouped by Education and Sex

Grade	Males	Females
Junior High	19.1	19.8
Senior High	28.7	30.4
College	44.1	45.9
Graduates	61.0	63.0

Note. $N = 2,886$.

1. THEORY AND RESEARCH

own controls. From ages 10 to 48, moral judgment showed stage progression step by step as predicted by the theory. Several other longitudinal studies using the Kohlberg measure with mixed gender groups (but shorter time spans) replicate the findings (e.g., Kohlberg, 1984).

A 10-year longitudinal study of the DIT was reported in Rest (1986). There were the usual findings of gains in moral judgment with age, but it was also found that education is a far more powerful predictor of moral judgment development than merely chronological age, per se. The general trend is that as long as subjects continue in formal education, their DIT scores tend to gain; when subjects stop their formal education, then their DIT scores plateau. Consequently, if you wanted to predict the DIT scores of adults, you would do best by knowing their education level, not age or gender.

McNeel (this volume) reports a summary of studies showing the effect of college on DIT scores. His analysis from many samples of colleges shows that the college experience is very effective in promoting DIT gains. In fact, when compared with gains on other variables (such as gains in verbal abilities, math, self-concept, attitudes), the gains in moral judgment are among the largest, most impressive gains of all tested variables influenced by the college experience.

What is it about formal education that produces this effect? Formal education must indirectly stand for some special experience, some special psychological conditions that produce growth in moral judgment. After several studies (see Rest, 1986, 1988), the following picture emerges:

> The people who develop in moral judgment are those who love to learn, who seek new challenges, who enjoy intellectually stimulating environments, who are reflective, who make plans and set goals, who take risks, who see themselves in the larger social contexts of history and institutions and broad cultural trends, who take responsibility for themselves and their environs. On the environmental side of the equation, those who develop in moral judgment have an advantage in receiving encouragement to continue their education and their development. They profit from stimulating and challenging environments, and from social milieus that support their work, interest them, and reward their accomplishments. As young adults, the people who develop in moral judgment are more fulfilled in their career aspirations, have set a life direction of continued intellectual stimulation and challenge, are more involved in their communities, and take more interest in the larger societal issues. This pattern is one of general social/cognitive development. (Rest, 1986, p. 57)

Therefore, the reason that formal education is a powerful predictor of moral judgment is because, generally speaking, those individuals who choose to go to college are more invested in their own development (than those who don't go to college), and the college environment stimulates and reinforces their development.

In summary, there is plentiful evidence for developmental trends on both the MJI and DIT. When age and education are separated, education is by far the more powerful variable.

Developmental Hierarchy (Who Says That "Higher is Better"?)

Some philosophers have criticized Kohlberg for arguing that "later stages are more advanced because they come later in a sequence" (see discussions in Modgil & Modgil, 1986). Such a claim would be committing the "naturalistic fallacy." Finding that stages occur in sequence (evidence for which was given earlier) does not argue that the later stages are better (in the sense of logically or philosophically more justifiable). A simple refutation of such a claim is that everything that comes later is not necessarily better—for example, in old age people loose hair and teeth, but this is not better than the earlier state.

First, something should be said about the sense in which higher stages are meant to be better. Following Piaget, "better" does not mean that a higher stage subject has more raw intelligence (brain power) or higher moral status, nor does it mean that those at higher stages are entitled to more of the world's goods and privileges. Rather, higher stages are said to be better conceptual tools for making sense out of the world and deriving guides for decision making. It is the same sense of "better" when we say that being able to do long division is better than only being able to do sums. Having the conceptual tools of long division enables us to solve math problems that would be difficult to do if we did not have those concepts.

Second, a series of studies (Rest, 1974; Rest, Turiel, & Kohlberg 1969; Walker, deVries, & Bichard, 1984) addresses the issue of a developmental hierarchy of moral judgment stages (i.e., is higher really better?). In addition to moral judgment measures, new measures of comprehension and preference were devised. Prototypic-stage arguments were written for each of the stages (e.g., for the Heinz story, a Stage 1 argument was written, a Stage 2 argument, Stage 3, etc.). Each argument was typed on a 3 × 5 card. Subjects were shown the cards one at a time and were asked to read the argument, then paraphrase the gist of the argument in their own words. If the subjects could successfully paraphrase the argument using different words, then they were credited with comprehending that argument. In this way it was possible to derive comprehension scores for each of the stages (10 arguments were written for each stage; if a subject successfully paraphrased all 10 cards, then that subject was credited with perfect comprehension for that stage). Note that this measure of comprehension is different from the usual measure of moral judgment in that the comprehension measure is an inventory of concepts that the subject *understands*, whether or not the subject actually *uses* these concepts to drive a recommendation for action; it is not like the MJI or DIT, which indicates the concepts that the subject *uses* to decide moral solutions.

In these studies we found that comprehension for the stages was cumulative—that is, if subjects had high comprehension for Stage 4, say, then they also had high comprehension for Stages 3, 2, and 1. Further, we found that comprehension tended to be high up to the subject's own stage (as assessed by the usual Kohlberg procedure) but as the comprehension statements were written at higher than the subject's own stage, then accuracy decreased. In other words, a subject tested on the MJI at Stage 3, say, would have high comprehension scores for Stages 1, 2, and

1. THEORY AND RESEARCH

3, but comprehension scores would drop for Stages 4, 5, and 6. This is evidence that the stages become increasingly difficult. It is consistent with the claim that higher stages are more complex, take more things into account, and widen the scope of concerns and problems addressed.

Although subjects were looking at the cards for comprehension, we also asked them to rate the adequacy or persuasiveness of the argument on a simple 1 to 5 rating scale (1 = *not adequate or persuasive,* 5 = *highly persuasive and adequate*). This is our measure of *preference* for the stages. We found that even though subjects could comprehend the arguments below their own stage, they did not give them high preference ratings. For instance, even though a subject had scored Stage 3 on the MJI, and had high comprehension of Stages 1, 2, and 3, that subject tended to give the cards with Stages 1 and 2 very low ratings. Preference went up as we came to arguments at the subject's own stage (in this case, Stage 3). For the arguments below the subject's own stage, subjects said things like, "That is simple-minded," or "I used to think that way, but I don't anymore," or "This sounds like a young kid." Subjects could give refutations of the lower stage arguments and tell why they were inadequate.

In summary, who says higher stages are better? *Subjects do themselves.* As people outgrow old ways of thinking—as they see them as too simplistic and inadequate—they still understand them but don't prefer them. Higher stages of thinking are preferred until that stage in turn becomes replaced by a newly comprehended stage. Kohlberg was struck by the parallelism between his theory of why lower stages were less adequate and the reasons that actual subjects gave for rejecting lower stages. This parallelism is what Kohlberg referred to as the *complementarity hypothesis,* and it provides important empirical support for the theoretical claim that "higher is better." Simply put, when subjects comprehend two stages, they prefer the higher stage and reject the lower for the same reason that Kohlberg gives in his theory for why a higher stage is better.

An experimental study by McGeorge (1975) reveals a second kind of empirical support. McGeorge's study argues that comprehension sets an upper limit upon the stage used in moral judgment (as measured by the DIT), but preference sets a lower limit upon the stages that are accepted. McGeorge asked subjects to take the DIT twice. In one treatment condition (*Fake High* condition), on the first testing he asked subjects to take the DIT in the standard way, according to the usual instructions; in the second testing subjects were asked to fake high: "Please assist us by trying to fill in the questionnaire so that it records the highest, most mature level of social and ethical judgment possible. Fill in the questionnaire as someone concerned only with the very highest principles of justice would fill it in." In the *Fake Low* condition, subjects were asked to take the DIT once in the standard way, but the second time, they received the instructions, "Please assist us by trying to fill in the questionnaire so that it records the lowest, most immature level of social and ethical judgment possible...." Table 1.6 shows the results of McGeorge's study: It is easy to fake downward, but subjects do not improve their scores by faking upward.

TABLE 1.6
Faking High and Low on the DIT

Standard	
	Fake High
44.0	40.0
	Fake Low
44.3	16.7

In the Standard condition, subjects are already giving their conception of the most fair, most just, highest levels of moral judgment. Comprehension limits how high they can go. Therefore in the *Fake High* condition they do not improve their scores. But in the *Fake Low* condition, subjects understand well what is below their own thinking, and can easily select DIT items that are less adequate, less mature, and more childish than their own current level, if asked to do so.

A third line of evidence that higher scores in moral judgment are more developmentally advanced comes from the fact that moral judgment scores correlate with other developmental scales (e.g., those of Perry, Loevinger, Hunt, Selman, Piaget) and predict to desirable behavior (see Thies-Sprinthall & Sprinthall, 1987; and sections on "Correlations" and "Links to Behavior").

In summary, there is evidence for a developmental hierarchy of moral judgment stages.

Cross-Cultural Studies and Universality

How generally does Kohlberg think his stage theory applies to all people the world over? It is almost axiomatic that different people have different moral values. So why isn't the claim of universality so obviously wrong that it is laughable?

Once again Kohlberg follows Piaget's lead. Piaget, focusing on the physical world, admits that the physical world looks very different to an Eskimo child, to a child in New York City, and to a child in the Amazon rain forest. Yet each child comes to organize a picture of the physical world in terms of basic conceptions of length, density, causality, directionality, and so on. Such conceptions are so fundamental that they are the basic categories for everyone, regardless of whether one lives in the frozen north, in New York City, or in the Amazon rain forest.

Likewise, Kohlberg argued that certain conceptions are so fundamental to human interaction in groups that they are relevant regardless of one's particular culture. Given that humans all live in groups and have to find ways to get along with each other, certain considerations are always relevant (such as the power of others, the possibility of exchanging favors, the fact that bonds of affection and enduring relationships exist among people, the fact that there are social norms and established practices in groups, etc.). Kohlberg agreed that the specific morals of cultures are ever-changing, but that beneath these surface differences are deep, structural conceptions that are always relevant. Kohlberg would argue that his six stages depict these deep, structural conceptions.

1. THEORY AND RESEARCH 19

One can argue for and against universality for a long time. Even if one accepts the distinction between surface appearances and deep structures, there is still the question of whether the deep structures, as portrayed in the six stages, are the *only* set of deep structures for organizing morality. Instead of arguing this issue in the abstract, let us consider some data.

Studies have been carried out in over 40 countries, although Fig. 1.1 presents data from just 6 countries. Notice, however, that the 6 countries in this figure represent both Western and non-Western countries. Age and education are represented on the *x*-axis, and DIT P-scores are represented on the *y*-axis. The different

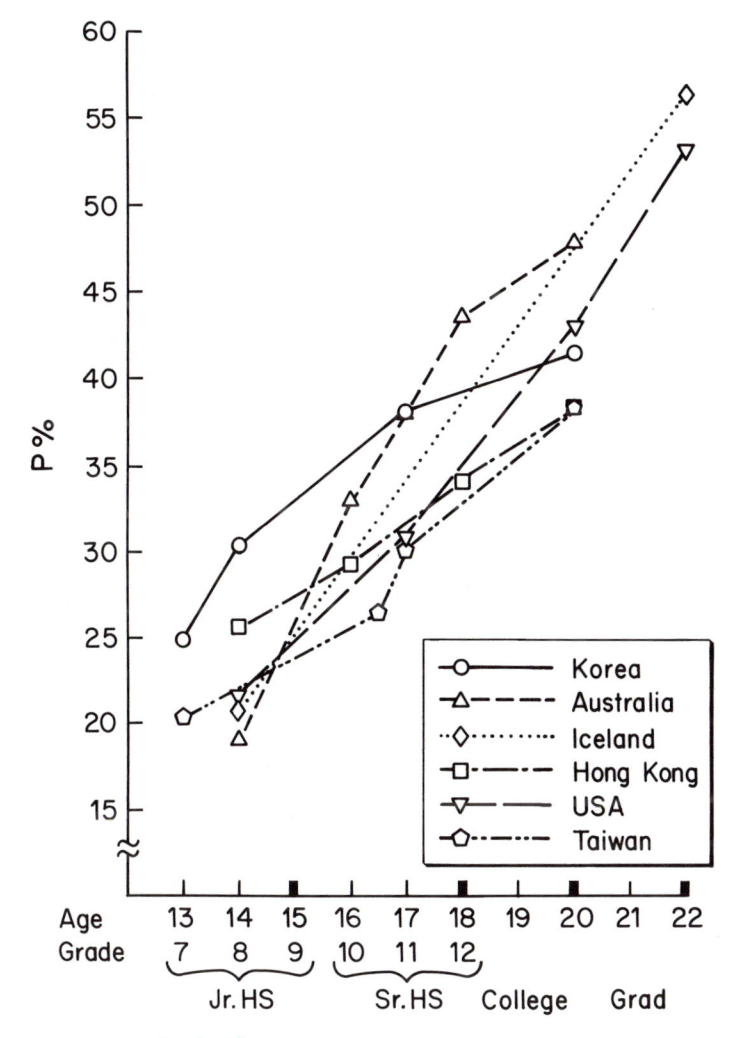

FIG. 1.1. Cross-cultural studies of age/education trends in moral judgment. From Rest, 1986, p. 408, published by Praeger Publishers, an imprint of Greenwood Publishing Group, Inc., Westport, CT. Reprinted by permission.

countries are represented by the different lines connecting boxes, triangles, circles, and so on. Note two things: First, in every country, DIT scores increase with age/education. The similarities are more striking than the differences among these countries. Second, the United States is represented in terms of the upside-down triangle; notice that the United States. is in the middle of the pack at all age/education levels. It is *not* the case that the United States is shown to be superior and all the rest of the world is shown as inferior. Some critics have claimed that Kohlberg defined his stages so that U.S. men would look good and everybody else would be "less developed." If Kohlberg set out to do this, he did not do a very good job.

Some qualifications should be made to these data in Fig. 1.1: (a) The samples from the various countries are not randomly chosen, large national samples. We do not know how representative the samples are of the national populations. (b) The instruments used in many of the cross-cultural studies involve translations of the DIT. Translating a test is a very vexing enterprise, and we do not know the equivalence of test scores from various translated tests. (See Rest, 1986, chap. 4 for further discussion of cross-cultural studies.)

Much of the work in this volume explores the usefulness of the DIT with different subgroups and subsamples in the United States—a less stringent test of the universality hypothesis, but nevertheless inquiring into the general usefulness of the psychological model in a variety of social settings. Rather than putting the question in terms of the cross-cultural generality of the Kohlberg approach, its usefulness is examined in a variety of professional, real-life settings.

Educational Interventions

The central question here is, "Can development of moral judgment be stimulated by deliberate educational intervention?" Previous meta-analyses of 56 moral intervention programs (Rest, 1986, chap. 3) found that moral education programs were effective in promoting DIT gains (experimental groups showing statistically higher gains than nontreated, comparison groups). Often in social science accounts, the strength of an intervention is reported in terms of a statistic, *effect size*.[7] The effect size reported in the meta-analysis was about 0.4—in the moderate range of effect sizes, but typical in power of the effectiveness of college programs (see Pascarella & Terenzini, 1991). Furthermore, the meta-analysis indicates that older subjects (i.e., graduate and professional school subjects rather than junior high school subjects) are especially receptive to moral education programs designed to foster moral judgment development. Hence, in contrast to the view that college or professional school is too late to attempt moral education, the evidence shows that such educational programs are not at all too late.

The chapters in this book add much to what is known about moral education programs. Bebeau (chap. 7) discusses a decade-long program that she developed

---

[7]Effect size is calculated as the difference between a pretest and posttest average for a sample divided by the standard deviation of the pretest.

1. THEORY AND RESEARCH

for dentistry. Sprinthall (chap. 5) discusses many types of intervention programs designed by counselors. Duckett and Ryden (chap. 3) describe their program for nurses that not only has as a goal to promote growth in moral judgment, but also growth in other components as well. McNeel (chap. 2) shows that a developmental program for college faculty produces gains in the students of that particular faculty member.

Correlations

The concept of *convergent* validity implies that a measure should be correlated with theoretically similar measures. *Divergent* validity implies that a measure should not be correlated with theoretically dissimilar measures. The DIT typically correlates in the 0.6 to 0.7 range with other measures of moral thinking, such as the MJI and the Comprehension of Moral Concepts test. On the other hand, the DIT is nonsignificantly correlated with Social Desirability and most personality trait measures (e.g., MMPI, Locus of Control, Allport-Vernon-Lindzey Values, Self-Esteem, Anxiety). The DIT is moderately correlated with aptitude and IQ measures (generally in the 0.2 to 0.5 range)—and we would expect this modest correlation with other cognitive measures, given the cognitive nature of moral judgment. Similarly, the DIT is moderately correlated with measures of liberal–conservative political attitudes and with other developmental variables (e.g., Perry, Loevinger, Hunt, cited previously). The DIT is slightly correlated with socioeconomic status and with religious conservatism. (See Rest, 1979, 1986, for references to specific studies and further discussion.)

There is the additional question of whether the DIT shows certain correlational patterns because it is "piggy-backing" on some other variable. In other words, how do we know that the patterns we observe in DIT are not due to shared variance with some other variable (such as IQ or Liberal–Conservative Attitudes)? What information is there in a DIT score beyond that contained in an IQ score (or measure of verbal fluency or political attitude)?

In Rest (1979), the issue of the distinctiveness of moral judgment (and in particular, the DIT) is discussed at some length; several studies are summarized there and more recent replications have been carried out since then. Suffice it to say that several kinds of studies have shown that the DIT carries useful and distinct information beyond that given by measures of aptitude or political attitude.

In summary, the correlational patterns of moral judgment scores support *convergent–divergent* validity of the DIT and its distinctiveness.

Links to Behavior

Does moral judgment predict to real-life behavior? Several hundred studies have addressed this issue (see Blasi, 1980; Rest, 1986, chap. 5). In general, these reviews reveal that moral judgment is statistically linked with hundreds of measures of behavior; however, the linkage is not strong (typical are correlations of 0.3–0.4).

Thoma (chap. 12) focuses on general issues in relating moral judgment to behavior, and describes a strategy of research involving a *moderator* variable, the Utilizer Score, that increases the power of the correlations of the DIT to behavioral measures. Ponemon and Gabhart (chap. 6) discuss how DIT scores relate to fraud detection in accountants. Duckett and Ryden (chap. 3) discuss how DIT scores predict to clinical performance ratings of nurses. Self and Baldwin (chap. 8) discuss how moral judgment scores predict to clinical performance ratings in medical doctors. Chang (chap. 4) discusses how DIT scores predict to school teachers' professional performance. Bredemeier and Shields (chap. 10) discuss how moral judgment relates to athletic performance.

Therefore, the facts regarding the relation of moral judgment to behavior are that there is a persistent statistically significant relation, but that the power of the relation is at a modest level. These facts lead to the view that moral behavior is determined by several psychological processes acting together, and that moral judgment is only one of these. If only one determinant is measured, then it should be *consistently* linked to behavior, but be only *modestly* correlated, since the other determinants are allowed to vary randomly. Hence, in order to build powerful predictions to behavior, all determinants have to be measured simultaneously—something that is not done when we correlate only moral judgment with behavior.

THE FOUR COMPONENT MODEL

Many people who read Kohlberg's work say that he may have been on to something interesting in his six stages, but that the six stages aren't everything in the psychology of morality. Another way of putting this is to say that there is more to moral development than moral *judgment* development, and there is more to moral judgment than the six stages.

Many people may be surprised to hear that Kohlberg agreed. He also saw moral judgment as only part of the psychology of morality (e.g., Kohlberg cited in Modgil & Modgil, 1986). There is widespread agreement that there are more components to morality than just moral judgment. The trick, however, is to identify more precisely what else there is in morality, and how all these pieces fit together.

My view of the major determinants of moral behavior (the Four Component Model) came to be formulated while I was doing a general review of the morality literature. The morality literature encompasses not only the cognitive-developmental research, but also research on morality from social learning, behavioristic, psychoanalytic, and social psychological approaches (Rest, 1983). It became clear that all these researchers were not talking about the same thing. I had to argue either that a lot of this work really had nothing to do with morality, or that the various approaches were talking about different aspects of morality—hence, morality was a multifaceted phenomenon. The Four Component Model (see Table 1.7) is not just pure speculation; there are research examples of each of the components (See also Rest, 1984, 1986 for further elaboration of the Four Component Model.)

1. THEORY AND RESEARCH

TABLE 1.7
Four Psychological Components Determining Moral Behavior

1. Moral sensitivity
   (Interpreting the situation)
2. Moral judgment
   (Judging which action is morally right/wrong)
3. Moral motivation
   (Prioritizing moral values relative to other values)
4. Moral character
   (Having courage, persisting, overcoming distractions, implementing skills)

In addition to being a framework for viewing disparate literatures, the Four Component Model is presented here as a theory of what determines moral behavior. Rather than dividing morality into cognition, affect, and behavior—as many contemporary accounts of moral development do (as if these were the basic psychological elements)—the Four Component Model starts with the question, "What must we suppose happens psychologically in order for moral behavior to take place?" We wind up with at least four distinct processes.[8]

An intuitive understanding of these four components may come more easily if we talk about four different kinds of moral failure—that is, different reasons why a person might *fail* to behave morally. After talking about deficiencies, we then do a flip-flop to the positive side, imagining what it takes to succeed in performing a moral act.

Component I: Moral Sensitivity. Imagine a person who fails to act morally because it just didn't occur to him or her that something he or she might be doing (or could do) would affect other people. For example, a teacher in the classroom might be unaware that he is giving more attention and encouragement to the boys in class than the girls. If someone pointed out this biased behavior, the teacher might be embarrassed because he was not intending to be biased. The teacher is just not interpreting the situation adequately.

Moral sensitivity is the awareness of how our actions affect other people. It involves being aware of different possible lines of action and how each line of action could affect the parties concerned. It involves imaginatively constructing possible scenarios, and knowing cause-consequence chains of events in the real world; it involves empathy and role-taking skills. Bebeau (chap. 7) describes her research program on moral sensitivity in the context of the dental profession. Duckett and Ryden (chap. 3) talk about moral sensitivity in the context of nursing. Bredemeier and Shields (chap. 10) discuss moral sensitivity in the context of sports.

Component II: Moral Judgment. This is the component that Kohlberg's work advanced and that the DIT purports to assess. Once the person is aware of

---
[8]The number 4 is not important here. There may well be more than four, but I would argue there are at least these four distinctions. Bredemeier and Shields (chap. 10) talk about 12 components.

possible lines of action and how people would be affected by each line of action (Component I), then Component II judges which line of action is more morally justifiable (which alternative is just, or right).

Deficiency in Component II comes about from overly simplistic ways of justifying choices of moral action. For instance, acts of terrorism justified in terms of revenge for previous wrongs may be shortsighted, counterproductive, and targeted at innocent people.

Notice that the dilemmas used to study moral judgment (like the Heinz dilemma) have already defined the possible lines of action for the actor and how parties will be affected by the action. Therefore, our measures of moral judgment (Component II) cannot be used to study Component I. The gist of the previous discussion has been to argue that moral judgment is important, but it is not the only determinant of moral behavior.

Component III: Moral Motivation. How are we to account for the most notoriously evil people in the world (e.g., Hitler, Stalin, etc.)? Their moral failure is unlikely to be due to deficiencies in awareness of what they were doing (Component I), or because they couldn't figure out what would be the fair thing to do (Component II). Rather, Hitler and Stalin set aside moral considerations in pursuit of other values. For example, Hitler could not be deterred by "bourgeois morality" in pursuit of the Reich that would last 1,000 years. The Reich was more important than morality. Another value completely compromised moral values.

Component III has to do with the importance given to moral values in competition with other values. Deficiencies in Component III occur when a person is not sufficiently motivated to put moral values higher than other values—when other values such as self-actualization or protecting one's organization replace concern for doing what is right.

Researchwise, not too much has been done regarding the measurement or empirical testing of Component III. (See, however, discussions of Component III in chaps. 7 and 10.)

Component IV: Moral Character. This component involves ego strength, perseverance, backbone, toughness, strength of conviction, and courage. A person may be morally sensitive, may make good moral judgments, and may place high priority on moral values, but if the person wilts under pressure, is easily distracted or discouraged, is a wimp and weak-willed, then moral failure occurs because of deficiency in Component IV (weak character). Psychological toughness and strong character do not guarantee adequacy in any of the other components, but a certain amount of each is necessary to carry out a line of action.

In summary, moral failure can occur because of deficiency in any component. All four components are determinants of moral action. In fact, there are complex interactions among the four components, and it is not supposed that the four represent a temporal order such that a person performs one, then two, then three, then four—rather the four components comprise a *logical* analysis of what it takes to behave morally. Duckett and Ryden (chap. 3) discuss some ideas for educational programs, attending to all four components. Bredemeier and Shields (chap. 10) also discuss viewing moral behavior in terms of all components.

This then is a summary of theory and research behind the chapters that follow. The chapters have a common interest in extending the general ideas into specific, real-world contexts. What is striking about these chapters is how the researchers have gone different ways, invented new strategies, and explored different lines of inquiry. In most cases a new line of research in one field could be tried in other fields. The authors hope that by bringing together these chapters from various professions, there will be cross-fertilization of the work in one profession to other professions.

REFERENCES

Bebeau, M., & Brabeck, M. (1989). Ethical sensitivity and moral reasoning among men and women in the professions. In M. Brabeck (Ed.), *Who cares?* (pp. 144–163). New York: Praeger.

Blasi, A. (1980). Bridging moral cognition and moral action: A critical review of the literature. *Psychological Bulletin, 88*, 1–45.

Colby, A., & Kohlberg, L. (1987). *The measurement of moral judgment* (Vols. 1–2). New York: Cambridge University Press.

Colby, A., Kohlberg, L., Gibbs, J., & Lieberman, M. (1983). A longitudinal study of moral judgment. *Monographs of the Society for Research in Child Development, 48*(1–2, Serial No. 200).

Habermas, J. (1979). *Communication and the evolution of society.* London: Heineman.

Gilligan, C. (1982). *In a different voice.* Cambridge, MA: Harvard University Press.

Kohlberg, L. (1973). Continuities in childhood and adult moral development revisited. In P. B. Baltes & K. Schaie (Eds.), *Life-span developmental psychology: Personality and socialization* (pp. 93–120). New York: Academic Press.

Kohlberg, L. (1981). *The philosophy of moral development* (Vol. 1). San Francisco: Harper & Row.

Kohlberg, L. (1984). *The psychology of moral development* (Vol. 2). San Francisco: Harper & Row.

Kohlberg, L. (1986). A current statement on some theoretical issues. In S. Modgil & C. Modgil (Eds.), *Lawrence Kohlberg: Consensus and controversy* (pp. 485–546). Philadelphia: The Falmer Press.

Kurtines, W., & Grief, E. (1974). The development of moral thought: Review and evaluation of Kohlberg's approach. *Psychological Bulletin, 81*(8), 453–470.

McGeorge, C. (1975). The susceptibility to faking of the Defining Issues Test of moral development. *Developmental Psychology, 44*, 116–122.

Modgil, S., & Modgil, C. (Eds.). (1986). *Lawrence Kohlberg: Consensus and controversy.* Philadelphia: The Falmer Press.

Pascarella, E. T., & Terenzini, P. T. (1991). *How college affects students.* San Francisco: Jossey-Bass.

Power, C., Higgins, A., & Kohlberg, L. (1989). *Lawrence Kohlberg's approach to moral education.* New York: Columbia University Press.

Puka, B. (1991). Toward the redevelopment of Kohlberg's theory: Preserving essential structure, removing controversial content. In W. M. Kurtines & J. L. Gewirtz (Eds.), *Handbook of moral behavior and development: Vol. 1. Theory* (pp. 373–393). Hillsdale, NJ: Lawrence Erlbaum Associates.

Rawls, J. (1971). *A theory of justice.* Cambridge, MA: Harvard University Press.

Rest, J. R. (1974). The hierarchical nature of moral judgment. *Journal of Personality, 41*, 86–109.

Rest, J. R. (1979). *Development in judging moral issues.* Minneapolis: University of Minnesota Press.

Rest, J. R. (1983). Morality. In P. H. Mussen (series Ed.) & J. Flavell & E. Markman (Vol. Eds.), *Handbook of child psychology: Vol. 3 Cognitive development* (pp. 556–629). New York: Wiley.

Rest, J. R. (1984). The major components of morality. In W. Kurtines & J. Gewirtz (Eds.), *Morality, moral behavior, and moral development* (pp. 24–40). New York: Wiley.

Rest, J. R. (1986). *Manual for the Defining Issues Test.* Minneapolis: Center for the Study of Ethical Development, University of Minnesota.

Rest, J. R. (1986). *Moral development: Advances in research and theory.* New York: Praeger Press.

Rest, J. R. (1988). Why does college promote development in moral judgment? *Journal of Moral Education. 17*(3), 183–194.

Rest, J., Turiel, E., & Kohlberg, L. (1969). Level of moral judgment as a determinant of preference and comprehension made by others. *Journal of Personality, 37,* 225–252.

Thies-Sprinthall, L., & Sprinthall, N. A. (1987). Experienced teachers: Agents for revitalization and renewal as mentors and mentor educators. *Journal of Education, 69*(1) 65–79.

Thoma, S. J. (1986). Estimating gender differences in the comprehension and preference of moral issues. *Developmental Review, 6,* 165–180.

Walker, L. (1991). Sex differences in moral reasoning. In W. Kurtines & J. Gewirtz (Eds.), *Handbook of moral behavior and development* (pp. 333–364). Hillsdale, NJ: Lawrence Erlbaum Associates.

Walker, L., deVries, B., & Bichard, S. L. (1984). The hierarchical nature of stages of moral development. *Developmental Psychology, 20,* 960–966.

Chapter 2

College Teaching and Student Moral Development

Steven P. McNeel
Bethel College

MORAL DEVELOPMENT AS AN AIM OF HIGHER EDUCATION

U.S. colleges were originally founded with some form of moral education as a primary goal. Nucci and Pascarella (1987) reported that the central goal of the curriculum and even the entire college environment was to develop sensitivity to moral responsibilities, to teach ethical thought and action, and to develop students' character. These goals make it clear that higher education in the United States was originally a whole-person education with emphases that sound very similar to Rest's (chap. 1) four components of morality: moral sensitivity, moral judgment, moral motivation, and moral character.

In the late-19th and early-20th centuries, however, the rise of disciplinary specialization led to a fragmentation of knowledge and to much less concern with "broader questions of human values and morality" (Nucci & Pascarella, 1987, pp. 271–272). In the social sciences, "the earlier conviction that ethics and social science were inseparable" gave way to "an emphasis on 'value-free' inquiry" (Sandin, 1989, pp. 219–220). Later, the general education movement sought to recover the earlier view that moral education was the responsibility of the curriculum and the entire college environment, but this effort has had only limited success due to a lack of interest in, or an antipathy toward, the kind of whole-person education that full-bodied moral education necessitates (Sandin, 1989).

More recently, however, it has become increasingly clear that moral issues are integrally bound up in the content of the various disciplines, and that an adequate higher education will require "ethics across the curriculum." Although college and university mission statements have always retained allusions to the college or university's role in moral education, it has become obvious that higher education must effectively implement, and not just speak of, these lofty goals. Thus, leading U.S. educators have argued strongly that an improvement in the teaching of ethics is essential in U.S. colleges and universities (e.g., Bok, 1988)

The Cognitive-Developmental Approach

The cognitive-developmental approach to moral development (reviewed in chap. 1) has wisdom to offer college educators in their task of enhancing moral development. First, the cognitive developmentalists have focused on moral judgment. Although morality is clearly more than moral judgment (the Four Component Model in Table 1.7 reflects this view), the cognitive component would certainly be expected to fit well in an educational environment that emphasizes cognitive growth.

Second, growth in moral judgment appears to occur through mechanisms that fit nicely in a college or university community, at least when there is a liberal arts focus. According to Lawrence Kohlberg's theory, growth in moral judgment (movement to higher stages) is presumed to take place through cognitive accommodation: "Change in one's cognitions comes from experiences that do not fit one's earlier (and simpler) conceptions. Cognitive disequilibrium is the condition for development" (Rest, 1986, p. 32). Liberal arts education has a central purpose consistent with this view of moral judgment growth: the purpose of bringing students into contact with a highly diverse range of facts and views about the world. Many of these, whether encountered through literature, philosophy, sociology, nursing, or whatever discipline, address the complexities and dilemmas that arise as different people seek to live cooperatively in the world. Students learn to see things from the other person's viewpoint and to appreciate systems different from their own. According to Kohlberg (1976), it is precisely such experiences of expanded role taking that provide the key for growth in moral judgment; these experiences provide cognitive disequilibrium that leads to growth in moral judgment. Thus, it is reasonable to expect a liberal arts education to facilitate moral judgment growth.

Rest (chap. 1) summarizes many studies that reveal that increased education is, in fact, generally associated with higher levels of moral judgment. Pascarella and Terenzini (1991, chap. 8) reviewed a number of studies on moral judgment development during college and conclude that there is a significantly positive effect, but that it is unclear how strong the effect is. This chapter reviews studies that have become available since their review and gives a clearer but still preliminary answer to the question of how strong the impact of college is on moral judgment development.

Differential Effects by Type of College Education

It has been suggested that some types of higher education may not accomplish well the liberal arts goals previously described, including moral judgment growth. A first example is vocationally oriented higher education. Among small college liberal arts faculty there has been concern in the last two decades about possible negative effects of more vocationally oriented majors such as business, or perhaps nursing. These worries seem akin to the concerns in the late 19th century (mentioned earlier) that an emphasis on teaching technical competence in a narrow area was associated with less concern about broader questions of human values and morality. In support of these worries, the literature in some vocational areas, such as business (e.g., Scott, 1988; Sims & Sims, 1991) and education (e.g., Goodlad, Soder, & Sirotnik, 1990), argued that there is an ethical crisis in these disciplines.

Although some educational approaches in the vocational areas may exist that do not encourage principled thinking, it seems possible to integrate vocational education with a broader liberal arts focus. This might be done, for instance, by addressing the values issues naturally raised in the discipline and bringing to bear relevant wisdom from other disciplines such as the sciences, the social sciences, and philosophy. This chapter includes a description of some differences in moral judgment growth as a function of college major, including less growth in certain vocational areas, and considers some possible reasons for these differences.

A second type of higher education may not accomplish well the liberal arts goal of moral judgment growth. Some have suggested that a conservative Christian focus may be associated with lower levels of moral judgment. Rest (1979, 1986) summarized some of this evidence from conservative Christian churches and from a fundamentalist seminary, and there is more recent evidence that a Bible college education may inhibit the development of moral judgment (Shaver, 1987). The mechanism is presumably an ideological, answer-oriented approach to education that operates against the development or expression of autonomous principled thinking in moral dilemmas. That is, because of a focus on given answers, a Christian higher education might not develop in students what Western philosophers call *the moral viewpoint*, the emphasis on making moral judgments out of basic universalizable principles, such as justice, or the valuing of human life and dignity.

However, it seems possible to have Christian higher education that does not lean in the direction of ideology or indoctrination but instead is characterized by genuine truth seeking (see McNeel, 1991). Holmes (1975) demonstrated that an adequate world view includes simultaneous commitment to one's own world view (where else would one start?) and openness to other perspectives (how else would one grow?). A higher education with this joint commitment would embody liberal arts goals, including many of the moral goals typically sought by colleges in the first half of U.S. history. Colleges such as those of the Christian College Consortium seek to implement such an integration by maintaining a joint commitment to a conservative theology and to open-minded examination of their own and alternative perspectives (Christian College Consortium, 1979). Holmes (1991) suggested that in such colleges "ethics is everybody's business," and as a means of implementing this integration he proposed eleven objectives for moral education. These objectives essentially detailed some of the specifics of Rest's Four Component Model of morality: moral sensitivity (consciousness raising and consciousness sensitizing); moral judgment (moral imagination, ethical analysis, and moral decision making); moral motivation (values analysis, values clarification, and values criticism); and moral character (becoming a responsible agent, developing virtue, and achieving moral identity).

EFFECTS OF COLLEGE ON MORAL JUDGMENT

Moral Judgment Growth at Bethel College

Given the appropriateness of moral judgment as a liberal arts college outcome variable, at Bethel College we decided to institute longitudinal and cross-sectional studies of the moral judgment growth of our students across their entire 4-year college experience. For a number of years, we administered the Defining Issues Test (DIT) to all incoming freshmen during their welcome-week orientation. We then followed up a random sample of each of these cohorts with a DIT testing in the spring of their senior year, 4 years later. For several years, an additional sample of seniors who transferred into the college was also tested in order to provide more complete cross-sectional samples.

One goal was to provide an adequate database for summative evaluation of this college outcome. Bethel College is a Christian liberal arts college with a strong commitment to an evangelical faith and to the openness of the liberal arts; thus we felt that moral judgment growth should be one important outcome of a Bethel education. A second goal was to use the information in a formative way, to help faculty and administration understand better where our students are on the developmental dimension of moral judgment. The overall purpose was to provide faculty and administration the opportunity and understanding necessary for them to modify their teaching or programs in ways that would be more powerfully educative on this developmental dimension, central to the mission of the college. A later section describes how this was done through the SPECTRUM faculty development program (Scholars Pursuing Educational Competencies to Reach Undergraduate Maturity), and through cooperative research with individual departments.

The results (see McNeel, 1992, for details) supported the contention that there is very strong longitudinal growth in moral judgment across students' 4 years of college: DIT principled reasoning increased from 35.7 to 46.4 in the combined longitudinal cohorts ($n = 216$ students who met the DIT consistency checks in both freshman and senior testings). The cross-sectional samples showed nearly identical results (Ns of 920 and 433). Consistent with other DIT research, there were no significant gender differences in principled reasoning, or very minimal differences favoring females. Furthermore, males and females did not grow at significantly different rates during their college experience.

The strength of this *college experience effect* can be assessed by calculating the *effect size* (*d*) used by Pascarella and Terenzini (1991) in their analyses of college effects: freshman-to-senior change divided by freshman standard deviation. Bowen (1977) has proposed the following rules of thumb for interpreting effect sizes: *small* = 0.10–0.39, *moderate* = 0.40–0.69, *large* = 0.70–0.99, and *very large* = 1.00 and above. By these standards, the effect sizes for the longitudinal (0.92) and cross-sectional (0.93) samples were quite large.

Meta-Analysis of College Effects: Comparison of College Types

In order to place these results in a larger context, I conducted an extensive literature search to identify other college and university samples that covered the entire 4 years of college experience and that provided sufficient information to calculate effect sizes (see McNeel, 1992). Twenty-two samples from 12 colleges or universities (7 liberal arts colleges, 3 universities, and 2 Bible colleges) met the criteria, providing a limited but substantial database (see Table 2.1). The results were striking because they show large average effect sizes for liberal arts colleges (longitudinal = 0.79, n = 6; cross-sectional = 0.81, n = 7), with the lowest liberal arts college effect size being moderate, d = 0.55. Although the number of institutions is extremely small, it is worth noting that there was a large or moderate average effect size for universities (longitudinal = 0.80, n = 2; cross-sectional = 0.48, n = 3) and no effect or a moderate average effect size for Bible colleges (longitudinal = 0.02, n = 1; cross-sectional = 0.48, n = 2).

The results also provided further support for the emerging view that, although a conservative Christian ideology may sometimes inhibit growth in principled reasoning (see earlier discussion in this chap.), this does not generally occur in a conservative Christian context with a truly liberal arts focus. Most of the liberal arts colleges in the meta-analysis have a conservative Protestant heritage and a strong commitment to developing students' personal Christian faith, and yet they revealed very strong growth profiles in principled reasoning. This is in contrast to the moderate growth or nongrowth in the Bible college samples. Thus, contrary to the suggestions of earlier research, it seems that growth in principled reasoning can occur alongside deeply held conservative Christian commitment (Clouse, 1990; McNeel, 1991).

Finally, the meta-analysis highlighted a paucity of freshman-to-senior studies, particularly in university and Bible college contexts. This lack of data is particularly troubling because the minimal university cross-sectional evidence (n = 3) raised questions about whether the growth profile in universities is as strong as it is in liberal arts colleges. The weaker cross-sectional effects in universities may be due to the specific universities or to additional sources of variability in cross-sectional designs, such as selection or mortality (i.e., students dropping out of college).

TABLE 2.1
Longitudinal and Cross-Sectional Percent Principled Reasoning for 4-Year Freshman–Senior Comparisons, With Effect Size (d)[a]

College/University	Longitudinal Results					
	Fr	Sr[b]	N	SD	Change	d
Liberal Arts Colleges:						
This study	35.7	46.4	216	11.62	10.7	.92
Alverno sample A[c]	35.6	47.4	70	11.53	11.8	1.02
Bethel[d]	37.3	47.7	28	14.39	10.4	.72
Houghton, Messiah, & Wheaton[e]	37.2	46.8	74	10.58	9.6	.91
Wheaton[f]	41.5	52.4	44	17.22	10.9	.63
Alverno sample B[c]	42.8	50.9	70	14.53	8.1	.56
Bible Colleges:						
Columbia Bible[f]	33.4	33.2	54	12.73	−0.2	.02
Universities:						
U Calif., Irvine[g]	36.9	48.1	95	13.26	11.2	.84
West Point[h]	34.4	43.3	104	11.83	8.9	.76

College/University	Cross-Sectional Results[i]					
	Fr	Sr[b]	N	SD	Change	d
Liberal Arts Colleges:						
This study	34.8	45.3	920(433)	11.28	10.5	.93
Alverno[c]	35.2	49.2	70 (53)	10.56	14.0	1.33
Bethel[d]	33.4	42.9	360 (36)	11.69	9.5	.81
Christian Col. A[j]	35.4	39.8	30 (30)	7.50	4.4	.59
Christian Col. B[j]	37.0	44.0	35 (30)	12.83	7.0	.55
Christian Col. C[j]	38.6	48.0	34 (33)	9.21	9.4	1.02
Mainline Col.[k]	43.4	51.1	57 (46)	13.34	7.7	.58
Wheaton[l]	41.5	52.2	119 (58)	15.48	10.7	.69
Bible Colleges:						
Columbia Bible[l]	32.4	36.7	212 (46)	14.89	4.3	.29
Bible Col. B[m]	30.3	39.8	39 (32)	13.98	9.5	.68
Universities:						
U of Iowa[d]	37.8	46.8	112 (40)	17.54	9.5	.51
U Calif., Irvine[g]	41.4	44.4	85 (56)	14.82	3.1	.21
West Point[n]	34.4	42.6	167 (47)	11.5	8.2	.72

[a]In each case, following Pascarella and Terenzini (1991, p. 15), effect size is the senior minus freshman difference divided by the freshman standard deviation.

[b]The freshman–senior differences in each sample were significant ($p < .01$), except for Columbia Bible college (n.s.) and Christian College A ($p < .03$, one-tailed). Statistical tests were not reported for Columbia Bible and University of California, Irvine cross-sectional results.

[c]Mentkowski and Straight (1983). Longitudinal sample A is traditional aged college students; longitudinal sample B is older students. Longitudinal sample is from p. 178; cross-sectional sample is from p. 160.

[d]McNeel (1991, p. 317); standard deviations provided by the author.

[e]Burwell, Butman, and Van Wicklin (1992, Table 1B).

[f]Shaver (1987, pp. 214–215).

[g]Loxley and Whiteley (1986, pp. 280, 275).

(continued)

2. COLLEGE TEACHING AND STUDENT MORAL DEVELOPMENT 33

TABLE 2.1 (continued)

[h]Bridges and Priest (1983, p. 29). In this very complex study, these 104 subjects came from four samples tested varying numbers of times (and at different times) during the 4 years of college. These 104 subjects included all subjects tested at the very beginning of their college experience (i.e., prior to basic training) and again in the spring of their senior year (some were tested at other times as well). The means presented here were calculated from the means and Ns given for the four groups. The sample's representativeness cannot be determined clearly from the report. The authors give no freshman standard deviations for their longitudinal samples, so the freshman standard deviation from their very large ($N = 616$) and most complete freshman sample (their Table 24) is used here to calculate effect size.

[i]The first N is the freshman sample size; senior sample size is in parentheses.

[j]Buier, Butman, Burwell, and Van Wicklin (1989, p. 74).

[k]From a quality liberal arts college in the upper Midwest associated with one of the mainline protestant denominations. The data are from an anonymous database assembled by the author.

[l]Shaver (1985, pp. 123, 126).

[m]From a small conservative Bible college. The data are from an anonymous database assembled by the author.

[n]Bridges and Priest (1983, p. 30). These results are for the freshmen (1977) and seniors (1981) who were tested only once during their college experience. Hence this is a cross-sectional sample in the sense that the two groups contained different people, but testing times were separated by nearly 4 years. This sample's representativeness cannot be determined clearly from the report.

However, it is also possible that the large longitudinal university effects are at least partly limited to the two samples studied. The lack of growth in the one Bible college studied longitudinally is consistent with earlier research suggesting that a conservative Christian environment may inhibit growth in moral judgment, or it may only represent that particular Bible college. However, the moderate cross-sectional effect in Bible colleges may suggest that growth in moral judgment is not incompatible with religiously conservative Bible colleges. Clearly, further studies are called for in both university and Bible college settings, as well as in a broader range of liberal arts colleges.

Comparison With Other College Outcome Variables. As detailed in McNeel (1992), the average liberal arts college and longitudinal university effect sizes of about 0.80 are among the largest average effect sizes for the many college impact variables that have been studied (Pascarella & Terenzini, 1991). They noticeably exceeded the average college effects on (a) cognitive variables such as general verbal (0.56), quantitative skills (0.24), oral (0.60) or written (0.50) communication skills; (b) self- and relational skills, such as personal adjustment (0.40), self-esteem (0.60), independence (0.36), interpersonal relations (0.16), and intellectual orientation (0.30); and (c) all values and attitude issues studied (effect sizes ranging from 0.10–0.50). The average principled reasoning effect size equals the effect size for subject matter knowledge (0.84) and for authoritarianism (− 0.81) and is exceeded only by the effect sizes reported for critical thinking (1.00), use of reason (1.00), and ability to deal with conceptual complexity (1.20).

The implications of these results concerning moral judgment growth in college are limited by the relatively small number of colleges and universities with adequate data ($N = 12$). However, they provide a preliminary qualification to Pascarella and Terenzini's (1991) conclusion that the impact of college on moral judgment is of uncertain size: This analysis suggested that 4 years of college has a very powerful effect on growth in principled reasoning, at least for liberal arts colleges.

College Major and Principled Reasoning Growth. The Bethel College data were analyzed by the student's college major wherever sample size warranted doing so (McNeel, 1992). Although each individual major showed statistically significant growth, some majors showed significantly sharper growth profiles than others. This differential growth resulted in the various majors having significantly different principled reasoning scores as seniors, when they had not differed significantly as freshmen. Effect sizes were calculated, and they were especially large for psychology (1.48) and nursing (1.47), with English (1.26), all others (1.15), and social work (1.01) also showing very large effect sizes. Other majors showed less strong growth. The highest growth took place in majors that focus on understanding humans in all their diversity and/or majors that include a central integration of ethical considerations within the content of a professional course of study. These results seem generally consistent with theory and research on factors influencing moral development (Rest, 1986).

In contrast, education and business, two majors perceived by students to be vocationally oriented, had only moderate effect sizes (see McNeel, 1992, for details). In fact, the moderate effect size for these two majors taken together (0.58) was only about half of the very large effect size of the remaining majors (1.10). This weaker effect was associated with significantly lower senior principled reasoning scores for these two majors (40.2) than for the remaining majors (49.4). Thus, the seniors in these two majors showed moral judgment more like that of college freshmen (average principled reasoning in the range of 34 to 42) than like that of their fellow seniors (average principled reasoning in the range of 43 to 52). Finally, freshmen with high principled reasoning scores showed different growth profiles across the 4 years if they majored in business or education, rather than other disciplines: Business or education majors were much more likely to show significant decreases in principled reasoning.

These data are consistent with the literature mentioned earlier, which suggested that there may be a moral development problem nationally in the areas of business and education. However, it is worth noting that in our samples, the growth profiles in these two majors were moderate, not low. If further research at other colleges confirms this moderate effect, then perhaps the "crisis language" used by some authors may be a bit overblown, even though the data still may give reason for concern.

In any case, interpreting the lower growth profiles in business and education is problematic because of the correlational research design. The lower growth may be due to factors inherent in these two disciplines or their curricula, such as, perhaps, lack of a central integration of ethical considerations with the content of the curriculum. However, the lower growth could also be due to differences in the way the disciplines are taught, differences in the personal qualities of students who choose these majors (including the academic qualifications or the values of incoming students), differences in the extracollege environmental demands on students who select these majors (including, perhaps, pragmatic parental pressure to get a job), or many other factors.[1] Further research will be needed to sort through the range and variety of potential explanations. However, because these two disciplines are very important in the community life of the nation, the only moderate growth profiles of business and education students are of great potential significance. Longitudinal studies at other colleges and universities are needed to assess whether their students show similar longitudinal differences due to college major.

ACTION RESEARCH IN THE COLLEGE/ UNIVERSITY CONTEXT

Historically, scientists have distinguished between basic and applied research. Although this distinction makes a certain sense, it can be drawn too sharply, and often the goals of both can be accomplished simultaneously. In the sciences, for example, the applied program to develop an atomic bomb led to significant theoretical advances, as did the U.S. space program. Similarly, in the social sciences, there can be a kind of *action research* that serves to advance practical goals in the immediate organizational context, while still being likely to yield research results of theoretical significance. In contrast to much scientific orthodoxy that argues for "value-free" science, action research is done from an explicit value orientation and with the goal of benefiting the subjects under study (Jacobs, 1974; Tax, 1975). Such a view of research is consistent with the value-laden expressions in colleges' mission statements. In an *age of accountability* in higher education, this kind of research is likely to prove an attractive alternative to many colleges and universities.

At Bethel College, we have implemented a moral judgment research program with these action research qualities. We accomplished this through identifying issues of both practical and theoretical importance (e.g., the impact of off-campus learning experiences) through working cooperatively with individual departments on research of significance to them, through implementing and evaluating a promising method of teaching ethics, and through assessing the impacts of a program designed to enhance faculty understanding of student development. The

---

[1]Different growth profiles in groups can sometimes be partially explained through examining input variables, such as ACT or SAT test scores, on which the groups might differ as they enter college. Pascarella and Terenzini (1991) dealt with this and other important topics relevant to understanding the causal influences on change scores in longitudinal research. We are currently beginning to analyze such data in order to clarify the meaning of the differential growth among majors.

goal of the research was program improvement, in order to deliver a more powerful education to our students. Because of this goal, the research program was carried out independently of the Academic Dean's office: We felt that faculty and staff apprehension regarding evaluation would be minimized if the research program had no connection with an office that was closely concerned with person evaluation. A research program characterized by cooperation also seemed critical, because research on moral judgment may feel threatening to, or judgmental of, some people, and program improvement is unlikely to be implemented effectively by a group of faculty or staff who feel threatened. Thus, opportunities for cooperative research were offered to various departments, and collaborative research programs have developed where the departments showed interest.

Some Issues of Practical and Theoretical Significance

One advantage of establishing an extensive longitudinal database is that growth can be related to other available databases. This gives at least preliminary answers to important questions that have both practical and theoretical importance for higher education. Three examples illustrate this point.

Off-Campus Learning Experiences. Early research at Bethel suggested that students' plans (stated during freshman orientation) for participating in an off-campus learning experience while at college were predictive of their growth profiles in moral judgment over the next 2 years. This finding was not surprising, for it is consistent with the literature suggesting that experiential learning can be powerfully educational (e.g., Borzak, 1981). However, because plans and actual experience are not the same thing, we designed a test of whether the same effect occurred as a function of actual experience. In a recent study, seniors who had been tested as freshmen filled out an additional questionnaire reporting on the nature of their college experiences. Included were questions regarding three types of experiences: (a) required off-campus learning experiences; (b) nonrequired off-campus learning experiences; and (c) participation in out-of-state (and usually cross-cultural) programs, such as a semester studying in England, Costa Rica or Washington, DC, or a January term in Israel, Ecuador, or the Philippines.

The results showed that participation in out-of-state programs was significantly associated with a very sharp growth profile (average principled reasoning scores from 32.6 as freshmen to 47.9 as seniors; $d = 1.42$), although lack of participation was associated with less strong growth (33.6–42.9; $d = 0.94$). Similarly, students who participated in a nonrequired off-campus learning experience that involved a large time investment showed a very strong growth profile (31.8–48.6; $d = 1.56$). Those with learning experiences that required only a small to moderate time investment showed a less strong but still large growth profile (33.8–46.3; $d = 1.12$). However, students who had no such learning experience during their college years showed only moderate growth (34.2–40.1; $d = 0.66$). In contrast to these results,

2. COLLEGE TEACHING AND STUDENT MORAL DEVELOPMENT

participation in required off-campus learning experiences did not relate to increased growth profiles.

These data are fascinating, because they support the idea that off-campus learning experiences can be powerful stimuli for growth in moral judgment. However, careful analyses are still needed in order to draw firm conclusions regarding causality. For example, those who choose off-campus learning experiences voluntarily may already be on sharper growth profiles, independent of the experiences they subsequently have. (However, the groups do not begin their freshman year with different principled reasoning.)

The data seem to suggest that choice is important in students' learning from their off-campus experiences. This notion is not surprising given the *inconsistency mechanism* that the cognitive developmentalists propose as the means for stage advancement (or growth in principled reasoning). Cognitive dissonance theorists have shown that attitude–behavior inconsistency leads to attitude change only when people perceive that they have freely chosen the counterattitudinal behavior. A similar restriction may operate in moral judgment growth: The inconsistency between students' experiences and their current way of thinking about moral issues may only motivate change in students' way of thinking (growth in principled reasoning) if they feel they have freely chosen their experiences.

This does not necessarily mean that required experiences cannot motivate moral judgment growth. It only means that students must perceive significant choice on their part; they must own the experience and choose to grow from it. Cognitive dissonance researchers have long experience creating experiments in which everyone ends up choosing a counterattitudinal behavior, and yet the participants feel that they have freely chosen the behavior. Perhaps educators can study the approach of such experimentalists in order to design required (or almost required) educational experiences that will be more powerfully educating because students will be able to feel freedom of choice.

Out-of-Class Contact With Professors. A second example of a research issue with important practical and theoretical implications concerns the role of student contact with professors outside of class. Small liberal arts colleges often tout the easy access their students have to professors. Research supports the value of this access. For example, Gaff and Gaff (1981) stated that "the relationships that made the greatest difference in the lives of students extended beyond the classroom [and were] characterized by a good deal of intellectual excitement, and conversations usually ranged beyond the narrow bounds of coursework" (p. 649).

Does such out-of-class contact with professors relate to amount of growth in moral judgment during the 4 years of college? A recent study addressed this question. Students who reported no such contact during their college experience had significantly lower growth in principled reasoning (33.6–38.3; $n = 0.44$) than the very strong growth of those who reported at least some out-of-class contact (33.2–47.5; $d = 1.44$).

From the viewpoint of moral judgment theory, it may be that professors are able to have a strong impact on students' moral judgment growth because of their maturity and expertise relevant to difficult moral issues with which students might be struggling. If this maturity and expertise is available to students in a personal and nonthreatening way, it might help them to choose their own growth more readily than they would through their more normal struggle with the diverse moral considerations the issues raise. This view does not deny the central cognitive-developmental idea that growth in moral judgment takes place through the person's constructing a new and better way of understanding the world morally. In fact, it is consistent with it because the research revealed that people are attracted to (somewhat) higher moral reasoning modeled for them (see the discussion of developmental hierarchy in chap. 1). Gentle and nonauthoritarian interaction between faculty and students out of class may embody the very conditions that will maximize students' moral growth.

Relationships to Other Personal Competencies of College Students.

A third example of a research area that has both practical and theoretical implications is the relationship between moral judgment growth and other whole-person student qualities that colleges claim to enhance. Colleges and universities are now being required by accrediting agencies to specify the student outcomes that they facilitate (e.g., communicating, valuing, problem solving), and many colleges are even designing integrated curriculum programs targeted to particular outcomes. The program at Alverno College, begun 20 years ago, is an excellent example of this approach.

Given the focus on student outcomes, it would seem important to understand how the various dimensions of student outcomes relate to one another. Consider the relationship between moral judgment and college students' sense of self-chosen identity. Burwell, Butman, and Van Wicklin (1992) reported data from Houghton, Messiah, and Wheaton colleges, showing that growth in principled reasoning is correlated with progress in developing one's own sense of identity, the Eriksonian stage of psychosocial development most directly relevant to the traditional college years. Specifically, students who advanced in their ego-identity status (Marcia, 1980) from their freshman to senior years also showed strong growth in principled reasoning (41.2–52.7). In contrast, students who persisted in *identity foreclosure* (an identity they had not made their own through reflective decision making or a period of crisis) showed little developmental advance in principled reasoning (38.4–39.1).

From an applied viewpoint this finding has potential importance. It suggests that students' sense of self-chosen identity may play an important role in their ability to grow in moral judgment. If so, then the whole-person focus of many liberal arts colleges on helping students find themselves (choose their own identity in a reflective way) is an important part of the college's impact on students' moral maturing. From the viewpoint of moral development theory, this finding also has important implications. It suggests that personal qualities that Rest (chap. 1) sees as an important part of Component III (moral motivation) are also important in the growth of Component II (moral judgment). Identifying the linkages between components of morality is an important theoretical elaboration that needs to be done, and this elaboration should in turn bring about a greater practical understanding of how to enhance moral development. Again, however, developing these understandings depends on establishing and maintaining an adequate longitudinal database for use in testing hypotheses. This is a goal to which colleges and universities should be able to wholeheartedly commit themselves.

Departmentally Focused Research

Nursing. Student nurses preparing for the workplace have a particular need to develop a high level of moral judgment, due to the potential consequences of nurses' actions for others. Thus, an effective nursing program should enhance nurses' moral judgment. At Bethel, in a relatively new baccalaureate nursing program, relevant ethical content had been integrated throughout the nursing curriculum, but little had been done to evaluate the actual moral development growth of nursing students. Consequently, a cooperative project with the nursing department was designed to meet this need. In addition to the data already reported, 3 additional cohorts of nursing students took the DIT in their freshman and senior years, and in three years all junior nursing students also took the test, including transfers from other colleges.

Consistent with the results cited earlier in this chapter, students in this study (see McNeel, Schaffer, & Juarez, 1993) showed extremely strong growth in principled reasoning across the 4 college years (35.5–50.8; $d = 1.46$). The data comparing transfers with nontransfers is particularly interesting. Although nontransfers showed as much growth during their first 2 years of college as is typical across 4 years of college (about 12 points), they still showed additional moderate growth during their last 2 years (45.3–51.2; $d = 0.48$), when they were centrally involved in taking nursing courses. This is in contrast to data of Mentkowski and Straight (1983), in which growth during the second 2 years was less strong than that of the first 2 years (students of all majors, not just nursing).

The power of the last 2 years, during which time students were focusing on nursing courses and clinicals, is further supported by the transfer data. Transfers began their junior year significantly behind nontransfers in principled reasoning (36.8 vs. 45.3), but during their nursing education program (in their junior and senior years) they were able to catch up to their nontransfer colleagues (49.5 vs. 51.2). Thus, the transfers showed almost as much growth in principled reasoning during the junior and senior years, when they were taking primarily nursing courses (36.8–49.5; $d = 1.38$), as the nontransfers did during their entire 4 years of college. While these dramatic results cannot be confidently attributed to the nursing program per se, they are certainly suggestive of an effective program.

A final item of interest concerns the correlation between principled reasoning and students' performance in their senior clinical experience (McNeel et al., 1993). Two 2-year cohorts of seniors were examined. In the earlier cohort, there was no significant relationship between principled reasoning and clinical performance. In contrast, in the later cohort, when the program was more fully developed and fine-tuned, the correlation was positive and significant [$r(51) = 0.23$]. This finding replicates the results reported by Sheehan, Husted, Candee, Cook, and Bargen (1980) in a medical school setting and by Duckett and Ryden (chap. 3) on a university nursing program. Although this correlation is not high, it does support the practical importance for nurses of growth in moral judgment.

Business. Recently, a research effort has begun in cooperation with the business department at Bethel College. The need for such an effort became clear when the longitudinal analyses consistently showed that business students had lower (but still moderate) growth profiles in moral judgment across the 4 years of college. These data seemed to support the view in the country at large that there is an ethical crisis in business and in the education of business students, which is at least partly rooted in inadequate cognitive development in the area of morality (e.g., Baxter & Rarick, 1987). This crisis in business ethics has led to calls for enrichment in moral education (e.g., Scott, 1988; Sims & Sims, 1991). The Bethel business department has begun by simply asking how their students are similar to and different from the remainder of students at the college.

The department is answering this question by use of a recent longitudinal moral judgment study. This study used a senior questionnaire that included Davis' (1983) Interpersonal Reactivity Index, a measure of several types of empathy (including *Perspective Taking*—a cognitive component of empathy, and *Empathic Concern*—an affective component of empathy).

Some preliminary results from this project can be cited. First, consistent with the longitudinal results reported earlier, business students had significantly lower growth in principled reasoning than all other majors combined. Second, the seniors' questionnaire showed that the senior business students were significantly lower on *Empathic Concern*, the affective component of empathy, although they did not differ on *Perspective Taking*, the cognitive component. Thus, the business students were less likely to say that statements like the following described them well: "I often have tender, concerned feelings for people less fortunate than me" and "When I see someone being taken advantage of, I feel kind of protective toward them."

These results on empathy suggest a possible explanation for the lower growth in moral judgment on the part of business students. Pascarella and Terenzini (1991) suggested that "for most developmental writers, the capacity for empathy with others represents a major determinant of higher level individual development" (p. 46). If this is so, then it is possible that business students less often meet the empathic prerequisites necessary for growth in moral judgment. One implication is that implementing empathy training in a business education program might be an effective way to enhance students' growth in moral judgment. (Empathy training has similarities to the approach of *deliberate psychological education*, which emphasizes social role taking; see chap. 5 by Sprinthall). This could perhaps be done through courses or components of courses that focus on business as a tool to help meet the needs of the disadvantaged in society. Such an approach would allow students to experience empathy for the unfortunate, without requiring them to give up on the obvious need for a business to make a profit. Given the data already cited on the impact of off-campus learning experiences, the most effective vehicles for this approach might be internships or direct experiences that acquaint students with both the clients and the internal workings of effective business ventures of this type. For example, business students could be taken to Mississippi to help rural woodcutters organize cooperatively owned businesses to enhance their bargaining power and thus their ability to earn a wage that could support a family.[2]

Course Interventions: Penn's Direct Approach

A wide range of educational programs and interventions have shown that peer discussion of controversial moral dilemmas facilitates modest growth in moral judgment (Rest, 1986, chap. 3). Dilemma discussion gives people practice in moral problem solving and provides the opportunity for individuals to discover, understand, and appreciate higher level moral arguments from their peers, leading to growth in moral judgment.

However, Penn (1990) argued that there is a more effective and powerful way to enhance moral judgment than by requiring people to discover completely for themselves the power of principled moral thinking. We don't require people to discover calculus for themselves, he argued. Instead, we teach them the concepts. Why wouldn't it also be more effective and efficient to directly teach the component skills of moral judgment, for example, skills of logic, role taking, and justice operations (Penn, personal communication, 1990)? Penn's argument is supported by Rest's (1986, chap. 3) review, which showed that dilemma discussion programs are particularly effective when they include exposure to Kohlberg's theory, a condition that more directly teaches justice operations. Penn described a course designed to directly teach the several skills involved in moral judgment, and he cited quasi-experimental data showing that the course has a very powerful effect.

To test the generality of Penn's approach, I designed a general education course for senior students based centrally on his materials (Penn, 1992a, 1992b). This course is one of many that students can select to fill a required senior general education slot. I have taught the course two separate semesters, each time administering the DIT on the first and last days of class. The results from 28 students (McNeel, 1994a) showed that there was a strong growth in principled reasoning (from 41.7–50.6; $d = 0.65$). This modest effect size is very impressive since it is about 80% of the average effect size associated with 4 years of liberal arts college (reported earlier in this chap.), and because it took place in just 3½ months.

Two additional points are important. First, the course appeared to be powerful only for a portion of the students. About one third of the students showed sharp gains in moral judgment, whereas the remainder showed only modest average gains at best. Penn (personal communication, 1991) reported a similar pattern among his students. Second, the gains were much sharper among business and education

---

[2]Thanks to Professor Robert Weaver for this idea, which comes from his consulting experience.

students taking the course than among the remaining students. Average growth among the former was 12.4 points ($d = 0.98$) compared to only 5.9 points among the latter ($d = 0.39$), even though both groups started at the same level of principled reasoning. This is important because, as reported earlier, business and education students were precisely the type of students who did not otherwise grow strongly in moral judgment during college. There remain important questions (e.g., is the result partly a testing effect?), but it seems that Penn's direct approach to teaching principled thinking can work well when used by other teachers and with other populations. And it works well with students who have tended not to grow as sharply during college.

MORAL DEVELOPMENT OF COLLEGE TEACHERS

There has been little systematic research examining the moral judgment level of a wide-ranging sample of college teachers (although there have been studies of public school teachers; see chap. 4). This is a strange lack because it seems reasonable to suppose that teachers' ability to create environments that would facilitate students' growth in moral judgment might be limited by the extent to which teachers themselves were characterized by principled reasoning.

As an initial attempt to remedy this lack of information, McNeel (1994b) administered the DIT to faculty from two Christian liberal arts colleges, who were participating in three faculty workshops on the teaching of ethics across the curriculum, or on enhancing faculty understanding of student development during the college years. Although these faculty members did not constitute a random sample from their colleges, their disciplines were broadly representative of the range of disciplines in liberal arts colleges of this size. Furthermore, there was significant monetary remuneration for participating in each workshop, making it less likely that only those interested in ethics would participate.

The results from 39 faculty showed an average principled reasoning score of 56.1, higher than is typical for college seniors (see McNeel, 1992), equal to that shown by liberal protestant seminarians (55.5), and somewhat below Rest's (1979) *expert* group (65.2) of moral and political philosophy graduate students. Clearly, these faculty should be capable of serving as good models of principled thinking for their students. However, when the faculty group was divided into thirds by level of moral judgment, we find some reason for concern: The lower third showed an average principled reasoning score (37.2), scarcely above that typical of incoming freshmen (McNeel, 1992).

How powerful can a faculty person be as a moral educator if he or she thinks about moral issues at the level of college freshmen? This question strongly suggests the need for follow-up research to discover whether these results are characteristic of Christian liberal arts colleges or of other types of colleges as well. If they are typical, then, given the moral component of the mission of colleges and universi-

2. COLLEGE TEACHING AND STUDENT MORAL DEVELOPMENT 43

ties, a significant faculty development problem may exist for those faculty characterized by low principled reasoning.

Developing Faculty to Develop Students

Research shows that students' moral judgment can be enhanced by various methods of moral education. These methods include dilemma discussion, *deliberate psychological education*, as discussed in chapter 5, and the more direct and targeted approach of Penn (1990). A strength of these methods is that they produce significant increases (or even striking increases, in the case of the Penn approach) in the moral judgment level of students. However, they all have the weakness that they often are implemented as specific courses. This is a weakness because many colleges will be unable to require all students to participate in such tightly targeted moral education experiences; the result is that many students may receive little enrichment in the area of moral education.

An alternative approach is to target the teachers (college professors) rather than the students, and to do so in a way that makes it likely that their courses will become more powerful developmental experiences for their students. One method for doing this is through teaching professors developmental instruction, "the intentional design of courses, classroom pedagogies, and assessment strategies to address the developmental levels of college students in ways that will facilitate maturation" (Nevins & McNeel, 1992, p. 12). An admirable collegewide program of this sort is the curriculum focused on student competencies at Alverno College (Mentkowski & Straight, 1983). However, many colleges may wish to consider interventions that do not involve total reorganization of the college.

At Bethel College, in each of 3 separate years, a year-long faculty development program was implemented that had the objective of introducing faculty to developmental instruction concepts and models that could be used in their classes as they saw fit. The program was titled Scholars Pursuing Educational Competencies To Reach Undergraduate Maturity (SPECTRUM; Lawyer, Nevins, Fauth & Eitel, 1984).[3] Participation in SPECTRUM's summer *intensive phase* workshop and year-long *extensive phase* was voluntary, but faculty were given a substantial stipend for their participation. Faculty in a wide range of disciplines chose to participate, and eventually, well over half of the college faculty participated. During the summer, they studied models of how students develop during the college years (including Kohlberg, Perry, Gilligan, Erikson, King and Kitchener, and Kolb; see Nevins & McNeel, 1992, for details). Whenever possible, we provided data from our own students, including DIT data, to help the faculty see where our students are on these developmental dimensions. In addition, general concepts such as maturational levels, developmental transformations, individual differences (including learning styles), and a balance between challenge and support were

---

[3]This student-focused faculty development program was funded cooperatively by Bethel College and the Bush Foundation.

presented and discussed. Faculty were also given extensive time for folding these models and concepts into their own experience-based understanding of college students. The goal here was to provide conceptual models that were new to them, but at the same time to respect the considerable expertise and understanding that they had developed over years of teaching.

Each faculty participant chose a target course to revise in light of what he or she had learned, and released time was given by the college to carry out the revisions. In addition, faculty met in small groups for support and new ideas as they taught their newly designed target courses. Respect for faculty expertise and choice was implemented throughout: How to apply developmental models to their classrooms was never dictated, nor were faculty directed to focus on facilitating development in moral judgment. Results (Nevins & McNeel, 1992) showed that faculty were very enthusiastic about the program: They "...felt they had grown in appreciating students' developmental differences, seeing students more as individuals, and understanding more clearly why students function as they do, and ...reported more positive attitudes toward developmental instructional models and increased their commitment to facilitating student growth in the classroom." These attitudinal changes continued over at least the next year, and they were associated with "changes in methods, structure, or classroom activities in their target courses" (p. 16).

Did these changes on the part of the faculty relate to student growth in moral reasoning? This question was answered in the affirmative through an unusual quasi-experimental evaluation (McNeel, Nevins, & Engholm, 1992; Nevins & McNeel, 1992). Students were divided up according to the amount of contact they had with SPECTRUM-trained professors, and their growth in DIT principled reasoning across the freshman and sophomore years was compared. Two types of contact were examined separately: contact with SPECTRUM target courses, and contact with SPECTRUM-trained professors in their nontarget courses.

The key results are shown in Fig. 2.1. Students with little contact with SPECTRUM-trained professors in the professors' target courses showed a very low growth profile (average principled reasoning scores of 40.9 and 43.6 at the beginning of the freshman and end of the sophomore years; $d = 0.33$). Those with moderate contact showed sharp growth (36.4 and 49.8; $d = 1.26$), whereas those with high contact showed moderate growth (34.1 and 41.2; $d = 0.67$). Although the high contact group did not grow as sharply as the moderate contact group in principled reasoning, the DIT D-score measure also showed significant growth, suggesting that this group also experienced some developmental advancement in the lower stages. Amount of contact with SPECTRUM-trained professors in the professors' nontarget courses was also related to student growth in principled reasoning during the freshman and sophomore years: Low contact was associated with only moderate growth (36.4–41.6; $d = .44$) and moderate contact was associated with very sharp growth (36.8–51.2; $d = 1.57$).

McNeel et al. (1992) analyzed a number of potential competing explanations for the differential growth profiles in this quasi-experimental design. Possible confounds included ceiling effects, statistical regression, selection of different

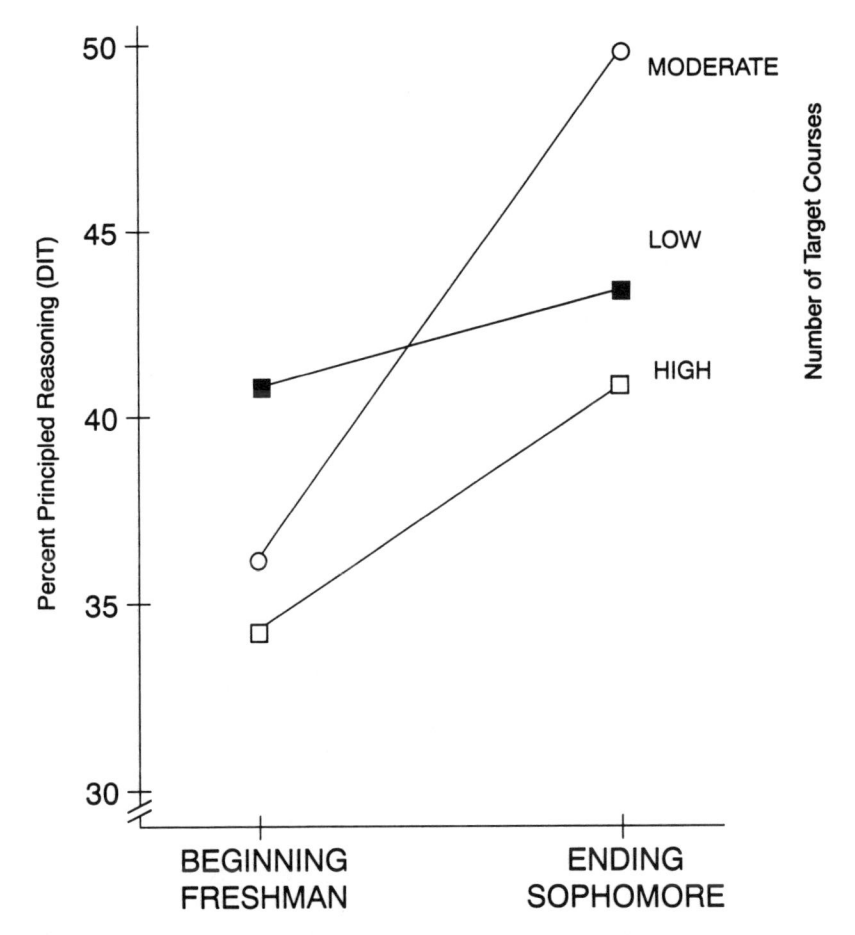

FIG. 2.1. Longitudinal mean principled reasoning as a function of student contact with SPECTRUM faculty development target courses.

students into the various contact groups, a student selection by maturation interaction, and even the possibility that faculty who were better teachers selected themselves into the SPECTRUM program. The best conclusion seemed to be that SPECTRUM faculty development did in fact facilitate growth in student moral reasoning. This program provided a workable and relatively inexpensive way to develop faculty to function as more powerful moral educators.

ASSESSING COLLEGE STUDENTS' MORAL SENSITIVITY

Although it is important to help college students grow in their moral judgment capability, a powerful college education should facilitate growth on all dimensions of morality. However, some of Rest's components of morality (chap. 1) are much less well researched and require the development of adequate measurement instruments. This is true of moral sensitivity, Component I in Rest's Four Component Model. Based on Bebeau's pioneering work (Bebeau, 1985; Bebeau, Rest, & Yamoor, 1985), we constructed an entirely new measure of moral sensitivity for use with college students (McNeel, Frederickson, Talbert, & Lester, 1992). This test focuses directly on students' ability to identify moral issues in dilemmas common to college students. That is, it assesses students' ability of moral perception (rather than the ability of moral judgment), and it does so in contexts familiar and meaningful to college students.

We created four complex and realistic 8–10 minute audio-taped radio dramas in which a variety of ethical issues were embedded. The dramas were based on in-depth interviews with college seniors that identified categories of realistic and meaningful dilemmas they had experienced during their college years. The 4 dramas focused on the following clusters of issues: (a) cheating, learning problems, and racism; (b) pressure for sex, date rape, depression, and codependency; (c) grieving a parent's death, autonomy and identity, career decisions, and parental pressure; and (d) alcohol abuse and its consequences, irresponsibility, and broken trust. These dramas may sound at first like prime-time soap operas—similar to "Beverly Hills 90210"—but they have turned out to be very convincing, effective stimuli.

Students took the test individually by listening carefully to each drama after being given instructions that "We are interested in what you notice and pay attention to." After hearing a given drama, students took the role of the central character's best friend and spoke into a tape recorder as though they were speaking directly to their friend. Nondirective, follow-up probe questions helped the students to express themselves on all the relevant issues they noticed in the situation. Coding manuals have been constructed that allow reliable and valid scoring of transcriptions of the tapes for recognition of various ethical/moral issues (see McNeel et al., 1992, for details).

The project is nearing completion, and sample results illustrate some of the important findings. First, we found a gender difference in moral sensitivity, favoring women, but only on some moral issues. Second, we found that perception of some moral issues was distressingly low, as in the case of recognizing that a date rape had occurred in the pressure-for-sex drama: 58% of the females recognized it, but only 22% of the males (these data were collected in spring 1991). Other findings along this line were that students generally showed insensitivity to the issue of promise keeping, and that a large number did not address the key issue of drinking and driving in the alcohol-abuse drama. Such findings as these are quite important, for they confirm what other evidence suggests, that there are specific areas in which sensitizing and consciousness raising are needed on college campuses (Holmes, 1991).

A final point is that the dramas proved valuable in generating enlightening classroom discussions, as well as in assessing moral sensitivity. An illustration comes from a class discussion that followed the pressure-for-sex drama. Several men felt that the central issue in the drama was that Jack was "being such a jerk" in pressuring Katie to have sex with him when premarital sex was contrary to her personal standards. Although this was certainly an important issue, it was very blatant in the drama; recognizing this issue did not require much sensitivity. Some women in the class argued strongly that the key issue in understanding the whole drama was the fact (less blatant, but still clear) that Katie had earlier been date raped by another student, Pete. They argued that once one perceived this, a whole set of issues in the drama, including evidence that Katie was experiencing significant depression, fell into place. This then made clearer what one's responsibilities (as Katie's best friend) were in the situation and what actions needed to be taken. This perspective seemed new and enlightening to the several men in the class who had focused narrowly on the single issue of pressure for sex. Thus, our experience is that the dramas can be used as effective educational stimuli to help students understand the need for moral sensitivity, and to see more clearly the microskills involved in being morally sensitive in specific situations.

CONCLUSIONS

The research reported in this chapter grows out of the assumption that moral development is a desirable and natural outcome of higher education that has a liberal arts focus. Good stewardship of limited resources suggests that colleges and universities should seek to understand better the conditions that maximize moral development. At Bethel College, we have examined moral development as a function of a variety of aspects of the college environment. The goal was simultaneously practical and theoretical: to understand better how to deliver a more powerful education to our students, both through the formal curriculum and through the broader aspects of college life, and to advance our understanding of the processes of moral development. This work is a case study of the kind of research being conducted in a number of colleges of the Christian College Consortium (for more detail, see Burwell et al., 1992; McNeel, 1994c).[4] Other institutions, especially Bible Colleges and universities (where there is a paucity of data on moral development), are urged to develop action research programs that address important questions concerning the institution's impact on their students' moral development.

REFERENCES

Baxter, G. D., & Rarick, C. A. (1987). Education for the moral development of managers: Kohlberg's stages of moral development and integrative education. *Journal of Business Ethics, 6,* 243–248.

Bebeau, M. J. (1985). Teaching ethics in dentistry. *Journal of Dental Education, 49,* 236–243.

---

[4]This research was sponsored by a grant to the Christian College Consortium from the Pew Charitable Trusts.

Bebeau, M. J., Rest, J. R., & Yamoor, C. M. (1985). Measuring dental students' ethical sensitivity. *Journal of Dental Education, 49*(4), 225–235.
Bok, D. (1988). Responding to the calls for reform. *Currents, 14*(4), 10–15.
Borzak, L. (Ed.). (1981). *Field study: A sourcebook for experiential learning.* Beverly Hills, CA: Sage.
Bowen, H. W. (1977). *Investment in learning: The individual and social value of American higher education.* San Francisco, CA: Jossey-Bass.
Bridges, C., & Priest, R. (1983). *Development of values and moral judgments of West Point cadets* (Report No. USMA–OIR–83–002). West Point, NY: United States Military Academy, Office of Institutional Research.
Buier, R. M., Butman, R. E., Burwell, R., & Van Wicklin, J. (1989). The critical years: Changes in moral and ethical decision making in young adults at three Christian liberal arts colleges. *Journal of Psychology and Christianity, 8*(3), 69–78.
Burwell, R., Butman, R., & Van Wicklin, J. (1992). *Values assessment at three consortium colleges: A longitudinal follow-up study.* Houghton, NY: Houghton College. (ERIC Document Reproduction Service No. ED 345 635)
Christian College Consortium. (1979). *Foundations of Christian higher education.* Arden Hills, MN: Author.
Clouse, B. (1990). Jesus' law of love and Kohlberg's stages of moral reasoning. *Journal of Psychology and Christianity, 9*(3), 5–15.
Davis, M. H. (1983). Measuring individual differences in empathy: Evidence for a multidimensional approach. *Journal of Personality and Social Psychology, 44*(1), 113–126.
Duckett, L., Waithe, M. E., Boyer, M., Schmitz, K., & Ryden, M. (Eds.). (1990). M*CSL building: Developing a strong ethics curriculum in nursing using Multi-Course Sequential Learning.* Minneapolis: University of Minnesota School of Nursing.
Gaff, J. G., & Gaff, S. S. (1981). Student–faculty relationships. In A. W. Chickering & Associates (Eds.), *The modern American college: Responding to the new realities of diverse students and a changing society* (pp. 642–656). San Francisco, CA: Jossey-Bass.
Goodlad, J. I., Soder, R., & Sirotnik, K. A. (1990). *The moral dimensions of teaching.* San Francisco, CA: Jossey-Bass.
Holmes, A. F. (1975). *The idea of a Christian college.* Grand Rapids, MI: Eerdmans.
Holmes, A. F. (1991). *Shaping character: Moral education in the Christian college.* Grand Rapids, MI: Eerdmans.
Jacobs, S. E. (1974). Action and advocacy anthropology. *Human Organization, 33*(2), 209–215.
Kohlberg, L. (1976). Moral stages and moralization: The cognitive-developmental approach. In T. Lickona (Ed.), *Moral development and behavior: Theory, research and social issues* (pp. 31–53). New York: Holt, Rinehart & Winston.
Lawyer, J., Nevins, K. J., Fauth, L., & Eitel, L. (1984). *SPECTRUM: A faculty development program grant reapplication.* St. Paul, MN: Bethel College.
Loxley, J. C., & Whiteley, J. M. (1986). *Character development in college students. Volume II: The curriculum and longitudinal results.* Schenectady, NY: Character Research Press.
Marcia, J. (1980). Identity in adolescence. In J. Adelson (Ed.), *Handbook of adolescent psychology* (pp. 159–188). New York: Wiley.
McNeel, S. P. (1991). Christian liberal arts education and growth in moral judgment. *The Journal of Psychology and Christianity, 10*(4), 311–322.
McNeel, S. P. (1992). *Moral maturing in college.* Manuscript submitted for publication.
McNeel, S. P. (1994a). *Integrating psychology and philosophy in the teaching of ethics: A replication of Penn's direct approach.* Unpublished manuscript, Bethel College, St. Paul, MN.
McNeel, S. P. (1994b). *Moral maturity in Christian college faculty.* Unpublished manuscript, Bethel College, St. Paul, MN.
McNeel, S. P. (1994c). Assessment of dimensions of morality in Christian college students. In D. J. Lee, & G. G. Stronks (Eds.), *Assessment in Christian higher education: Rhetoric and reality.* Lanham, MD: University Press of America.

McNeel, S. P., Nevins, K. J., & Engholm, K. (1992). *Enhancing student moral reasoning through the SPECTRUM faculty development program* (Tech. Rep. No. 17). St. Paul, MN: Bethel College.

McNeel, S. P., Frederickson, J., Talbert, B., & Lester, B. (1992, November 12–14). *Understanding difficult situations: Preliminary report of a moral sensitivity test for college students.* Paper presented at the annual conference of the Association for Moral Education, Toronto.

McNeel, S. P., Schaffer, M., & Juarez, M. (1993). *Growth in moral judgment among baccalaureate nursing students.* Unpublished manuscript, Bethel College, St. Paul, MN.

Mentkowski, M., & Straight, M. J. (1983). *A longitudinal study of student change in cognitive development, learning styles, and generic abilities in an outcome- centered liberal arts curriculum.* Milwaukee, WI: Alverno College, Office of Research and Evaluation. (ERIC Document Reproduction Service, No. ED 239 562)

Nevins, K. J., & McNeel, S. P. (1992). Facilitating student moral development through faculty development. *Moral Education Forum, 17*(4), 12–18.

Nucci, L., & Pascarella, E. (1987). The influence of college on moral development. In J. Smart (Ed.), *Higher education: Handbook of theory and research* (Vol. 3, 271–326). New York: Agathon.

Pascarella, E. T., & Terenzini, P. (1991). *How college affects students: Findings and insights from twenty years of research.* San Francisco, CA: Jossey-Bass.

Penn, W. Y., Jr. (1990). Teaching ethics—A direct approach. *Journal of Moral Education, 19*(2), 124–138.

Penn, W. Y., Jr. (1992a). *A logic primer: Skills for critical reasoning.* Unpublished manuscript, St. Edward's University, Austin, TX.

Penn, W. Y., Jr. (1992b). *Seeds of justice: A study of principled moral reasoning* (3rd ed.). Unpublished manuscript, St. Edward's University, Austin, TX.

Rest, J. R. (1979). *Development in judging moral issues.* Minneapolis: University of Minnesota Press.

Rest, J. R. (1986). *Moral development: Advances in research and theory.* New York: Praeger.

Sandin, R. T. (1989). *Values and collegiate study.* Atlanta, GA: Mercer University.

Scott, W. G. (1988). Profit at any price: The moral failure of business schools. In J. R. Schermerhorn, J. G., Hunt & R. N. Osborn (Eds.), *Managing organizational behavior.* New York: Wiley.

Shaver, D. G. (1985). A longitudinal study of moral development at a conservative religious liberal arts college. *Journal of College Student Personnel, 26,* 400–404

Shaver, D. G. (1987). Moral development of students attending a Christian, liberal arts college and a Bible college. *Journal of College Student Personnel, 28,* 211–218.

Sheehan, T. J., Husted, S. D., Candee, D., Cook, C. D., & Bargen, M. (1980). Moral judgment as a predictor of clinical performance. *Evaluation and the Health Professions, 3,* 393–404.

Sims, R. R., & Sims, S. J. (1991). Increasing applied business ethics courses in business school curricula. *Journal of Business Ethics, 10,* 211–219.

Sloan, D. (1980). The teaching of ethics in the American undergraduate curriculum, 1876–1976. In D. Callahan & S. Bok (Eds.), *The teaching of ethics.* New York: Plenum Press.

Tax, S. (1975). Action anthropology. *Current Anthropology, 16*(4), 514–517.

Chapter 3

Education for Ethical Nursing Practice

Laura J. Duckett
Muriel B. Ryden
School of Nursing, University of Minnesota

THE NEED FOR ETHICS EDUCATION IN NURSING (Issues, Issues Everywhere)

Advances in technology and the growing complexity of the health-care delivery system present nurses with recurrent situations that pose ethical problems. Breakthroughs such as organ transplantation occur in medical treatment; epidemics such as AIDS and teenage pregnancy continue; exposures to clients who lack access to health care arouse troubling concerns about justice; and pressures for cost containment require difficult decisions regarding allocation of resources. The wrenching ethical decisions brought about by these trends add to the ethical issues nurses historically have faced in their day-to-day care of patients. Since the founding of modern nursing by Florence Nightingale in the mid-1800s, nurses have been instructed to undergird their practice with strong moral values. To help overcome the Sairey Gamp image of the venal, drunken women who "nursed" the sick, as described by Charles Dickens in *Martin Chuzzlewit* (Cook, 1913), Nightingale carefully selected Protestant deaconesses, Catholic sisters, and a few "ladies" to take with her to the Crimean War zone. Having been well educated in classical studies, she believed that intelligence, education, and strength of character were essential ingredients for the professional practice of nursing (Barritt, 1973). These characteristics remain critical for nursing practice today.

Situations That Require Ethical Decisions

Situations with ethical implications that nurses confront fall into at least three categories. First are situations in which moral principles and compassion for clients provide unequivocal direction as to the course of action that should be taken. For example, a psychiatric nurse–practitioner clearly is obligated not to exploit a patient being counseled in order to meet the nurse's own sexual needs.

A second type of situation, is one in which a group of expert nurses and moral philosophers might readily agree on an ethical course of action, whereas the student or novice nurse might be confused by seemingly conflicting principles and loyalties. In these cases, the experts would maintain that one principle clearly supersedes the other in importance. For instance, when students are presented with the case example of a nurse whose friend co-worker consistently comes to work under the influence of alcohol, some students suggest alternatives that give precedence to the principle of loyalty (as they define it) to the friend. They try to find ways of protecting patients without getting the friend in trouble. Some students fail to recognize that protecting the friend from experiencing the consequences of the unhealthy and unsafe behavior enables the behavior to continue, places the immediate well-being of the friend (avoiding sanctions) above long-term well-being (treatment and recovery), and threatens the safety of current and future patients of this nurse.

The third type of situation presents a true dilemma to the ethicist and to the highly ethical practitioner. In such a situation, in which two or more ethical standards are clearly relevant, a panel of expert clinicians and moral philosophers might disagree as to which of the competing standards should take precedence. An exemplar is the case of Hilda Wanglie, whose family insisted on continued aggressive life-prolonging treatment that most health-care providers considered to be futile. Here client/family autonomy, best-interest standards, and stewardship of resources competed for precedence.

Documents such as the Florence Nightingale Pledge and early versions of the American Nurses Association Code illustrate the historic importance of ethics to nursing practice and reflect efforts to guide the practice of nursing in its apprenticeship era. Ethical practice during this period was characterized by loyalty and obedience to physicians and hospital administrators. With the development of nursing as a discipline with a growing body of knowledge on which to base professional practice, nurses were faced with the need to develop skills in both autonomous and collaborative ethical decision making and a code that would guide this professional practice.

Preparing Students for Ethical Decision Making

How best to prepare nursing students for ethical decision making and action has been problematic for nursing educators. At the same time that the need for improved ethics education was becoming more pronounced, many baccalaureate nursing programs replaced curricula that had been based on the medical model (e.g., units

3. EDUCATION FOR ETHICAL NURSING PRACTICE

on medicine, surgery, pediatrics) with integrated curricula organized around key concepts central to professional nursing practice (e.g., health, chronicity, pain, and loss). Although this has led to a more holistic way of viewing clients and their nursing care, it has produced some gaps and overlaps in content areas in curricula (Dison, 1985). One such gap repeatedly identified by nurses and moral philosophers is ethics (Aroskar, 1977; Benoleil, 1983; Bindler, 1977; Evers, 1984; Muyskens, 1982; Purtilo & Cassel, 1981; Steinfels, 1977).

The importance of systematically including ethics in nursing curricula and the rich opportunities for teaching and learning about ethics that are inherent in the student experience were documented by Dison (1985). She interviewed 32 baccalaureate nursing students from 5 midwestern states and 26 new graduates, who had completed nursing programs in 8 states, to determine the recurring ethical dilemmas experienced by nursing students. Using a questionnaire based on 25 dilemmas identified by these students and recent graduates, Dison surveyed 995 senior students from 96 baccalaureate nursing programs in 42 states. Respondents were asked to rate the importance of each dilemma, the frequency with which the issue had been experienced, and the context in which the student had become aware of the issue. Her findings clearly identified the variety and prevalence of ethical issues encountered by nursing students.

ETHICS IN NURSING CAN BE TAUGHT AND LEARNED (Faculty Can Lead Students to the Fountain of Knowledge and Help Them to Drink)

The nature of nursing practice, which affects the health and well-being of others, challenges nursing educators to prepare graduates who are morally sensitive and ethically literate. Rest (1988b) asserted that "although there may be important precursors to adult ethical behavior, and although there may be important characterological dispositions that already need to be established in professionals before age 20, nevertheless, to function ethically in professional situations requires special education and preparation" (p. 25).

What Should be Learned?

There are several different aspects of ethics that can be learned. Ethical knowledge has been identified as one of four fundamental ways of knowing in nursing (Carper, 1978). The other three are empirics, the science of nursing; esthetics, the art of nursing; and personal knowledge. Although most nursing curricula reflect an emphasis on the body of *scientific* knowledge, Carper pointed out that an ethical pattern of knowing required an understanding of a body of *moral* knowledge. Such a body of knowledge can be taught. Nursing students need not be expected to complete a full program in moral philosophy. However, knowledge of the best-known and most influential moral theories, and the principles and values those theories embody, is essential for providing students with formal grounding for making ethical decisions in their professional practice. This also gives them a language for communicating about ethical issues with professional colleagues.

In addition to learning a body of moral knowledge, students must also learn to think critically (Jones & Brown, 1991). Students' skills in critical thinking about clinical problems can be foundational for the process of moral reasoning about the ethical aspects of health care. Educators agree that moral theories can be learned and critical thinking skills can be further enhanced.

The third and perhaps most important aspect of ethics that can be learned is an enhanced awareness of circumstances in which values, duties, rights, principles, and/or needs are in conflict. Educators can build on already developed sensitivities to the rights and values of others through discussion of case studies and real clinical situations that students have encountered. Faculty can help students increase their awareness of the ethical implications of situations about which they may have only an undefined, gut-level sense of discomfort. Faculty can also provide insights into nursing situations in which students are completely unaware of the existence of conflicting values or violations of principles, such as justice and autonomy.

Although moral knowledge, critical thinking, and perceptiveness are all essential for ethical practice, they may not be sufficient. The fourth aspect of ethics that can be learned is how to effectively implement a moral decision. For example, skill developed in interpersonal communication, assertiveness, and conflict resolution can greatly facilitate moral action.

Ethics education in nursing is possible for students whose prior development has been such that they are capable of normal moral emotions such as empathy, care, concern, and love. Moral theory can be learned; sensitivity and reasoning skills can be enhanced; and effective ways of implementing moral choices can be mastered.

Common Curricular Approaches to Ethics Education in Nursing (Different Strokes for Different Folks)

Ethics education in the health professions has tended to follow one of three basic models: (a) a discrete ethics course offered by a philosophy or theology department as a requirement or an elective; (b) a discrete ethics course within the discipline as a requirement or an elective; or (c) ethics content integrated into one or more core courses. All of these approaches have been problematic to some degree. We offer an alternative.

Discrete Courses (What Does This Have to do With Being a Nurse?).
Courses taught by philosophers or theologians, whether within other departments or within nursing, tend to be very abstract. Often they do not include specific,

3. EDUCATION FOR ETHICAL NURSING PRACTICE

realistic applications to nursing. What is gained in terms of a broad, liberal education in moral philosophy is offset by a loss of perceived relevance to the immediate student experience. When an ethics course is developed for health sciences students, it is often taught by a philosopher who lacks intimate knowledge about the ethical problems students face on a daily basis. If nursing classes and clinical seminars do not provide linkages to such an ethics course, students may not be able to transfer and apply the moral knowledge they have gained.

Integration (It's Supposed to Be Here Somewhere, but I Can't Find It).
Some schools employ the third model, integration, with ethics included in various courses in the curriculum. This approach has potential value, but can be fraught with hazards. For example, many nursing faculty are not prepared to teach ethics. Occasional guest lecturers may provide fragmented aspects of the domain of moral knowledge. The inclusion of ethics content may depend on the degree of faculty interest in teaching the course. Faculty members with their own agendas of vital content may not find time to include ethics in more than a token way. If no coordination exists among courses, some content may be duplicated, while other important areas remain untouched. If integration means that ethics teaching is everyone's responsibility, it may end up being no one's responsibility.

The Multi-Course Sequential Learning Approach (Why Just Sit There When You Can Do Something?)

Because of dissatisfaction with all three of the approaches to the teaching of ethics previously described, a model called Multi-Course Sequential Learning (MCSL) was developed, implemented, and evaluated at the University of Minnesota School of Nursing with support from a 3-year grant from the Fund for the Improvement of Postsecondary Education (FIPSE), U.S. Department of Education. MCSL is a curricular approach that weaves an identifiable strand of content—in this case, ethics—throughout a curriculum by including the content in a vertical course, with units embedded in existing courses across various levels of a program. A carefully constructed MCSL (pronounced "muscle") provides a strong content fiber running through the curriculum. Important characteristics of a MCSL include the following:

1. The content domain is precisely identified.
2. The content is carefully sequenced from course to course in the various levels of the program so as to provide a good fit with student development and to build on previous learning, while preventing omissions and undesirable duplication.
3. The course is given visibility as an entity.
4. Student learning in the MCSL is specifically evaluated, based on achievement of stipulated objectives.
5. A defined group of faculty is given responsibility and accountability for the MCSL.

This model is described more fully in prior publications (Duckett et al., 1990; Duckett, Waithe, Boyer, Schmitz, & Ryden, 1993; Ryden, Duckett, Crisham, Caplan, & Schmitz, 1989).

In addition to core content units in selected courses throughout the curriculum, augmentation content contributes to the Ethics MCSL. *Augmentation* is defined as enlarging, extending, or enhancing. Prior analysis of the curriculum had revealed that certain content related to ethics was an integral part of many courses, although it was not identified as such. Augmentation involves accentuating the ethical aspects of existing content so that these aspects are not lost to students, who are not yet able to transfer and apply concepts without faculty assistance. The Ethics MCSL at the University of Minnesota, with the combination of core units and augmentation, provides the equivalent of a traditional 4-quarter credit course.

Who Should Teach Ethics to Nursing Students? (Not Everyone Can Teach All of It but Everyone Can Help)

The question of the qualifications for teaching ethics to nursing students is a concern of both nurses and philosophers (Aroskar, 1977; Rosen & Caplan, 1980). Expert knowledge of moral philosophy and of nursing is desirable, but not often found in one individual. At a minimum, expertise in one discipline and conversant familiarity with, and respect for, the discipline in which one lacks expertise is needed. A crossdisciplinary effort can provide the best of both worlds, and some schools of nursing have at least one nursing faculty member who has a special interest in nursing ethics and has completed a degree or minor in biomedical ethics or philosophy.

At the University of Minnesota School of Nursing, we have developed several types of faculty roles for implementing the Ethics MCSL. The first could be thought of as the *person(s) responsible and accountable for the Ethics MCSL;* this role is currently enacted by the authors. We are regularly assigned teaching responsibility for the MCSL, which includes coordinating with faculty assigned to teach specific courses in the curriculum to ensure that the Ethics MCSL units are implemented effectively according to a master plan.

The role of *cross-disciplinary guest expert* has been used very successfully in implementing the Ethics MCSL. In our university setting, we have access to colleagues who are philosophers to teach the unit dealing with ethical theory, and colleagues with expertise in the clinical application of biomedical ethics to teach units such as aggressive versus limited treatment. In each case in which a colleague from another discipline has been involved, it has been to help implement a specific planned piece of the Ethics MCSL. Therefore, these classes taught by guests are part of a coherent whole, not disconnected fragments.

Faculty members teaching in specific courses play additional important roles in teaching the Ethics MCSL. They serve as *reinforcers* of ethics content when they refer back to the Ethics MCSL unit as they teach subsequent units in the course.

They also serve as *advisors* to the ethics faculty, helping to keep the Ethics MCSL well-connected to the courses in the curriculum and to the students' day-to-day experiences. When these advisors, or the ethics faculty, determine that changes are needed, revisions are made to units in the Ethics MCSL. However, the effects of changes on the entire Ethics MCSL must be considered when modifications are made in any one unit.

The last role, and perhaps the most important one, if ethical knowledge is to lead to ethical professional practice, is that played by the clinical teacher. This person is the *facilitator* who helps students apply ethical knowledge to their day-to-day clinical experiences. An effective approach to assist clinical faculty in the role of facilitator is to co-lead a clinical conference with one of the ethics faculty. The ethics faculty member knows exactly what the students have learned about ethics in the classroom during the current and previous quarters, and the clinical instructor serves as the expert who has knowledge about the clinical setting and the clients that is essential for good ethical decision making and action. A description of strategies used for classroom sessions and clinical conferences can be found in a handbook (Duckett et al., 1993) and in a series of journal articles (Pederson, Duckett, Maruyama, & Ryden, 1990; Ryden, Waithe, Crisham, Caplan, & Duckett, 1989; Waithe, Duckett, Schmitz, Crisham, & Ryden, 1989).

Helping Faculty Prepare to Assume the Various Roles in Teaching Ethics (I Know It's Important and I Would if I Could)

For many of us who did not study ethics as a part of our formal education, it is a personal responsibility and a challenge to find ways to increase our knowledge and skill in this important domain. As part of the Ethics Education Project at the University of Minnesota, the project staff conducted annual workshops for nursing faculty. At these workshops, faculty members were given current information about the development and implementation of the Ethics MCSL, an approach they had formally approved before the FIPSE grant was submitted. To further their own knowledge development in ethics and to inform themselves about what students were learning in the Ethics MCSL, faculty participated in abbreviated versions of some of the Ethics MCSL classroom and clinical conference activities and were given overviews of others. Small groups of faculty identified ethical problems encountered in various clinical settings and developed paradigm cases for use in clinical conferences (Waithe et al., 1989). They also developed specific plans for using the paradigm cases during clinical conferences.

During the final year of external funding, a representative group of nursing faculty participated in a national conference, "The Care–Justice Puzzle: Education for Ethical Nursing Practice," held at the University of Minnesota. This provided an opportunity to discuss ethics education with nursing faculty from 26 states and Canada.

Educators who are interested in strengthening ethics within their curriculum may find it helpful to determine how faculty in their school or department perceive their own knowledge and comfort level regarding ethics. We found that a simple survey provided us with valuable information for use in planning faculty development workshops (Duckett et al., 1993).

The Theoretical Underpinnings for Ethics in Nursing (The Intersection of Moral Philosophy, Developmental Psychology, and Nursing)

The emerging discipline of nursing has been focused to a great extent on a scientific way of knowing, but the profession of nursing has long been characterized by caring practitioners (Leininger, 1990). Nursing scholars are struggling to define the ethic of nursing. Activities of nurse researchers in the area of ethics have been reviewed by Gortner (1985), Ketefian and Ormond (1988), and Ketefian (1989). Ethics in nursing can be viewed as the intersection of three overlapping disciplines: nursing, philosophy, and moral psychology.

The discipline of moral philosophy encompasses knowledge about the most powerful ethical theories of Western and non-Western civilizations. Although individuals and communities may be greatly influenced by particular theologies, the ethical theories that are foundational for ethics education in public institutions in our pluralistic society are philosophical rather than theological in nature. The particular philosophical stance upon which U.S. social structure is founded is one that is tolerant of individuals whose moral convictions may come from a variety of theological traditions.

The discipline of moral psychology is the second domain from which nursing draws. Whereas moral philosophy is prescriptive (i.e., the science of what a person ought to do, morally speaking), moral psychology is descriptive (i.e., the science of what happens and how when people engage in moral reasoning and take moral action). Within the field of psychology, moral psychology has been studied from various theoretical perspectives, particularly from the social learning and cognitive developmental perspectives.

MORAL REASONING IN NURSES AND NURSING STUDENTS

Studies: What Conclusions are Valid?

Drawing on moral psychology, a number of nursing researchers have studied the development of moral reasoning in nurses (e.g., Crisham, 1981a; Felton & Parsons, 1987; Gaul, 1987; Ketefian, 1981, 1989; Ketefian & Ormond, 1988; Mayberry, 1986). In these studies, moral reasoning has been measured primarily by the

Defining Issues Test (DIT) developed by Rest (1979), or the Nursing Dilemmas Test (NDT), developed by Crisham (1981b) to parallel the DIT. The contributions and limitations of the NDT, and selected published studies that used it, are discussed by Ketefian and Ormond (1988).

A review of studies of nurses' moral reasoning and issues related to using the DIT with nurses was published recently (Duckett et al., 1992). The article was written to address inaccuracies and misperceptions about measures of moral reasoning and the previously published moral reasoning scores of nurses. The purposes were to (a) clarify information about the DIT that is critical for researchers who use the instrument; (b) critique research and other literature dealing with the moral reasoning of nurses and nursing students; and (c) compare the DIT scores for nurses and nursing students reported by other researchers with normative data. The authors concluded that

1. There is a need for greater scientific rigor in studies of moral reasoning among nurses.
2. There is a need for greater accuracy in interpreting and reporting moral reasoning scores.
3. Moral reasoning of nurses, like that of other groups previously tested, tends to increase with more formal education.
4. Nurses' scores are usually equal to, and sometimes higher than, scores of other groups with similar academic credentials.

The Tension Between Proponents of the Care and Justice Traditions (Must We Take Sides?)

In a movement away from a focus on justice-based moral reasoning, some nurses have joined feminists in challenging the relevance of the work of Kohlberg and Rest to women. Drawing on the work of Gilligan (1982a, 1982b) and Noddings (1984), nursing scholars who espoused an ethic of caring as primary to nursing viewed it as subjective, feminine, and connected—a way of counteracting the justice ethic, which they viewed as medical, masculine, objectifying, and distancing (Watson, 1988). According to Watson, the field of nursing ethics is now commonly referred to as the "Ethics of Caring." Benner and Wrubel (1989) argued that caring as a moral art is primary for nursing practice.

The need for nursing to utilize scientific and ethical theorizing to bring about change in practice was asserted by Beckstrand (1978). In her discussion of the development of nursing ethics as a field of inquiry, Fry (1989) pointed out that Beckstrand's argument for the use of scientific theory in nursing has been accepted widely, but no formal theories of ethics for nursing practice have been developed. Fry considered the value foundations of nursing ethics to be derived from the nature of the nurse–patient relationship, and asserted that the value of caring ought to be central to any theory of nursing ethics, and that such a theory need not endorse typical frameworks of justification that are characteristic of theories of biomedical ethics. More recently, a middle-range theory of caring was empirically developed by Swanson (1991) from phenomenological studies in three perinatal contexts. The theory delineated five caring processes: *knowing, being with, doing for, enabling,* and *maintaining belief.*

An integrative theory of nursing ethics that synthesizes caring and justice has yet to be developed. In today's highly technical health-care system, there seems to be general agreement that nurses must be rational, logical thinkers who can critically apply scientific knowledge in practice. There also seems to be consensus that human caring is the essence of nursing's historical legacy. We need to consider whether there is merit in limiting rational objectivity to the scientific way of knowing in nursing, or whether an ethical way of knowing can incorporate both the tradition of justice that draws on long-established modes of moral reasoning, as well as nursing's tradition of caring.

Integrating Caring and Justice in Education for Ethical Nursing Practice (Putting Them Together Makes Our Practice Whole)

Although development of skill in making moral judgments is heavily emphasized in the ethics education literature, we believe that the ultimate outcome of ethics education of nurses should be moral behavior. A breadth of perspective that places moral reasoning alongside other important moral processes is depicted in Table 1.7 by Rest's (1982, 1984, 1986) Four Component Model of moral action. Within this framework, both justice and caring can be viewed as central to ethical action (Rest, 1990). In chapter 1, Rest describes the four components necessary for moral action. The following discussion of these components highlights the interrelationships with caring.

Moral Sensitivity. In making an interpretation of the particular situation in which there is a moral problem, persons who have empathy and can take the perspective of others, and who care for others—even people who are quite different from themselves—are likely to exhibit high levels of moral sensitivity. Perspective taking, empathy, and genuineness have been taught and practiced in interpersonal relationship courses in baccalaureate nursing programs for many years. Students also learn through role playing and actual clinical experiences that a caring approach is what makes the other techniques really work in the real world. In the Ethics MCSL curriculum, these aspects of the two interpersonal communications courses are considered to be augmentation for the Ethics MCSL units in other courses.

Moral Reasoning. A person must be able to reason about a situation and make a judgment about which course of action is morally right, thus labeling one possible line of action as what ought morally to be done in that situation. According to Kohlberg (1976) and Rest (1979, 1986), as people advance to Stages 5 and 6 of moral reasoning, they use ethical principles, especially the principle of justice, to weigh conflicts among stakeholders' claims. Reasoning that takes relationships and contextual considerations into account is a strength of the caring tradition. The ability to use principled thinking to consider what is right for persons other than those with whom one is in a caring relationship is a strength of the justice tradition.

Moral Commitment or Motivation. A person must give priority to moral values above other competing values so that the person intends to do what is, in his or her judgment, morally right. Both a strong desire to do what is most morally defensible and a strong caring for other humans may be necessary in order for a professional person to put aside a possible action that would serve self-interest in favor of the most ethical alternative action. For instance, there will be times when a nurse perceives, accurately or not, that taking the most morally defensible action will bring her into conflict with a hospital or nursing administrator, a more experienced nursing colleague, or a physician, in such a way that her job security could be threatened. Will she be able to take the moral action despite the perceived threat?

Moral Character. In nursing students, as in other populations, there is likely to be diversity in what Rest describes in chapter 1 as moral character (e.g., ego strength, perseverance, toughness, strength of conviction, and courage). Many past experiences from infancy onward no doubt influence the development of moral character. Can the professional education process also be influential, or is it too late by the time students are in professional school? Experience suggests that there is probably some threshold level of moral character that a beginning nursing student must possess in order to further develop these attributes during professional education, but there are no empirical data to shed light on this speculation. From observations of students participating in the Ethics MCSL, it appears that engaging students in discussions with other students and faculty who clearly exhibit these attributes provides the students who have less courage, ego-strength, toughness, and perseverance, with positive role models whom they may attempt to emulate.

Implementing the Moral Decision (a Fifth Component). Rest describes the preceding four components as psychological processes that must occur in order for moral behavior to occur. Our work with nursing students suggests that another component is also essential. However, this fifth component involves interpersonal processes, rather than purely psychological processes. Individuals must execute the moral decisions to which they have committed. Implementing a moral decision could be done in a rational, but cool, distant, or autocratic manner. Or, moral action could be taken in a manner that illustrates interpersonal warmth, empathy, compassion, and connectedness. Assertive communication, or conflict-resolution techniques that may be needed to accomplish the moral act, will be more successful if the communication is also calm, caring, and respectful. Skillful implementation of moral decisions increases the probability that the underlying moral objective will be accomplished.

These five components—moral sensitivity, moral reasoning, moral commitment/motivation, moral character, and interpersonal implementation skills—have been used as a guide to structuring the content domains within the Ethics MCSL. The whole model is introduced to the students in the first core course in the nursing curriculum. They are encouraged to view the components as highly interrelated, and not representing a strictly linear process. However, because moral sensitivity seems conceptually prerequisite to moral action, primary goals for entering students are development or enhancement of moral sensitivity and skill in moral reasoning. Learning experiences in the senior year continue the focus on those two components, but, in addition, challenge students to develop commitment, character, and interpersonal implementation skills. Specific teaching–learning strategies and client situations used in conjunction with the Rest model have been published elsewhere (Duckett et al., 1993; Waithe et al., 1989).

Student Gains in Moral Reasoning (Show Me That It Works!)

As part of an overall effort to assess curricular outcomes of students in the undergraduate program at the University of Minnesota School of Nursing, all students entering since fall 1987 have been given a pretest of moral reasoning (the DIT), and those who have graduated, to date, have been posttested. The groups admitted to the program prior to fall 1989 entered as sophomores. Beginning fall 1989, students entered the revised upper division baccalaureate program as juniors. All of these students participated in the Ethics MCSL, described elsewhere (Duckett et al., 1993, 1990; Ryden et al., 1989). Students took the entry DIT during orientation or scheduled class time, and the exit DIT during scheduled class time.

Table 3.1 includes longitudinal DIT data for four groups of students. Groups A and B entered the nursing program as sophomores; and Groups C and D entered as juniors. All students who took both the entry and exit DIT, and who had valid scores on both, were included in the table. Very few students have failed to take the entry DIT tests, but larger numbers have been absent from class when the exit tests were given. In the cases in which students were absent at the time they were to be tested, reasonable efforts were made to administer the tests at a slightly later date; however, there were no penalties for the students who never completed the tests. The tests were sent to Rest (1988a) for scoring; a student's data set had to pass all of the checks built into the computerized scoring program in order to yield a score that was considered valid. For three of the four subgroups, significant gains occurred in DIT scores between entry and exit tests.

The finding that three of the four groups showed significant growth in moral reasoning from entry to exit assessment is encouraging. It is not possible, however, to conclude whether the significant changes in DIT P% mean scores should be attributed to additional experiences in college, to the undergraduate nursing curriculum in general, to the ethics curriculum, or to a combination of all three. Rest (1979) presented evidence that intellectual milieu is associated with moral judg-

3. EDUCATION FOR ETHICAL NURSING PRACTICE

TABLE 3.1
Defining Issues Test (DIT) P% Scores from Four Groups of Baccalaureate Nursing Students: Longitudinal Data

Group	A	B	C	D
Entry Test Date	Fall 1987	Winter 1988	Fall 1989	Fall 1990
Entry DIT P%:				
$\bar{x}$	46.6	41.8	43.4	46.0
SD	13.9	12.2	13.8	12.2
Range	20–72	17–62	13–75	23–73
Exit DIT P%:				
$\bar{x}$	53.2	43.7	51.1	50.3
SD	16.6	12.7	12.9	14.5
Range	17–87	25–70	22–77	17–82
n[a]	32	27	48	48
t test[b]	4.08	.84	4.42	2.31
p value	.0003	.41	.0001	.0260

[a]The number reported is the number of students who had both a valid entry P% score and a valid exit P% score.
[b]Comparison of entry mean P% scores with exit mean P% scores using a paired t test.

ment, and suggested that moral judgment differences may be interpreted in terms of enriched versus impoverished environments. The Ethics MCSL and, to some degree, the previous nursing curriculum, included learning activities that have been suggested as experiences that foster moral development. These students were exposed to ethics content and were encouraged to examine their views and allow their perspective to be challenged by others. According to Rest, this process leads to more complex and advanced thinking, that is, higher principled reasoning scores.

Group B, the one group of students who did not show significant change from entry to exit DIT testing, is an interesting and somewhat atypical group. They had the lowest entry DIT P% mean score, and the lowest exit mean score. This group was the last to be admitted as sophomores prior to the implementation of the undergraduate program curriculum revision. They were admitted at a time when the number of applicants to the program had reached the lowest point in many years. There were 8 students in the entry group who had valid pretests, but were lost to longitudinal follow-up, 6 of whom left the program, and 2 of whom had invalid posttests. It is noteworthy that the six who left without graduating had a mean entry DIT score of 48.2, which was higher than the 41.8 mean of the total group.

The exit scores, except for the one atypical group, are above the norm for college students (42.3–45.9, depending on the sample) and below the norm for graduate students (53.3–63.0) reported by Rest (1988a). Our students were all graduating seniors at the time they took the exit tests; therefore, they had experienced at least 4 years of college, the entire nursing curriculum, and the entire Ethics MCSL.

A full-length manuscript in progress includes details about the DIT data and relationships between the DIT scores and other variables, such as credits earned prior to graduation, age, and other standardized test scores. Work in progress also includes examination of predictors of entry and exit DIT scores, and exploration of variables associated with particularly high and low DIT scores. The relationship between moral reasoning and clinical performance is described in the next section. Of concern to the authors are students who have low entry DIT scores. Should they be admitted to the program? (Currently the DIT is given only to students already admitted.) If admitted, do they need an intervention that is different and more intense than the regular Ethics MCSL? Of even greater concern to us are students, albeit a small number, who graduate with low DIT scores.

The Relationship Between Moral Reasoning and Clinical Performance (What Is the Bottom Line?)

Of Rest's four components of moral action, the body of knowledge about nurses' moral reasoning, as described in the preceding section, is perhaps the most extensive. However, with respect to ethics, the ultimate concern for both the profession of nursing, as well as the clients for whom nurses care, is not the level of nurses' skill in moral reasoning; it is ethical practice by nurses.

Excellence in clinical performance has always been the hallmark of a good nurse (Krichbaum, Rowan, Duckett, Ryden, & Savik, 1994). We were stimulated to explore the link between moral reasoning and the clinical practices of our students by a study in which the relationship between the moral reasoning of pediatric residents and their clinical performance was examined (Sheehan, Husted, Candee, Cook, & Bargen, 1980). The study compared medical faculty ratings of the clinical performance of residents with the residents' DIT scores. The investigators found that the moral reasoning ability of 244 pediatric residents was a predictor of their clinical performance. The authors concluded that high moral reasoning virtually excludes the possibility of poor clinical performance, and that the very highest level of clinical performance is rarely achieved by those at the lowest level of moral thought.

The process used to assess students' moral reasoning scores upon entrance into our program was described earlier. We also obtained faculty ratings of the clinical performance of students who comprised the last class to enter the program as sophomores. Ratings were requested from the clinical teachers in seven practica in the junior and senior years. Clinical performance was measured using the Clinical Evaluation Tool (CET), an instrument developed to assess students' clinical performance across settings at various levels of the program. The reliability and validity of the CET is described by Krichbaum et al. (1994). The average CET scores for both the junior and senior years were computed. Then an average score was determined for the combined junior- and senior- year ratings.

Other variables included as candidates for prediction of clinical performance were age at admission; prior number of credits; scores on the ACT, an instrument widely used to assess academic aptitude; grade point average (GPA) on admission; and scores on an ethical theory test taken during the second quarter of the program. Of the 85 students completing the DIT at admission, a complete data set was available for 48. Attrition was due to students leaving the program ($n = 17$), invalid moral reasoning scores ($n = 5$); and missing CET ratings ($n = 15$). No significant differences were found between the group on whom complete data were available and those with missing data on any of the following variables: age at admission, admission GPA, number of credits prior to entry, and ACT composite scores.

The zero order correlations between the variables are shown in Table 3.2. All the variables were found to have a significant positive association with the mean of the combined junior and senior CET score. Because this combined score was derived from a linear combination of the junior and senior mean CET scores, the high correlations between the various CET scores is to be expected. Similarly, it is logical that the number of credits at entry would be highly correlated with age at admission. The DIT P% score at entry and age at admission are the variables most strongly associated with the combined CET score.

A stepwise multiple linear regression of the mean CET scores for the combined junior and senior years showed that the DIT P% score, which entered at Step 1, accounted for 34% of the variance; age, which entered at Step 2, accounted for an additional 12%. (See Table 3.3.) The other variables did not enter the equation.

These findings support the relationship between moral reasoning and clinical performance that was found by Sheehan et al. (1980). The data also suggest that there are important relationships between age, academic experience, and clinical performance of nursing students. If these findings are replicated with larger, more diverse groups, there might be future implications for the recruitment and admission of students to nursing programs, where performance on academic aptitude tests and/or GPA have been the primary criteria for admission.

Data from subsequent classes in the revised curricula are incomplete. An early look suggests less strong associations between moral reasoning and clinical performance than we found among the 48 students described earlier. This may be due to difficulties in securing a sufficient number of valid CET ratings for each student. Also, teaching in clinical courses now involves more preceptors and temporary clinical faculty, who are not as experienced in teaching and evaluating students as the full-time faculty. Completing the CET for each student is voluntary; some faculty choose not to rate students.

SUMMARY

The recognition within nursing of the importance of ethics to professional practice, and the belief that aspects of ethics can be learned, have led to various approaches to ethics education. Preparation for ethical practice (moral action by nurses) can include a synthesis of nursing's tradition of care, moral sensitivity, moral reasoning based on the justice tradition, and moral commitment. Evaluation of progress in moral reasoning in students who experienced ethics education via Multi-Course Sequential Learning showed that three of four groups made significant increases in DIT scores from the point of entry to the point of exit from the program. Examination of the relationship between moral reasoning and clinical performance in a subsample of these students revealed that the DIT was a strong predictor of clinical performance.

TABLE 3.2
Pearson Correlations Among Measures of Clinical Performance and Selected Predictor Variables (*n* = 48)

Variable	1	2	3	4	5	6	7	8	9
1. Age at admission	1.00	***.69	**.33	**.37	.23	.17	**.36	**.39	***.48
2. Credits prior to entry		1.00	.20	**.32	.17	.02	.22	**.40	***.38
3. Admission GPA			1.00	***.42	.20	*.26	.17	*.31	*.29
4. ACT composite score				1.00	***.45	**.34	**.37	*.26	**.42
5. DIT P% score at entry					1.00	.22	***.48	***.42	***.58
6. Ethical theory score						1.00	**.32	.21	**.35
7. Mean Jr. CET[a] score							1.00	.18	***.87
8. Mean Sr. CET score								1.00	***.64
9. Mean Jr./Sr. CET score									1.00

[a]The CET is the Clinical Evaluation Tool. The score equals the sum of the ratings on the 10 items.
*.05 ≥ *p* > .01. **.01 ≥ *p* > .001. ***.001 ≥ *p*.

TABLE 3.3
Summary of Stepwise Multiple Linear Regression of Mean CET Scores for the Junior and Senior Years Combined on the Predictor Set ($n = 48$)

Predictors[a]	$\bar{x}$ CET Score Junior & Senior Years					
	b	se_b	b*	t	prob. t
DIT P% score at entry	.14	.03	.50	4.44	.0001
Age at admission	.29	.09	.36	3.24	.002
Intercept	29.13	2.31			

$R^2 = .46$ adjusted $R^2 = .44$ $F = 19.51$ prob. $F = .00001$

Note. Unstandardized multiple regression coefficient = b. Standardized multiple regression coefficient = b*. All values included in the table are for the final step of the stepwise multiple regression.

[a]Criterion for entry was prob. $t \leq .05$. Values are given for predictor variables that entered the equation. Variables that did not enter the equation were ACT composite score, admission GPA, credits earned prior to entry, and score on the ethical theory test.

ACKNOWLEDGMENTS

We gratefully acknowledge the contributions of P. Crisham, PhD, RN; M. Rowan, PhD, RN; K. Schmitz, MPH, RN; J. Rest, PhD; and M. E. Waithe, PhD to the ideas presented in this chapter. They were collaborators during the Ethics Education Project supported by the Fund for the Improvement of Postsecondary Education (FIPSE) described in this chapter and were coauthors of earlier publications. Without their creative ideas, day-to-day work with students, and contributions to disseminating the work during a series of workshops, there would be much less to share with the readers of this chapter.

REFERENCES

Aroskar, M. A. (1977). Ethics in the nursing curriculum. *Nursing Outlook, 25,* 260–264.
Barritt, E. R. (1973). Florence Nightingale's values and modern nursing education. *Nursing Forum, 12*(1), 6–47.
Beckstrand, J. (1978). The need for a practice theory as indicated by the knowledge used in the conduct of practice. *Research in Nursing and Health, 3,* 175–179.
Benner, P., & Wrubel, J. (1989). *The primacy of caring.* Menlo Park, CA: Addison-Wesley.
Benoliel, J. Q. (1983). Ethics in nursing practice and education. *Nursing Outlook, 31*(4), 210–215.
Bindler, R. (1977). Moral development in nursing education. *Image, 9*(11), 18–20.
Carper, B. (1978). Fundamental patterns of knowing in nursing. *Advances in Nursing Science, 1*(1), 13–23.
Cook, S. E. (1913). *The life of Florence Nightingale* (Vol. 1). London: Macmillan.

Crisham, P. (1981a). *Moral judgment of nurses in hypothetical and nursing dilemmas.* Unpublished doctoral dissertation, University of Minnesota, Minneapolis.

Crisham, P. (1981b). Measuring moral judgment in nursing dilemmas. *Nursing Research, 30*(2), 104–110.

Dison N. (1985). *Dilemmas of baccalaureate nursing students.* Doctoral Dissertation, , University of Minnesota, Minneapolis.

Duckett, L., Boyer, M., Ryden, M., Crisham, P., Savik, K., & Rest, J. (1992). Challenging misperceptions about nurses' moral reasoning. *Nursing Research, 41*(6), 324–331.

Duckett, L., Ryden, M., Waithe, M. E., Schmitz, K., Caplan, A., & Crisham, P. (1990). Ethics education for professional students. *Thought and Action: The NEA Higher Education Journal, 6*(1), 77–84.

Duckett, L., Waithe, M. E., Boyer, M., Schmitz, K., & Ryden, M. (Eds.). (1993). *MCSL building: Developing a strong ethics curriculum in nursing using Multi-Course Sequential Learning* (2nd ed.). Minneapolis: University of Minnesota School of Nursing.

Evers, S. L. (1984, Autumn). Nursing ethics: The central concept of nursing education. *Nurse Educator,* pp. 14–18.

Felton, G. M., & Parsons, M. A. (1987). The impact of nursing education on ethical/moral decision making. *Journal of Nursing Education, 26,* 7–11.

Fry, S. T. (1989). Toward a theory of nursing ethics. *Advances in Nursing Science, 11*(4), 9–22.

Gaul, A. L. (1987). The effect of a course in nursing ethics on the relationship between ethical choice and ethical action in baccalaureate nursing students. *Journal of Nursing Education, 26,* 113–117.

Gilligan, C. (1982a). *In a different voice.* Cambridge, MA: Harvard University Press.

Gilligan, C. (1982b). New maps of development: New visions of maturity. *American Journal of Orthopsychiatry, 52*(2), 199–212.

Gortner, S. R. (1985). Ethical inquiry. In H. H. Werley & J. J. Fitzpatrick (Eds.), *Annual review of nursing research* (pp. 193–214). New York: Springer.

Jones, S. A., & Brown, L. N. (1991). Critical thinking: Impact on nursing education. *Journal of Advanced Nursing, 16,* 529–533.

Ketefian, S. (1981). Moral reasoning and moral behavior among selected groups of practicing nurses. *Nursing Research, 30,* 171–176.

Ketefian, S. (1989). Moral reasoning and ethical practice. In J. Fitzpatrick, R. L. Taunton, & J. Benoliel (Eds.), *Annual review of nursing research* (pp. 173–195). New York: Springer.

Ketefian, S., & Ormond I. (1988). *Moral reasoning and ethical practice in nursing: An integrative review.* New York: National League for Nursing.

Kohlberg, L. (1976). Moral stage and moralization: The cognitive-developmental approach. In T. Lickona (Ed.), *Moral development and behavior: Theory research, and social issues* (pp. 84–107). New York: Holt, Rinehart & Winston.

Krichbaum, K., Rowan, M., Duckett, L., Ryden, M., & Savik, K. (in press). *The Clinical Evaluation Tool: A measure of the quality of clinical performance of baccalaureate nursing students.*

Leininger, M. (1990). Historic and epistemologic dimensions of care and caring with future directions. In J. S. Stevenson & T. Tripp-Reimer (Eds.), *Knowledge about care and caring: State of the art and future developments.* Proceedings of a Wingspread Conference (pp. 19–31). Kansas City, MO: American Academy of Nursing.

Mayberry, M. A. (1986). Ethical decision making: A response of hospital nurses. *Nursing Administration Quarterly, 10*(3), 75–81.

Muyskens, J. L. (1982). *Moral problems in nursing.* Totowa, NJ: Rowan & Littlefield.

Noddings, N. (1984). *Caring: A feminine approach to ethics and moral education.* Berkeley: University of California Press.

Pederson, C., Duckett, L., Maruyama, G., & Ryden, M. (1990). Using structured controversy to promote ethical decision making. *Journal of Nursing Education, 29*(4), 150–157.

Purtillo, R. B., & Cassel, C. K. (1981). *Ethical dimensions in the health professions.* Philadelphia, PA: Saunders.

Rest, J. R. (1979). *Development in judging moral issues.* Minneapolis: University of Minnesota Press.

3. EDUCATION FOR ETHICAL NURSING PRACTICE

Rest, J. R. (1982). A psychologist looks at the teaching of ethics. *Hastings Center Report, 12*(1), 29–36.

Rest, J. R. (1984). The major components of morality. In W. M. Kurtines & J. L. Gewirtz (Eds.), *Morality, moral behavior, and moral development* (pp. 23–38). New York: Wiley.

Rest, J. R. (1986). *Moral development: Advances in research and theory.* New York: Praeger.

Rest, J. (1988a). *DIT manual: Manual for the Defining Issues Test* (Rev. 3rd ed.). Minneapolis: Center for the Study of Ethical Development, University of Minnesota.

Rest, J. (1988b, Winter). Can ethics be taught in professional schools? The psychological research. *Easier Said Than Done,* pp. 22–26.

Rest, J. (1990, October). *The Four Component Model for moral action: Implications for teaching professional students.* Paper presented at the conference, The Care-Justice Puzzle, Education for Ethical Nursing Practice, St. Paul, MN.

Rosen, B., & Caplan, A. L. (1980). *Ethics in the undergraduate curriculum.* Hastings-on-Hudson, NY: Hastings Center.

Ryden, M., Duckett, L., Crisham, P., Caplan, A., & Schmitz, K. (1989). Multi-course sequential learning as a model for content integration: Ethics as a prototype. *Journal of Nursing Education, 28*(3), 102–106.

Ryden, M., Waithe, M. E., Crisham, P., Caplan, A., & Duckett, L. (1989). Wrestling with the larger picture: Placing ethical behavior in clinical situations in context. *Journal of Nursing Education, 28*(6), 271–275.

Sheehan, T. J., Husted, S. D. R., Candee, D., Cook, C. D., & Bargen, M. (1980). Moral judgment as a predictor of clinical performance. *Evaluation and the Health Professions, 3*(4), 393–404.

Steinfels, M. O. (1977, August). Ethics, education, and nursing practice. *Hastings Center Report,* pp. 20–21.

Swanson, K. M. (1991). Empirical development of a middle range theory of caring. *Nursing Research, 40*(3), 161–166.

Waithe, M. E., Duckett, L., Schmitz, K., Crisham, P., & Ryden, M. (1989). Developing case situations for ethics education in nursing. *Journal of Nursing Education, 28*(4), 175–180.

Watson, J. (1988). Introduction: An ethic of caring/curing/nursing qua nursing. In J. Watson & M. A. Ray (Eds.), *The ethics of care and the ethics of cure: Synthesis in chronicity* (pp. 1–3). New York: National League for Nursing.

Chapter 4

School Teachers' Moral Reasoning

Fon-Yean Chang
National Pingtung Teachers College

TEACHING IS MORAL BY NATURE

Teachers have tremendous influence on the moral development of children. Parents entrust their children to teachers and believe that teachers behave ethically in the classroom, transmit values upheld by society, and serve as moral models for their students (Sirotnik, 1990). Today, the influence of schools and teachers increases as the influence of family, church, and community decreases.

The importance of ethics in teaching cannot be overstated. If the vulnerability of children is considered, ethical concerns become imperative for teachers, because teachers usually work in isolation and children are likely to feel helpless and are unable to recognize unethical treatment (Strike & Soltis, 1992). In a word, children tend to be victimized if teachers behave unethically.

From the early 20th century to the present, the moral aspects of teaching have been heavily emphasized (Kimball, 1991). Growing interest in the ethics of teaching is also reflected in the writings of educational philosophers. Sockett (1990) viewed teachers as moral agents in a pluralistic society. Goodlad (1990) argued that teaching is a high and noble calling. Kimball, agreeing with Goodlad, further claimed that to view teaching as a noble calling may be not only good and right, but also a timely strategy for elevating the teaching profession. Thomas (1990) stated that teaching involves a great deal of moral decision making, and that teaching is a moral enterprise because it is a social enterprise. He viewed teachers at the center of moral instruction and moral struggle, routinely facing the need to make moral choices because teachers spend long hours each day with children. Strike and Soltis (1986) and Strike (1990) mentioned that moral decision making in teaching is a daily occurrence for teachers. The moment the children come to school in the morning, moral choices begin and are continually made. To illustrate the moral nature of teaching, Strike cited many examples of common occurrences (Strike, 1988; Strike & Soltis, 1992). He stated there are five kinds of decisions made by teachers every day. Teachers (a) assign grades and make decisions based on these grades; (b) allocate resources, especially their own time, to students; (c) discipline or punish students; (d) broker or negotiate educational programs and other matters with and between parents, students, administrators, board members, and the community; and (e) make decisions about sensitive and vulnerable young people.

If it is true that teaching is moral by nature—teachers are forced to make moral decisions continuously—then the question arises: What can help teachers make sound decisions and perform ethically? Ethical codes of teaching and/or teachers' training programs are typically the first step. The ethical codes of teaching are made specifically for teaching and learning, and therefore provide general guidelines to teachers. However, as with other professional codes of ethics, teaching codes seem to have their limitations when applied to more complex and ambiguous situations. Most teachers' training programs offer courses in ethics, philosophy and/or educational philosophy, and expect these courses to build a sound knowledge base for teachers and lead them to perform ethically. Teachers, however, usually have difficulty in applying abstract philosophical theories to the concrete realities of day-to-day teaching. Teachers' training programs appear to do little to prepare teachers to be perceptive regarding the moral issues that arise in practice (Strike, 1990). Similarly, little is done to prepare teachers for decision making in situations where teachers must exercise moral judgment skills.

THE MORAL JUDGMENT OF TEACHERS

Research Findings

According to some empirical studies, the developmental level of moral judgments of preservice and inservice teachers is not satisfactory. Bloom (1976) found that the moral judgments of education students compared unfavorably with those of college students in other fields. Diessner (1991), after reviewing 30 studies, concluded that most teachers reasoned only at the conventional level measured by Kohlberg's interview format. In terms of the Defining Issues Test (DIT), Diessner concluded that most preservice and inservice teachers had P scores in the 40s, and that 30% to 50% of the time, teachers were at the principled level. This result implies that most teachers could recognize, but could not produce, postconventional thinking. In other words, their moral thinking is subject to change depending upon school leaders or the atmosphere of the schools in which they serve. In short, although teaching is moral by nature and teachers make moral decisions continuously, teachers do not seem to be well prepared for this aspect of their jobs.

4. SCHOOL TEACHERS' MORAL REASONING 73

Teachers' educators, realizing this, may consider adopting the theory of moral cognitive development to solve the problem.

According to Kohlberg (1976), moral development advances sequentially through six stages (see "The Six Stages," chap. 1). Each stage has its distinctive features. Kohlberg's theory has been well documented and widely researched (Rest, 1983). Based on Kohlberg's theory, Rest (1979) developed the DIT to measure moral comprehension and preferences. Since its development, the DIT has been shown to be an effective instrument in more than 1,000 studies. Among studies of moral reasoning, many concern teachers' attitudes and performances.

Brief Description of Research

Although the relationship between moral judgment and moral behavior has been of interest to many researchers, teachers' moral reasoning and its relationship with teaching has received researchers' attention only since the late 1970s. The major instruments used to measure teachers' moral reasoning are Rest's DIT and Kohlberg's Moral Judgment Interview (MJI); Pupil Control Ideology and the Minnesota Teacher Attitude Inventory are scales often used to assess teachers' attitudes toward teaching. Most of the samples for these studies are elementary school teachers. Preservice teachers serve as samples in a number of studies, and a few studies use junior or senior high school teachers as their subjects.

The researchers usually give several inventories to the subjects and relate moral judgment to other teaching variables. Some researchers (e.g., Johnston, 1985, 1989) have interviewed or observed the practices of small groups of teachers in actual settings, and correlated this data with teachers' moral reasoning. Researchers have also investigated students' responses toward their teachers (e.g., teacher support or classroom moral atmosphere) and related these responses to teachers' moral judgment. If student teachers are the subjects, on-site supervisors are usually asked to rate student teachers' performances, which are then related to the moral judgment of the subjects.

Research findings of the relationship between teachers' moral reasoning and teaching concern the following areas: discipline, teacher's role, relations with students, educational concepts understanding, and performance.

Moral Reasoning and Discipline

With very few exceptions (Conroy, 1987), most of the empirical research showed that teachers at higher levels of moral reasoning tended to hold a more humanistic–democratic view of student discipline. Teachers at lower moral reasoning levels tended to hold a custodial–authoritarian view of student discipline and were more interested in conformity-oriented behavior, such as keeping an orderly classroom and following rules (Bloom, 1978; Deal, 1978; Holt, Kauchak, & Person, 1980; Novogrodsky, 1977). Furthermore, teachers with higher moral reasoning were able to consider and accommodate different viewpoints about social–conventional issues, such as wearing uniforms and addressing teachers by their nicknames. In contrast, teachers with lower moral reasoning viewed social–conventional issues only from their own or the school's viewpoint.

Results also showed that moral reasoning was related to teachers' tolerance for students' disturbing behaviors. Teachers at principled moral levels tended to be tolerant of socially defiant behaviors, whereas teachers at the preprincipled moral levels tended to be bothered by socially deviant behaviors and behaviors against social–convention (Bailey, 1985).

In the same line, teachers' moral reasoning scores were associated with their conceptualization of rules. Teachers operating at lower levels of moral judgment saw rules primarily serving to maintain social order. Any infringement of a rule was viewed as a personal attack on the teacher. Teachers operating at higher levels of moral judgment, conversely, felt that rules were needed to ensure certain rights of students and their students were encouraged to take part in rule–making (Johnston & Lubomudrov, 1987; Lubomudrov, 1982). High moral reasoning teachers were also more willing to help students understand and reason about rules from different perspectives than were low moral reasoning teachers.

Moral Reasoning and Teacher's Role

The ways in which various teachers perceived their roles differed, and this difference was a function of teachers' moral reasoning. Results showed that teachers at higher moral reasoning levels tended to view their roles as more democratic and facilitative. In contrast, teachers at lower moral reasoning levels viewed their role as controlling and policing (Johnston & Lubomudrov, 1987; MacCallum, 1991).

Moral Reasoning and Relationships With Students

Concerning affective constructs, those teachers operating at higher levels of moral reasoning could better perceive students' feelings and needs, and maintained a more positive relationship with their students than teachers operating at lower levels of moral reasoning (Johnston & Lubomudrov, 1987; Novogrodsky, 1977). Additionally, compared to teachers with preprincipled moral reasoning, teachers with principled moral reasoning tended to create an intellectual and participative climate in the classroom (Holt et al., 1980).

Interview results also indicated that high school students taught by teachers at higher levels of moral judgment reported that they received more support from their teachers than did students taught by teachers at lower levels of moral judgment (Gerety, 1980). Consequently, although not perceived as more interesting or preferred by their students, high moral reasoning teachers were perceived as more friendly, cheerful, and admired by their students than lower moral reasoning teachers (Hilton, 1989).

Classroom moral atmosphere, as perceived by students, was a function of teachers' moral reasoning. Junior and senior high school students of higher moral reasoning teachers responded more positively to their classroom's moral atmosphere than did those students of lower moral reasoning teachers (Gerety, 1980).

Moral Reasoning and Understanding Educational Concepts

Teachers at higher moral reasoning levels showed that they could understand educational concepts more broadly and deeply way than the teachers at lower levels. For instance, the conceptualizations of "on-task" were different for teachers at different levels of moral reasoning. According to teachers at lower levels of moral reasoning, "on-task" meant working on the assignment given by the teacher, and whether children were "on-task" was decided by teachers' observing their students' behaviors. For teachers at higher levels of moral reasoning, on-task was defined differently for each child, depending on the student's characteristics and on the teacher's responses to the students (Johnston, 1985).

Similarly, teachers understood the concept *individualized instruction* differently. Low moral judgment teachers saw it as one way of helping students achieve some predetermined levels. High moral judgment teachers, on the other hand, saw *individualized instruction* as one way to adjust the curriculum to students' abilities and needs (Johnston, 1989).

In an interview of teachers regarding their understanding of the conventional curriculum, similar results were also obtained. Teachers at lower levels of moral reasoning saw themselves as the managers of students, materials, and district curriculum. Teachers at higher levels of moral reasoning, on the other hand, could see curriculum issues both from a broader social view and also in terms of individual student's interests. These high level moral reasoning teachers also argued that it was important to include students in curriculum planning so that the students could understand the meaning of learning and its significance to their lives (Wheaton, 1984).

Moral Reasoning and Teacher Performance

The relationship between moral reasoning and student teachers' performances has also been investigated in several studies. Student teachers' performances were found not to be related to their moral reasoning levels (Bergem, 1986; McNergney & Satterstrom, 1984; Thoma & Rest, 1987). Teaching competencies included in these studies were grouped as instructional competence, relationships with staff and school personnel, and communication skills and leadership.

There are several possible explanations for the nonsignificant relationship between moral reasoning and student teachers' performances. First, the student teachers were completing their internships in situations that were very different from those of regular teachers. The student teachers, in unfamiliar environments, were being rated by on-site supervisors. Learning how to survive or adapt to the new environment may have been more important than loftier goals. Second, their teaching performances were not based on self-reported data. Their performances were rated by individual on-site supervisors. A person's characteristics might be perceived very differently by others who do not know that person well, a fact that might have influenced the research findings. Third, unlike the variables noted in this section, teaching performances are more closely related to teaching knowledge or skills. That teaching performances are not shown to be related to moral reasoning is understandable, because moral reasoning is a reasoning process about moral issues and it is not relevant to teaching knowledge or skills.

These empirical findings revealed that except for teachers' competencies, moral reasoning is significantly related to teachers' conceptualizations of student discipline, teacher's roles, curriculum, and educational issues. Moral reasoning is also related to the teacher's relationship with students and to the intellectual and moral atmosphere of their classes. This implies that advanced moral reasoning allows teachers to reason about teaching issues more thoroughly and fundamentally, and thus to see the essential dimension of teaching. Based on this deeper understanding, teachers with advanced moral reasoning can be more empathic to students' needs and more willing to facilitate students' growth, respect students' rights, avoid taking students' challenges personally, and be more objective when dealing with problems caused by students. Consequently, teachers with high levels of moral reasoning can be more student centered and perform more humanely, democratically, and professionally.

THE DEVELOPMENT OF ETHICAL REASONING TESTS FOR SPECIFIC PROFESSIONS

The DIT and the MJI used to measure teachers' moral reasoning have surely contributed to the understanding of teachers' behaviors. However, in terms of understanding or predicting moral behaviors in each professional field, tests derived from real-life situations may work better than these hypothetical tests. Some researchers have taken this next step and developed ethical tests for their specific professions (Bebeau, 1985; Crisham, 1979; Hoffmann & Sprague, 1991; Plakans, 1990).

Rest (1986) also encouraged the development of such profession-specific ethical measures. He believed that although the DIT had been widely used and shown to be a useful instrument for measuring moral reasoning in general, it had only modest predictive ability for moral behavior. The long-term goal of the psychology of morality is to understand and predict moral behavior in real-life contexts.

4. SCHOOL TEACHERS' MORAL REASONING

Therefore, he suggested that researchers develop real-life moral dilemmas in each professional field.

The positive relationship between teachers' moral reasoning and teaching revealed by previous studies served to encourage development of a teaching-specific moral reasoning test, with which researchers can then more closely examine the relationship between teachers' moral reasoning and teaching.

A Specific Test for Teachers: The Development of the TTMR

Design and Method. Chang (1993) developed a teaching-specific moral reasoning test, the Test of Teachers' Moral Reasoning (TTMR). Two studies were conducted. The design of Study 2 was based mainly on the findings of Study 1. All subjects for both studies were from Taiwan. Study 1 was modeled after the DIT. Through extensive interviews, the TTMR was developed and used in Study 1. It comprised 7 stories and 15 consideration statements for each story (Chang, 1993). These stories were recurrent teaching dilemmas in school settings, and the statements represented possible considerations when one tried to make a decision about each of the teaching dilemmas. The following is an example of a dilemma that portrayed classroom theft:

> The communal fund of teacher Su's class was stolen again. It was the third theft in a month. Su is very sure that the thief is one of her students. During the first two thefts, Su spent a long time in class letting students know that stealing was wrong. She also let the thief have chances to confess in private. However, no one admitted the theft to Su. This time Su felt that it was necessary to let students learn the seriousness of stealing. Therefore, no matter how late it got, she decided to keep the students inside after school until someone confessed his or her misconduct. Long after school hours, no one had yet told Su that he or she was responsible for the theft.

After reading the dilemma story, subjects were asked to respond to consideration statements such as the following:

1. The principal's opinion of Su's method of catching the thief.
2. The fairness of punishing the whole class for the acts of a few.
3. Students' rights and their abilities to work with the teacher to investigate and judge the thefts.

The subjects were first asked to rate the importance (from *Great* to *No Importance*) of each of the consideration statements and to choose and rank the three most important of these statements from each story.

Unlike the DIT, the scoring scheme of the TTMR did not adopt Kohlberg's six-stage scheme (Kohlberg, 1976). Instead, Rest suggested dividing items into high or low levels.[1] This was because Kohlberg's scheme, which was designed to measure general moral development, might not have been suitable for a special group of highly educated subjects (teachers) reasoning about moral issues in a special area (teaching). Subtle differences in teachers' moral reasoning about teaching issues might not be detected by Kohlberg's scheme.

Compared with low level items (e.g., Statement 1), high level items (e.g., Statements 2 and 3) were more humanistic, democratic, and in accordance with educational principles.

A weighting scheme was used for scoring the ranking results. T tests were conducted to contrast the weighted scores for novice and expert teachers. The novice group was composed of teachers' college students. The expert group was composed of teaching faculty and experienced teachers, both selected by sociometric nominations as morally expert teachers. The expert group was expected to select more high level items and fewer low level items as important considerations than the novice group.

Results showed that t tests could differentiate these two groups. The expert teachers tended more than the novice group to endorse high level items and not to endorse low level ones. Readers interested in the complete report of findings are referred to the original work (Chang, 1993).

After Study 1, the researcher decided to delete two undifferentiating stories and maintain 12 consideration statements for each of the remaining five stories, because the statements seemed to be differentiating the expert group from the novice group. Except for the total number of stories and the total number of consideration statements, the revised TTMR looked very much the same as the one used in Study 1. This revised TTMR was used in Study 2.

In Study 2, the sample included 223 primary school teachers and 108 teacher college students. After finishing the TTMR, the primary school teachers were instructed to nominate two or three peer teachers whom they thought were fair, just, and capable of sound judgments. Thus, the primary school teachers were divided into morally expert and less morally expert groups according to the votes they got from the morality nomination by their peers. In a similar way, using sociometric

---

[1]In dividing the items into high or low levels, we assume the following: (a) Some types of moral thinking are higher or more defensible than others. If all moral thinking was at the same level, there would be no point in having courses in morality, because the purpose of moral education is to raise students' moral thinking from a low to a high level. (b) High or low level moral thinking is agreed on or accepted by persons with expertise in moral reasoning (e.g., professors of ethics). This high or low level of moral thinking is not an idiosyncratic or individual view. There is some agreement about what is better within society, or at least among these moral experts.

The conception of high or low moral thinking was tested in Studies 1 and 2. Findings from these two studies confirmed this conception. That is, the expert group tended more than the novice group to endorse high-level thinking and tended not to endorse low-level thinking. Additionally, the conception of high/low moral thinking was tested and supported by the results from the factor analysis. The clusters of the high and low level items from the researcher's conception (a priori approach) were similar to those from the factor analysis (factor-analysis approach). Results of all hypothesis testing from these two approaches did not vary much. Therefore, the conception of high/low level moral thinking is supported by the factor-analysis results.

nominations, the teachers were also categorized into popular and less popular groups.

The scoring scheme of the TTMR in Study 2 still used the high/low level scheme and the weighting scheme because they proved to be effective in differentiating the experts from the novices in Study 1. The key items in Study 2, nevertheless, were derived from two approaches. One was an a priori approach in which the key items were formed from the researcher's intuition based on her understanding of moral theory and her experiences in the teaching profession. The other approach was the factor-analysis approach in which the key items were derived empirically from a factor analysis. The factor-analysis approach was used to corroborate empirically the classification of items from the a priori approach. For each approach, 8 indices were derived.[2] The reason for having so many indices was to explore the data as thoroughly as possible in order to suggest the best indexing for the TTMR.

Hypotheses. Seven hypotheses were formed to test the revised TTMR and to compare the efficacy of the TTMR and the Chinese DIT.[3] The following are brief descriptions of each hypothesis, their rationales, and the statistical methods used to test the hypotheses. Hypotheses 1 and 2 tested the reliability of the TTMR.

Hypothesis 1: The TTMR items were internally consistent. Cronbach's Alpha was used to test this hypothesis. The researcher had tried out 16 indices to analyze the data. Results from Hypothesis 1 showed that the Cronbach's Alpha values did not differ much when including or excluding Story 4. Because the research was exploratory, the researcher then decided to test the subsequent hypotheses with the data, both including and excluding Story 4. Thus, the TTMR had two versions, the 4- and 5-story versions. As noted earlier, there were 16 indexing methods for the data analysis. Because there were two versions (4- and 5-story versions), the number of indices became 32, which was the product of 8 indices (4 single and 4 combination), two approaches (factor analysis and a priori) and two versions (4- and 5-story versions).

Hypothesis 2: The test and retest of the TTMR showed adequate stability. Pearson Product Moment Correlations were used to test this hypothesis. Validity testing was another concern. Hypotheses 3, 4, and 5 tested the validity of the TTMR.

Hypothesis 3: The TTMR was more associated with peer nomination of morality than peer nomination of popularity. The TTMR was a moral reasoning test; therefore, it should have been more associated with peer nomination of morality

---

[2] Index 1 was derived from some high-level key items in which the researcher had most confidence. Index 2 was derived from more high-level key items. Index 3 was derived from some low-level key items in which the researcher had most confidence. Index 4 was derived from more low-level key items. Indices 5, 6, 7, and 8 were the combinations of two single indices: Index 5 was the combination of Index 1 and Index 3; Index 6, the combination of Index 1 and Index 4; Index 7, the combination of Index 2 and Index 3; and Index 8, the combination of Index 2 and Index 4.

[3] The Chinese version of the DIT has unknown equivalence to the regular DIT.

than peer nomination of popularity. *T* tests of the correlation coefficients were used to test this hypothesis.

Hypothesis 4: The TTMR scores of the morally expert teachers were higher than those of the less morally expert teachers. The rationale was that those teachers nominated by their peers as morally expert teachers were expected to demonstrate higher level thinking in teaching issues than the less morally expert teachers. *T* tests were computed to test Hypothesis 4.

Hypothesis 5: The TTMR scores of the primary school teachers were higher than those of the teachers' college students. The rationale was that because these dilemma situations were recurrent in day-to-day teaching, teachers should have opportunities to encounter these real-life dilemmas in their teaching. They should develop mature thinking through reflection or discussion with their colleagues. On the other hand, teachers' college students lacked teaching experience even though they were in the teachers' training program. Thus, preservice teachers were not expected to make as sound judgments as practicing teachers. *T* tests were computed to test Hypothesis 5.

In addition to the reliability and validity testing, the researcher investigated (Hypotheses 6 and 7) the relationship between the TTMR (a profession-specific test, with intermediate-level concepts—see chapter 1) and the Chinese DIT (a general test, with more coarse-grained concepts). The intent in developing the TTMR was not simply to devise an equivalent version of the DIT with changed, more relevant content. The intent was to devise an instrument that would measure moral judgment at a different level than the DIT. Unfortunately, since the study was conducted in Taiwan in Chinese, the regular DIT was not appropriate for comparisons. Instead, a Chinese translation of the regular DIT had to be used, and not much research has been done with the Chinese version. Therefore the equivalence of the Chinese DIT with the regular DIT is unknown.

Hypothesis 6: The TTMR could better differentiate the morally expert teachers from the less morally expert teachers than could the Chinese version of the DIT. Discriminant function was computed to test Hypothesis 6.

Hypothesis 7: The Chinese version of the DIT and the TTMR were significantly correlated. It was hypothesized that these two tests were modestly correlated. These two tests should be correlated because they were both moral reasoning tests and their formats were similar. However, the correlation coefficient should not be too high. Hypothesis 7 could also be viewed as one way of testing the validity of the TTMR. Pearson Product Moment Correlations were used to test Hypothesis 7.

Findings

Results from all hypothesis tests showed that Index 1 from the factor-analysis approach for both the 4- and 5-story versions was the best index. In fact, the two versions did not differ much in validity and reliability. The 4-story version, therefore, was recommended because of the consideration of time subjects needed to finish the test. Again, readers are referred to the original work (Chang, 1993) for a complete report of the findings and further explanation. Results from the 4-story version of Index 1 in the factor-analysis approach are presented as follows:

1. *Reliability:* Hypotheses 1 and 2 were related to the reliability of the TTMR. The internal reliability coefficient for the TTMR was .7654. The 1-week test–retest reliability was .6152. These coefficients are all acceptable.
2. *Validity:* Hypotheses 3, 4, and 5 were relevant to the validity of the TTMR. All the p values from the 4-story version in these three hypothesis tests were significant, showing that the TTMR was more associated with peer nomination of morality than with peer nomination of popularity. The TTMR could significantly differentiate the morally expert teachers from the less morally expert teachers. The TTMR could also successfully differentiate primary school teachers from teachers' college students. All these findings support the validity of the TTMR.
3. *Relationship with the Chinese version of the DIT:* Hypotheses 6 and 7 dealt with the relationship between the TTMR and the Chinese version of the DIT. From the finding of Hypothesis 7, the correlation coefficient between the TTMR (the best index) and the Chinese DIT was .3084. This value indicated these two tests did not measure exactly the same areas of morality. Hypothesis 6 was about the differential effects of these two tests in the teaching area. The TTMR, a teaching-specific moral test, could differentiate the morally expert teachers from the less morally expert teachers. In contrast, the Chinese version of the DIT, a hypothetical general test, could not differentiate between these two groups of teachers. This finding showed that the TTMR is more differentiating than the Chinese DIT in the teaching area.

CONCLUSION

"Teaching is moral by nature" has been argued by educational philosophers. The results of empirical research indicate that teachers' moral reasoning is related to how they understand their practice. Teachers with higher moral reasoning can be more empowering to student learning and healthy social development than teachers with lower moral reasoning. These conclusions suggest that teachers' moral reasoning plays a crucial role in teachers' practice. Promotion of a moral reasoning component in teachers' training programs seems to be necessary for cultivating fully functioning teachers.

The TTMR shows that measurement of moral reasoning of teachers in a more profession-specific way is possible. With this instrument, researchers in the future can relate the TTMR with demographic variables of teachers, such as years of education completed, professional credits taken, student age levels served. The TTMR can also be related to teaching attitudes and behaviors; for example, to student discipline. Furthermore, using the TTMR, researchers can explore changes in the moral reasoning of teachers as they progress from preservice to practice. With such findings about the relationship between teachers' moral reasoning and their practice, teachers' behaviors can be better understood. Hopefully, application of these findings will significantly improve teachers' training programs, leading directly to the development of more fully functioning teachers.

REFERENCES

Bailey, D. A. (1985). *The relationship between stages of moral judgment and elementary classroom teachers' perceptions of disturbing students.* Unpublished doctoral dissertation, University of Missouri, Columbia.

Bebeau, M. J. (1985). Teaching ethics in dentistry. *Journal of Dental Education, 49*(4), 236–243.

Bergem, T. (1986). Teachers' thinking and behavior: An empirical study of the role of social sensitivity and moral reasoning in the teaching performance of student teachers. *Scandinavian Journal of Educational Research, 30,* 193–203.

Bloom, R. B. (1976, May). Morally speaking, who are today's teachers? *Phi Delta Kappan,* pp. 624–625.

Bloom, R. B. (1978). Discipline: Another face of moral reasoning? *College Student Journal, 12*(4), 356–359.

Chang, F. Y. (1993). *The development of a test of teachers' moral reasoning.* Unpublished doctoral dissertation, University of Minnesota, Minneapolis.

Conroy, B. J. (1987). Teachers' moral reasoning and their attitudes and behaviors regarding discipline. *Dissertation Abstracts International, 47*(11), 3917–3918A.

Crisham, P. (1979). *Moral judgment of nurses in hypothetical and nursing dilemmas.* Unpublished doctoral dissertation, University of Minnesota, Minneapolis.

Deal, M. D. (1978). *The relationship of philosophy of human nature, level of cognitive moral reasoning and pupil control ideology of graduate students in a department of curriculum and instruction.* Unpublished doctoral dissertation, Oklahoma State University, Stillwater.

Diessner, R. (1991). T*eacher education for democratic classrooms: Moral reasoning and ideology critique.* A seminar presented at the 16th annual conference of the Association for Moral Education, Athens, GA.

Gerety, M. A. (1980). A study of the relationship between the moral judgment of the teacher and the moral atmosphere in the classroom. D*issertation Abstracts International, 41,* 1952A.

Goodlad, J. (1990). The occupation of teaching in schools. In J. I. Goodlad, R. Soder, & K. A. Sirotnik (Eds.), *The moral dimensions of teaching.* (pp. 3–34) San Francisco: Jossey-Bass.

Hilton, J. B. (1989). *Teachers' moral reasoning and students' perception of teacher affect.* Unpublished doctoral dissertation University of South Carolina, Columbia.

Hoffmann, J., & Sprague, J. (1991). *Exploring alternate perspectives on fairness to help TAs develop course policies and manage student challenges.* Paper presented at the third national conference on TA Training and Employment, Austin, TX.

Holt, L., Kauchak, D., & Person, K. (1980). Moral development, educational attitudes and self-concept in beginning teacher education students. *Educational Research Quarterly, 5*(3), 50–56.

Johnston, M. (1985). How elementary teachers understand the concept of "on-task": A developmental critique. *Journal of Classroom Interaction, 21,* 15–24. Johnston, M. (1989). Moral reasoning and teachers' understanding of individualized instruction. *Journal of Moral Education, 18*(1), 45–59.

Johnston, M., & Lubomudrov C. (1987). Teachers' level of moral reasoning and their understanding of classroom rules and roles. *Elementary School Journal, 88,* 65–78.

Kimball, B. (1991). The liberal profession of teaching. *American Journal of Education, 100*(1), 106–118.

Kohlberg, L. (1976). Moral stages and moralization: The cognitive-developmental approach. In T. Lickona (ed.), *Moral development and behavior* (pp. 31–53). New York : Holt, Rinehart & Winston.

Lubomudrov, C. A. (1982). *Case studies of relationships among level of moral cognitive development, teachers' understandings of educational issues and teaching practices.* Unpublished doctoral dissertation, University of Utah, Salt Lake.

MacCallum J. A. (1991). *Teacher reasoning and moral judgment in the context of student discipline situations*. Paper presented at the annual meeting of the American Educational Research Association, Chicago, IL.

McNergney, R., & Satterstrom, L. (1984). Teacher characteristics and teacher performance. *Contemporary Educational Psychology, 9*, 19–24.

Novogrodsky, J. (1977). Teachers' moral development and their expressed attitudes toward students. *Dissertation Abstracts International, 38*, 2006A.

Rest, J. R. (1979). *Development in judging moral issues*. Minneapolis: University of Minnesota Press.

Rest, J. R. (1983). Morality. In P. H. Mussen (Series Ed.), J. H. Flavell and E. M. Markman (Vol. Eds.), *Handbook of child psychology: Vol. 3. Cognitive development* (pp. 556–62). New York: Wiley.

Rest, J. R. (1986). *Moral development: Advances in research and theory*. New York: Praeger.

Sirotnik K. A. (1990). Society, schooling, teaching, and preparing to teach. In J. I. Goodlad, R. Soder, & K. A. Sirotnik (Eds.), *The moral dimensions of teaching* (pp. 296–327). San Francisco: Jossey-Bass.

Sockett, H. (1990). Accountability, trust and ethical codes of practice. In J. Goodlad, R. Soder, & K. A. Sirotnik. (Eds.), *The moral dimension of teaching*. San Francisco: Jossey-Bass.

Strike, K. A. (1988). The ethics of teaching. *Phi Delta Kappan, 70*(2), 156–158.

Strike, K. A. (1990). Teaching ethics to teachers: What the curriculum should be about. *Teacher & Teacher Education, 6*(1), 47–53.

Strike, K. A., & Soltis, J. F. (1986). Who broke the fish tank? and other ethical dilemmas. *Instructor, 95*(5), 36–37.

Strike, K. A., & Soltis, J. F. (1992). *The ethics of teaching* (2nd ed.). New York: Teachers College Press.

Thoma, S. J., & Rest, J. R. (1987). Moral sensitivity and judgment in the development and performance of student teachers. *Moral Education Forum, 12*, 15–20.

Thomas, B. R. (1990). The school as a moral learning community. In J. I. Goodlad, R. Soder, & K. A. Sirotnik (Eds.), *The moral dimensions of teaching* (pp. 266–295). San Francisco: Jossey-Bass.

Wheaton, W. F. (1984). *An investigation of the relationship between cognitive developmental level, teachers' perception of role, and their understanding of issues related to the elementary curriculum*. Unpublished doctoral dissertation, University of Utah, Salt Lake.

Chapter 5

Counseling and Social Role Taking: Promoting Moral and Ego Development

Norman A. Sprinthall
North Carolina State University

ROLE TAKING: A NEGLECTED METHOD

In the 1960s, applied psychology was confronted with a professional dilemma. Research had shown that traditional approaches of counseling and psychotherapy had at best achieved only very modest positive effects (Smith & Glass, 1977). In fact, much earlier research had shown no effect whatsoever (Bergin, 1963; Eysenck; 1978, Levitt, 1967). Partly as a result of these findings some leaders within the psychological establishment called for what was then viewed as a radical change. Miller (1969), in his presidential address to the American Psychological Association, urged that psychologists concentrate on giving their skills away to the lay public. He said that we should select principles and practices from the armamentarian of applied psychology and teach the public how to employ such knowledge and skills on its own behalf. At the same time, Kohlberg (1974) and his associates had completed a major review of child, adolescent, and adult development and reached a stark conclusion. "Put bluntly there is no research evidence indicating that clinical treatment of emotional symptoms during childhood leads to predictions of adult adjustment" (p. 251). Kohlberg, LaCrosse and Ricks (1970) noted further that "the best predictors of the absence of adult mental illness and maladjustment are the presence of various forms of competence and ego maturity in childhood and adolescence rather than the absence of problems and symptoms" (p. 1274).

This same theme was echoed by Albee's (1982) comments on the need for a primary preventive approach for applied psychology rather than after-the-fact treatment on an individual basis from the intrapsychic paradigm. The way to avoid mental illness was to promote psychological development; prevention is always more effective than curing. At the same time, there was a serious effort in applied psychology to create a theoretical framework for human development. Allport (1968) always pointed out that most psychological theories of the day essentially conceptualized humans as reactive rather than proactive. Cognitive-developmental theory was clearly an example of the latter.

Emergent Cognitive-Developmental Theory

The work of theorists such as Flavell (1971), Loevinger (1966), Hunt (1974), and, of course, Kohlberg (1972), changed our basic understanding of the process of human growth and development. These theorists and others such as Perry (1970) and Heath (1977), although all working independently, came to remarkably similar conclusions, namely that humans have an intrinsic potential for growth through stages from lower order to higher order human functioning. This work provided applied psychologists with an important set of directing constructs, particularly if we were to take Miller's dictum to heart and give our skills away.

From Theory to Practice: The Difficult Transition

There is a major difference between pointing out new directions for practice and the successful implementation of those ideas. In fact with the single exception of Blatt's (1969) dilemma discussion approach, there were no examples of successful applications in the service of cognitive-developmental growth or of primary prevention at that time. During the late 1960s, a team of us at Harvard started to test a series of methods to teach psychology to high school students. We tried all of the traditional methods, such as large and small group discussions, field trips, analyses of films and novels, case studies, improvisational dance, and drama. In all cases, in spite of our best efforts, we could not detect any noticeable improvement on measures of psychological growth or in the qualitative analysis of written commentary. My colleague, Ralph Mosher, remarked wryly at one point after our third or fourth failure, "Well, once more we've snatched defeat from the jaws of victory." McClelland (1973), another colleague, had always noted that the best and most difficult way to understand any psychological phenomenon was to try to change it. Under these conditions, we were learning just how difficult it was to give psychology away (Mosher & Sprinthall, 1971).

Role Taking: A Promising Alternative

The colleague team decided that an innovative method was necessary. We were involved in graduate programs teaching counseling and teaching skills to graduate

5. COUNSELING AND SOCIAL ROLE TAKING 87

students. What would happen if we essentially took these same courses (with perhaps a slightly shorter reading list) and taught them to high school students? This would certainly fit Miller's dictum of giving our skills away to the public. It might also serve as an example of primary prevention. In this regard, Kohlberg suggested that we measure our outcomes with his instrument, the Moral Judgment Interview (MJI) and include Loevinger's (1966) index of Ego Development. We could clearly see the relationship between our course goals and ego development, but the question of moral judgment perplexed us. We were not using the dilemma discussion method or anything remotely connected with the usual Kohlberg dilemmas. Research, however, can mean exploring the unknown or at least what was unclear to us. We included both measures, but with some puzzlement over the moral judgment index. The first program in peer counseling (Dowell, 1971) provided convincing evidence that we were on the right track. The adolescents showed improvement in their level of ego maturity on Loevinger's index and on the MJI as well. The qualitative assessments of journals and other subjective observations all provided further validation. At this point, we had a long discussion with Kohlberg. He gently but persuasively directed us away from our attempt to bridge humanistic psychology with cognitive-developmental psychology and introduced us to George Herbert Mead (1934) and the theory of role taking. By placing students in important and real roles that required empathy and the iron discipline of listening (setting aside one's own ego), the students would improve on their perspective taking, not just intellectually but emotionally as well. He also introduced us to one of his graduate students, Selman (1971), who was outlining the relationship between role taking as an intermediate psychological process between intellectual understanding and moral judgment. As a result, we had a clearer understanding of the role taking methods, in this case peer counseling, and also the reasons why the high school students moved up on the assessments of growth.

Naturally, one study does not make for a definitive new model. The Harvard graduate programs in counseling and teaching, however, were closing. Thus, it was time to expand the role-taking research and to try it more broadly in other areas, in this case, first in Minnesota and more recently in North Carolina. These programs, under the general rubric of peer helping, followed the same procedures. A significant role-taking experience such as peer counseling, tutoring, teaching, child care, companions to elderly, and so on, was combined with careful reflection, journalizing, discussions, and readings on a weekly basis. At that time such an approach was considered quite unique for school programs. Role taking required a shift in emphasis from either conventional secondary school programs (Goodlad, 1984) or the use of simulations such as role playing. Instead, the adolescents actually learned to apply the skills of counseling, teaching, and child care in real-world activities. Piaget had always used the metaphor of a child as a physicist exploring the nature of time, space, and causality. We found that adolescents were natural psychologists exploring questions of understanding causes of behavior, or as we referred to it, "Learning psychology by doing psychology." The role-taking activities were selected as within the reach of teenagers and usually required at least one semester for each activity. Continuity and focus were essential in order to avoid the "bag of tricks" mode so common to programs such as *Values Clarification*. With carefully guided and graduated experiences in helping activities, the teenagers exhibited responsible performance in all these role taking programs.

Helping skills, then, were learned and applied in real-world settings. The praxis between acting and reflecting was also central to the growth process. In fact, one of the colleague teams in Minnesota actually demonstrated that role taking without continuity of reflection would not promote psychological growth (Exum, 1980). This reminded us that Dewey (1938) was right years ago, when he noted that experience by itself could be educative or miseducative. Without guided reflection, experiential learning could be as arid as passively listening to lectures.

Role Taking Outcomes: A Meta-Analysis

A meta-analysis of the role-taking studies indicated that the effect sizes were substantial on both measures of cognitive development. An important point here is to recognize that the role-taking programs avoided any confounding with the assessment methods. Rest (1986) suggested that a possible weakness of the moral dilemma discussion interventions concerns the use of dilemmas similar in format to the outcome measures. The role-taking programs in content and process were independent of the measures. Also, the role-taking research always followed the Campbell and Stanley (1963) dictum by employing more than one measure of the independent variable. The use of two measures with such different formats as the Loevinger index, the MJI and/or Rest's DIT provided cross-validation for the role-taking effects in addition to the qualitative analyses of student journals.

The results of the meta-analysis are presented in Table 5.1. The method advocated by Light and Pillemer (1984) was followed in comparing the posttest means between two groups and dividing the difference by the standard deviation of the control group. The average effect size then was weighted by the sample size (larger studies given more weight). In general, according to Sprinthall, Schmutte, and Sirois (1991), an effect size of + .20 can be considered as small, + .50 as moderate and above and + .80 as very significant. Thus, on an overall basis the effects were highly significant on the average. Also, the various measurements were combined according to a specific rationale. Perhaps most obviously, the assessment results employing either the Kohlberg MJI or the Rest DIT were grouped together. Both are measures of the same phenomenon even though the techniques are different. The MJI results were reported by the 600 point moral maturity scale where 200 equals Stage 2 and so on. The Rest results were reported using the recommended P index. Both Hunt and Loevinger, however, purported to measure different domains (e.g., ego vs. conceptual). The assessment method, none the less, is highly similar (e.g., open-ended sentence stems scored according to cognitive complexity). Also, these studies, to reduce a reactive testing effect from multiple measures, employed a shortened version of the Loevinger index, the first 18 items. Hunt presented six stems and required at least three sentences for each stem, also yielding the same amount of response patterns. We did use the 10-point metric for the

## 5. COUNSELING AND SOCIAL ROLE TAKING

Loevinger scales (e.g., 2 = Delta, 3 = Delta 3, 4 = Stage 3, etc.; and the 3-point metric for the Hunt scales e.g., 1.0, 2.0, 3.0 for parametric conversions to interval data).

A final point, the studies themselves were conducted in different sections of the country, with different types of schools and colleges; across socioeconomic levels; rural, urban, and suburban districts; and with students from majority and minority backgrounds. The patterns of change were similar across such differences. The replications, then, added to the validity of the approach in general. Where there were differences in the power of individual studies (e.g., Satterstrom, 1980; Tucker, 1977), a post-mortem revealed a weakness in the amount of significant role taking

TABLE 5.1
Social Role Taking: A Meta-Analysis of Moral Judgment and Ego Developmental Effects

Study		Kohlberg MJI or Rest DIT (Pscore) Posttest			Loevinger SCT[a] or Hunt CL[b] Posttest		
		Mean	SD	Effect	Mean	SD	Effect
Dowell (1971)	E	350	—	MJI	5.3	—	SCT
	C	280	82	+.85	3.3	1.09	+1.83
Rustad & Rogers (1975)	E	401		MJI	5.7		SCT
	C	295	55	+1.97	4.3	.89	+1.57
Mosher & Sullivan (1976)	E	345		MJI	7.21		SCT
	C	272	36.5	+2.02	5.57	1.40	+1.17
Tucker (1977)	E	44.2		P	6.00		SCT
	C	41.3	16.7	+.18	5.70	1.26	+.23
Hedin (1979)	E	40.2		P	5.48		SCT
	C	35.3	6.8	+.72	4.05	1.06	+1.35
Cognetta (1980)	E	39		P	6.05		SCT
	C	38	12.3	+.08	4.46	1.16	+1.37
Exum (1980)	E	No data available			7.06		SCT
	C				5.83	.98	+1.25
Satterstrom (1980)	E	48		P	2.0		CL
	C	48	19	.00	1.8	.42	+.47
Sprinthall & Scott (1989)	E	34.8		P	1.72		CL
	C	26.2	9.7	+.87	1.39	.27	+1.22
Sprinthall, Hall, & Gerler (1992)	E	33.3		P	6.70	SCT	SCT
	C	22.3	12.9	+.85	5.58	1.20	+.93
Reiman & Parramore (1993)	E	56.9		P	1.9		CL
	C	46.4	13.4	+.93	2.0	.61	−.16
Average Effect Size		($N = 10$)		+.85 MJI or DIT	($N = 11$)		+1.10 SCT or CL

Note. About half of the studies were quasi-experimental designs. A very large meta-analysis ($N = 500$ studies) by Cohen, Kulik, and Kulik (1982) found no differences in effect size by quasi versus true experimental designs.
[a]Sentence completion test.
[b]Conceptual level.

that was actually employed. These classes spent too much time in simulations rather than in actual role-taking experiences.

ROLE-TAKING STUDIES FOR ADOLESCENTS: A CLOSER LOOK

To provide a more detailed account of what is involved in the process of giving psychology away to the public, a more comprehensive description is presented. Two recent studies demonstrate the process and effects for both those individuals providing peer help and those on the receiving end.

Study 1

In the first program (Sprinthall & Scott, 1989), the goal was to involve high school females as math tutors for elementary school females. There has been so much information concerning female fear of success and the erosion of confidence in math skills that the choice of participants and focus was obvious. What might happen to the self-confidence and academic achievement of fifth-grade females if they received tutoring by adolescent females? And what might be the developmental stage impact upon the high school helpers?

The teenage helpers met each week as a group for training in tutoring methods (with heavy use of concrete manipulative materials for the elementary students). In addition to the skills training, the teenagers discussed their own feelings and thoughts about such helping and wrote weekly reflection entries in their journals. There were two sets of noteworthy results for (a) the elementary school-aged female tutees and (b) the senior high female tutors.

For the elementary school-aged females, the tutored group (about 40 minutes per week), improved both in skills and attitudes. They raised their national score on the California Achievement Tests (CAT) from the 50th to the 61st percentile. A control group improved only 4 points. In addition, the tutored group became more confident as self-directed learners. In psychological attribution theory, it has been found that males attribute success to their own efforts and failure to the environment. "If I get an A," a male might say, "it's cause I earned it: if I get a D, either the test isn't fair or the teacher couldn't teach the stuff." Self-confidence as a learner is retained. For females, on the other hand, the situation is reversed. Females tend to attribute success to luck and failure to self-inadequacy (Fennema, Wolleat, & Pedro, 1979).

Thus we were as interested in the attribution results as in the skills results. We weren't disappointed. The elementary-aged females changed positively in their attributions of success and failure. They felt more in charge of their own learning and reduced the tendency to blame themselves when faced with learning difficulties. Quite importantly, the girls in the control group showed a decrease in self-confidence and an increase in self-blame over the 6-month period. In that relatively short time, the erosion of perceiving one's self as an active learner in

5. COUNSELING AND SOCIAL ROLE TAKING

TABLE 5.2
California Achievement Math Score Gains and Math Attribution of Success
for Elementary School Females
CAT

	Experimental Group (N = 15) Tutored	Comparison Group (N = 15) Nontutored
Pretest	50.4	51.4
Posttest	61.8	56.6
Mean Gain	+11.46	+4.53
SD	8.93	8.92
	$t = 2.12, p < .02$	(28 ndf)
	Attributes of Success Due to Effort and Ability	
Pretest	26.3	24.6
Posttest	30.4	24.47
Mean Gain	+4.1	−0.13
SD	6.73	3.93
	$t = 2.09, p < .02$	(28 ndf)
	Attributes of Success Due to Task and Environment	
Pretest	29.3	29.27
Posttest	27.2	30.93
Mean Gain	−2.1	+1.66
SD	5.64	3.37
	$t = 2.25, p < .02$	

math had begun. For the tutored group, however, a relatively small amount of weekly tutoring had a two fold positive outcome in math skills and in their attributions. Table 5.2 presents the results.

The senior high females involved in helping also benefited. As one colleague put it, "We did not rob Patricia to pay Pauline." On both measures, moral development and conceptual complexity, the tutors improved, as noted earlier in the meta-analysis (Table 5.1). They became more self-directed, less peer dominated, more complex in problem solving and more principled in moral judgment. On the other hand, and most tellingly, a control group did not change. Those females participated in a helping experience as teacher's aides. They did not, however, meet for discussion dialogue, or engage in the reflective journal writing. This indicated that so-called *service learning*, or various kinds of volunteer work, may not have had any noticeable developmental impact without guided reflection. Thus, a relatively modest tutoring program provided evidence of two levels of outcomes. Both groups benefit. Control groups showed either no change or a decline in the psychological domains assessed.

Study 2

A second study (Sprinthall, Hall, & Gerler, 1992), patterned after the role-taking model, involved high school students as small group discussion leaders for middle school students. The early adolescents had one thing in common: their families had all recently experienced a divorce. Hetherington's (1984) research revealed that such family disruption had the greatest negative effect upon middle school pupils. Probably as a result of so many psychosocial changes, those students reacted the most negatively when parents separated. Early adolescence has often been considered the weakest link in the chain of development and the added stress of divorce probably accounts for the greater stress, anxiety, acting out, and withdrawal moods of that age group.

At the same time, some recent research (Ursone, 1990), has shown at least retrospectively that secondary school students experiencing a family divorce were reluctant to seek out professional school counselors. The vast majority of students in that sample remembered experiencing distress, yet avoided counseling assistance for fear of some stigma, such as being labeled *crazy*. They also reported, again in retrospect, that it would have been helpful to talk with somebody to gain some perspective and support.

From these two points, then, the model peer assistance program was set up. The high school students were trained for one semester in small group techniques and reviewed the emotional issues that arise when parents separate. After training, they worked in pairs coleading weekly meetings. Some 40 early adolescents had been identified by the school counselors in the stress of a divorce. Eight small groups of five students each were formed and met for a semester. The high school group leaders continued to meet with their supervisor for continued skill training in discussion techniques, planning, dialogue, and reflection through journal writing. The combination of action and reflection was continually stressed in these seminars.

For example, a student commented, "I really like coleading the group of students. Mostly I just feel good and comfortable about this class. I feel closer to the students in here than to anyone else in school...." Another commented, "Seems like I communicate better with these middle school students than with some of my high school friends" (Sprinthall et al., 1992, pp. 291–292). Such reflections helped deepen the group counseling experiences for the high school leaders.

The results were positive for both groups. The early adolescents made gains on self-concept and self-esteem as presented in Table 5.3. They were less morose and withdrawn. The discussions helped them realize that they were not responsible for the divorce, a common misperception at that age. Also, they improved in their ability to get along with the separated parent and, in some cases, with their new blended family. The teachers and counselors reported improved school performance. By far the most positive impact, however, was from the relationships that they formed with their new "big" brothers and sisters. Certainly anytime high school juniors and seniors paid positive attention to sixth and seventh graders, those squirrely teeny boppers were transformed. This study was no exception. There were clear signs in the journals and in verbal and nonverbal behavior that the middle schoolers felt important, significant, and affirmed by such contact.

The high school group leaders also demonstrated significant psychological growth. On the measure of ego development, they moved to the level of personal

TABLE 5.3
Ego Development and Locus of Control Gains for Middle School Students Experiencing Family Disruptions

	Mean	SD	Gain	t	p
			Ego Development		
Pretest ($N = 40$)	4.20	1.24	+.35	3.0	< .002
Posttest	4.55	1.36			
			Locus of Control		
Pretest	15.5	4.06	−2.27	3.27	< .001
Posttest	13.2	3.92			

Note. On the Nowicki-Strickland (1973), a drop indicates an increase in internal control. The Loevinger conversions were the same as noted e.g., $D = 2$, $D3 = 3$, $3 = 4$, $3/4 = 5$, etc.

autonomy, and on the measure of moral judgment, as noted in the meta-analysis (Table 5.1). Signs of psychological maturity were evident, derived from the leadership experience. It was, however, more than the experience itself. As was the case in the small group counseling course, these students also reflected on their learning each week, both in the seminar and in their journal entries. The students would comment particularly on their different feelings associated with being a teacher versus their usual role in secondary school classes. A control group of peer leaders minus the reflection sessions showed no similar gains in maturity, as was the case for the control group in the math tutoring study. Another outcome of these reflection seminar groups for the high school students was a sense of community. The high school students in both the math project and the model peer counseling program all mentioned the feelings of group participation. For the first time, they felt that they had gotten to know and understand their peers during the training classes. The usual subgroups, cliques, and isolates that Coleman (1961) had documented many years ago as endemic to secondary school, disappeared. The class of helpers became unified not only in purpose, but also in relationship to each other. Those single classes, then, served as small examples of what secondary schools can become, a place for development through a community with values more meaningful than good looks, fast cars, and athletics.

Central to the success of both programs was the acquisition of genuine counseling skills for the small group leaders. These same skills formed the core learning for individual tutoring. In the latter case, acknowledging the scared feelings vis-à-vis learning math was at least as important as the practice problem solving. Of course, not all school counselors or counseling psychologists were as comfortable in such an outreach setting as in regular classrooms and the heterogeneous make-up of such classes. From our experience, however, such an approach in regular classrooms is at the heart of the primary prevention model.

A second issue of instructional importance is the ability of the leader to understand the developmental balance between accommodation and assimilation. This is sometimes referred to as the problem of mismatching, constructive dissonance, or aiming at Vygotsky's (1978) zone of proximal growth. This means the leader must balance the intellectual and affective learning between creating a supportive atmosphere à la Carl Rogers (1961) and a challenging climate à la Albert Ellis (1962). An exclusive focus on either one does not induce growth. Developmental growth requires a person to give up the old way of problem solving, which is always painful (Perry, 1978); hence the need to challenge through a knowledge *perturbation*. At the same time, there is an equally important need to provide for periods of relaxed reflection and affective support (Furth, 1981). Unfortunately, most of the literature on cognitive-developmental interventions rarely mentions this instructional paradox (e.g., supportive yet challenging). Thus the leader does need to blend two apparently opposite counseling techniques in the social role-taking programs as a challenging Rogerian, or as a supportive rational emotive therapist. Otherwise, there is little reason to believe that a role-taking experience will result in cognitive structural complexity.

ROLE TAKING FOR ADULTS?

Originally, of course, cognitive developmental theorists had assumed that stage growth ceilinged out during early adulthood. In fact, Kohlberg himself graciously ate crow (Kohlberg & Kramer, 1969) when he and many developmentalists made the same fortuitous error. In reviewing longitudinal versus cross-sectional studies, they found that at least some adults continued to advance in stage and sequence. The most important current account of this process can be found in Lee and Snarey (1988). Such a theoretical revision posed another question, perhaps obvious. If we could promote stage growth for adolescents, would the same follow for adults? The conditions for psychological growth were clear: (a) a role-taking experience in helping; (b) guided reflection; (c) a balance between action and reflection; (d) continuity, or time on task of at least one semester; and (e) a classroom climate that was both supportive and challenging.

The first question focused on the process of adult development. It now seemed that adult growth was possible. Next was the question of a role-taking experience for teachers and/or counselors. In Minnesota we had tried some approaches with results that were modest, at best. Activities such as individualizing instruction, interviewing skills, and self-directed behavioral modification didn't quite produce the kind of cognitive structural change that we had seen with adolescents (Sprinthall & Bernier, 1979). The move to North Carolina, however, provided a new and more compelling opportunity for the role-taking method.

The State Department of Public Instruction there had mandated a program for first- and second-year teachers that called for a probationary period to be completed with an assessment check list of requisite teacher behaviors. There was, however, nothing in place in the schools to provide assistance to the novice teachers in developing the required effective teaching skills. In this case, Thies-Sprinthall (1984) had already demonstrated that experienced teachers could be educated as effective mentors through a role-taking program. Her program followed the train-

5. COUNSELING AND SOCIAL ROLE TAKING

ing guidelines closely. The role-taking was focused on the skills of so-called clinical supervision. She observed that although an experienced teacher might be quite adequate as a classroom instructor, more often than not such a teacher had few skills and very little knowledge, if any, on how to supervise a novice teacher. The only major change she made in the conditions for development was to expand the training program over a two-semester sequence, with the second semester as the time for the actual mentoring of the beginner. She found that the experienced teachers needed some time to relearn a greater repertoire of their own instructional skills and then to master the skills of clinical supervision.

With her colleagues Alan Reiman (Reiman & Thies-Sprinthall, 1993), she now was able to demonstrate the same positive effects upon the two domains of conceptual development and moral judgment for the experienced teachers. Also, their research indicated that the teachers changed considerably in their supervisory discourse. They demonstrated a greater ability with empathic listening skills from the program. This was yet another indicator of the Mead, Kohlberg, Selman contention noted earlier, namely that the role-taking skills involved in empathic communication (counseling skills) promoted interpersonal perspective taking. Learning to place one's self in another's shoes at both an intellectual and affective level generated moral development, regardless of age. The results of two studies on the cognitive developmental assessments with the experienced teachers are presented in Table 5.4.

Although the studies did not employ a contemporaneous control group, prior research by Rest (1986) indicated most clearly that adults in general do not change significantly on moral judgment in a 9-month time period. Also, it was shown that regular academic classes for teachers in graduate school did not impact either their moral- or ego- development level (Oja & Sprinthall, 1978; Sprinthall & Bernier, 1979). Thies-Sprinthall (1980) found that professional experience by itself had no noticeable effect on either the level of psychological development, or the supervisory behavior of teacher-supervisors. In fact, what she found was that a substantial number of supervising teachers were functioning at very modest levels of moral and conceptual development. Their supervisory behavior was to punish and de-

TABLE 5.4
Two Studies of Moral Judgment and Conceptual Level Effects and Listening Skill Acquisition for Experienced Teachers[a]

	Pretest	Posttest	t	p
Study 1 (Thies-Sprinthall, 1984)				
Rest DIT	41	53	2.46	< .04
Hunt CL	1.6	1.8	2.35	< .04
Listening Skills	1.28	2.58	3.80	< .01
Study 2 (Reiman & Thies-Sprinthall, 1993)				
Rest	33.7	44.4	2.81	< .04
Hunt CL	1.8	2.1	3.39	< .01
Listening Skills	1.10	2.70	4.40	< .01

[a]Assessed using a version of a 4-point accurate empathy scale.

value the innovative efforts of their student teachers. McKibbon and Joyce (1981) found that assessed developmental stage accurately predicted which teachers would be able to adopt and generalize innovative practice in their classrooms. Thus the role-taking studies indicate that it is possible to promote adult development in professional settings and that other research has indicated the importance of such efforts. This is really another version of the "higher is better" argument. If the task at hand involves complex human relationship skills such as accurate empathy, the ability to read and flex, to select the appropriate model from the professional repertoire, then higher order psychological maturity across moral, ego, and conceptual development is clearly requisite. In fact, a very recent study by Peace (1992) demonstrated similar gains in conceptual and moral judgment, as well as in accurate empathy in a sample of counselors being trained for the role of clinical supervisor for a beginning counselor. Thus, there is emerging evidence to support the contention of cognitive structural growth and professional skill acquisition by adult teachers and counselors through role taking.

IMPLICATIONS

Rest (1986) maintained that there are at least four interacting components (see chap. 1) that comprehend the complex relationship between moral judgment and moral behavior. His framework clearly suggests two issues if we wish to promote both judgment and behavior. First, we need an expanded theoretical framework beyond the rational analysis of moral issues. Second, and as a result of the idea of four components, we need to think more broadly about interventions. Certainly the dialogue dilemma method achieves positive results on moral judgment measures. The social role-taking procedures outlined here, however, have a broader perspective and an expanded scope. The role requirements insure that the participants will actually employ certain communication and helping skills in real-world situations. These activities are not simulations or role plays. Also, the guided reflection through weekly journal entries provides the opportunity for the instructor to individualize the feedback according to the current developmental level of the participant (Reiman, 1991). In this sense, then, the social role taking methods seem more potent as an intervention strategy for broad scale, multiple component growth than a discussion method. Through counseling skill acquisition in the context of role-taking and reflection, the broader goals of the four components appear more viable and less singular than the dilemma method by itself.

Certainly there has been great controversy originated, particularly by Gilligan (1982), which suggested that moral judgment theory and practice was too narrow, impersonal, and lacking in care. As a result, she posed a dichotomy between Kohlbergian justice (the cold, Kantian, categorical imperative) and her own version of gender-specific empathy. The social role-taking research over the past 20 years clearly indicates that such a separation is unnecessary. Learning higher order helping skills in the variety of forms exhibited in these programs nurtures humane behavior, ego and conceptual development, and moral judgment. The participants exhibit more personal autonomy, caring, and a greater understanding of Rawlsian democratic principles. Also, in none of these programs have we ever found any differences in the ability to learn the role-taking skills by gender. The only difference we found occurred at the outset, when we were teaching graduate students in one class and high school students in another. We found that the top half of the high school class performed more adequately than the bottom half of the graduate student class. Some graduate students were so concerned about theory that they had great difficulty in responding empathically to their clients.

A third issue of importance relates to the opening question of this chapter. Can we view social role taking as an important element for primary prevention in the service of Albee's dictum to promote human welfare? Professional organizations quite unfortunately seem to thrive and strive toward goals of exclusiveness, privilege, and ever-extended professional training. Bakan (1967) some years ago referred to this as the mystery–mastery complex. Keep the professional skills safely locked up within layers of professional certification requirements and wage legal wars against any challenge to this hegemony. And, unfortunately, Bakan was an accurate prophet as the current court cases among psychiatry, clinical psychology, and counseling training programs attest (Sprinthall, 1990). Thus, at the graduate level there is an urgent need for programs to focus on a developmental model. Clearly in such a complex arena as how to promote human growth and development there is a urgent need for more applied research for schools, colleges, community based counseling centers, and for training programs designed to produce a host of professional helpers. Role-taking programs require modification and expansion as a means of achieving the general goals of psychological maturity. The conventional or standard curriculum for schools, colleges, or professional training programs rarely, if ever, addresses the issues of human relationships and moral judgment. Some of the examples in this volume, including social role taking may point the way in a different direction.

REFERENCES

Albee, G. (1982). Preventing psychopathology and promoting human potential. *American Psychologist, 37*, 1043–1050.

Allport, G. (1968). *The person in psychology*. Boston, MA: Beacon.

Bakan, D. (1967). *On method*. San Francisco: Jossey-Bass.

Bergin, A. (1963). The effects of psychotherapy: Negative results revisited. *Journal of Counseling Psychology, 10*, 244–250.

Blatt, M. (1969). *The effects of classroom discussion programs upon children's level of moral development*. Unpublished doctoral dissertation, University of Chicago.

Campbell, D., & Stanley, J. C. (1963). *Experimental and quasi-experimental designs for research*. Chicago: Rand McNally.

Cognetta, P. (1980). *Cross-age teaching in secondary schools: A program for psychological development*. Unpublished doctoral dissertation, University of Minnesota, Minneapolis.

Cohen, P., Kulik, J., & Kulik, C. (1982). Educational outcomes of tutoring: A meta-analysis of findings. *American Educational Research Journal, 19*, 237–248.

Coleman, J. (1961). T*he adolescent society.* New York: The Free Press.

Dewey, J. (1938). *Experience and education.* New York: Macmillan.

Dowell, R. C. (1971). *Adolescents as peer counselors.* Unpublished doctoral dissertation, Harvard University, Cambridge, MA.

Ellis, A. (1962). *Reason and emotion in psychotherapy.* New York: Lyle Stewart.

Exum, H. (1980). Ego development: Using curriculum to facilitate growth. *Character Potential, 9,* 121–128.

Eysenck, H. (1978). An exercise in mega-silliness. *American Psychologist, 33,* 517.

Fennema, E. Wolleat, P., & Pedro, J. (1979). Mathematics attribution scale. *JSAS: Catalog of Selected Documents in Psychology,* (Ms. No. 1837).

Flavell, J. (1971). Stage-related properties of cognitive development. *Cognitive Psychology, 2,* 421–453.

Furth, H. (1981). *Piaget and knowledge.* Chicago: University of Chicago Press.

Gilligan, C. (1982). *In a different voice.* Cambridge, MA: Harvard University Press.

Goodlad, J. (1984). *A place called school.* New York: McGraw-Hill.

Heath, D. (1977). *Maturity and competence.* New York: Gardner.

Hedin, D. (1979). T*eenage health educators: An action learning program to promote psychological development.* Unpublished doctoral dissertation, University of Minnesota, Minneapolis.

Hetherington, M. (1984). Families in transition. In R. Parke (Ed.), *Review of child development research* (pp. 398–440). Chicago: University of Chicago Press.

Hunt, D. E. (1974). *Matching models in education.* Toronto: Ontario Institute of Studies in Education.

Kohlberg, L. (1971). Humanistic and cognitive developmental perspectives on psychological education: A critique. *The Counseling Psychologist, 1,* 74–82.

Kohlberg, L. (1972). The cognitive-developmental approach to moral education. *Humanist, 32,* 13–16.

Kohlberg, L. (1974). Counseling and Counselor Education. *Counselor Education and Supervision, 14,* 250–256.

Kohlberg, L., & Kramer, R. (1969). Continuities and discontinuities in children and adult moral development. *Human Development, 12,* 93–120.

Kohlberg, L., LaCrosse, J., & Ricks, D. (1970). The predictability of adult mental health from childhood behavior. In B. Wolman (Ed.), *Handbook of child psychopathology* (pp. 1271–1284). New York: McGraw-Hill.

Lee, L., & Snarey, J. (1988). The relationship between ego and moral development. In D. Lapsley & C. Power (Eds.), *Self, ego, and identity* (pp. 151–178). New York: Springer-Verlag.

Levitt, E. (1967). The undemonstrated effectiveness of therapeutic process with children. In B. Berenson & R. Carkhuff (Eds.), *Sources of gain in counseling and psychotherapy* (pp. 33–45). New York: Holt, Rinehart & Winston.

Light, R., & Pillemer, D. (1984). *Summing up: The science of reviewing research.* Cambridge, MA: Harvard University Press.

Loevinger J. (1966). The meaning and measurement of ego development. *American Psychologist, 21,* 195–206.

McClelland, D. C. (1973). Testing for competence rather than for "intelligence." *American Psychologist, 28,* 1–14.

McKibbon, M., & Joyce, B. (1981). Psychological states and staff development. *Theory Into Practice, 19,* 248–255.

Mead, G. H. (1934). M*ind, self, and society.* Chicago: University of Chicago Press.

Miller, G. Al. (1969). Psychology as a means of promoting human welfare. *American Psychologist, 24,* 1063–1075.

Mosher, R., & Sprinthall, N. (1971). Psychological education: A means to promote personal development during adolescence. *The Counseling Psychologist, 1,* 3–74.

Mosher, R., & Sullivan, P. (1976). A curriculum in moral education for adolescents. *Journal of Moral Education, 5,* 159–172.

5. COUNSELING AND SOCIAL ROLE TAKING

Nowicki, S., & Strickland, B. (1973). A locus of control scale for children. *Journal of Consulting and Clinical Psychology, 40*, 148–154.

Oja, S., & Sprinthall, N. A. (1978). Psychological and moral development for teachers. In N. A. Sprinthall & R. L. Mosher (Eds.), *Value development...as the aim of education* (pp. 117–134). New York: Character Press.

Peace, S. (1992). *A study of school counselor induction: A cognitive-developmental model.* Unpublished doctoral dissertation, North Carolina State University.

Perry, W. (1970). *Forms of intellectual and ethical development during the college years.* New York: Holt Rinehart & Winston.

Perry, W. (1978). Sharing the costs of growth. In C. Parker (Ed.), *Encouraging development in college students* (pp. 267–276). Minneapolis, MN: University of Minnesota Press.

Reiman, A. (1991). Charting the future of teacher induction. *Eastern Educational Journal, 21*, 6–10.

Reiman, A., & Parramore, B. (1993). Promoting preservice teacher development through extended field experience. In M. O'Hair & S. Odell (Eds.), *Diversity and teaching: Teacher education yearbook I* (pp. 111–121). Forth Worth, TX: Association of Teacher Educators.

Reiman, A., & Thies-Sprinthall, L. (1993). Promoting the development of mentor teachers: Theory and research programs using guided reflection. *Journal of Research & Development in Education, 26*, 179–185.

Rest, J. (1986). *Moral development.* New York: Praeger.

Rogers, C. (1961). *On becoming a person.* Boston: Houghton Mifflin.

Rustad, K., & Rogers, C. (1975). Promoting psychological growth in a high school class. *Counselor Education and Supervision, 14*, 227–285.

Satterstrom, L. (1980). *A matching model for differentiated supervision of student teachers.* Unpublished doctoral dissertation, University of Minnesota, Minneapolis.

Selman, R. (1971). The relation of role taking to the development of moral judgment in children. *Child Development, 42*, 79–91.

Smith, M., & Glass, G. (1977). Meta-analysis of psychotherapy outcome studies. *American Psychologist, 32*, 752–760.

Sprinthall, N. A. (1980). Psychology for secondary schools. The saber-toothed curriculum revisited. *American Psychologist, 35*, 336–347.

Sprinthall, N. A. (1990). Counseling psychology from Greyston to Atlanta: On the road to Armageddon? *The Counseling Psychologist, 18*, 455–463.

Sprinthall, N. A., & Bernier, J. (1979). Moral and cognitive development of teachers. In T.C. Hennessy (Ed.), *Value and moral education* (pp. 119–145). New York: Paulist Press.

Sprinthall, N. A., Hall, J., & Gerler, E. (1992). Peer counseling for middle school students experiencing family divorce. *Elementary School Guidance and Counseling, 26*, 279–294.

Sprinthall, N. A., & Scott, J. (1989). Promoting psychological development, math achievement and success attribution of female students through deliberate psychological education. *Journal of Counseling Psychology, 36*, 440–446.

Sprinthall, R. C., Schmutte, G., & Sirois, L. (1991). *Understanding educational research.* Englewood Cliffs, NJ: Prentice-Hall.

Thies-Sprinthall, L. (1980). Supervision: An educative or miseducative process? *Journal of Teacher Education, 31*, 17–30.

Thies-Sprinthall, L. (1984). Promoting the developmental growth of supervising teachers: Theory, research, programs and implications. *Journal of Teacher Education, 35*, 329–336.

Tucker, A. (1977). *Empathy training for undergraduate college students in a cross-cultural milieu.* Unpublished doctoral dissertation, University of Minnesota, Minneapolis.

Ursone, D. (1990). *Parental divorce during childhood.* Unpublished master's thesis, North Carolina State University, Raleigh.

Vygotsky, L. (1978). *Mind and society.* Cambridge, MA.: Harvard University Press.

Chapter 6

Ethical Reasoning Research in the Accounting and Auditing Professions

Lawrence A. Ponemon
Binghamton University, SUNY

David R. L. Gabhart
Bentley College

The concept of professional ethics is more than an external measure by which the profession can maintain a virtuous image. For many practitioners, it is a concept that implies a reasoning capability that permits the individual to render judgment unaltered by self-interest that could impair his or her professional responsibility. The ethical reasoning process is part of the individual's overall moral consciousness from which he or she deals with difficult conflict or dilemmas in everyday practice. Ethical choice is just one of many types of decisions that the accountant or auditor must render in order to be an effective member of this profession. In this chapter, we first discuss the ethical domain in the accounting and auditing profession,[1] and then relate the theory of ethical development to judgment by the use of one case study. The chapter concludes with a brief discussion of the professional implications of ethical reasoning theory and a review of recent empirical studies in the accounting and auditing field.

---

[1] *Accounting* refers to the process of organizing and preparing financial reports and financial statement information to be used by an organization's stakeholders and exchange partners. *Auditing* refers to the process of examining financial information to ascertaining that the financial statements were prepared and reported correctly.

THE ETHICAL DOMAIN IN ACCOUNTING AND AUDITING

Professional practice requires the accounting practitioner to deal with various individuals, entities, and organizations. Many times, such interactions will result in conflict of interest, causing the accountant to behave in a way that will compromise professional conduct according to the norms espoused by the firm or the profession. The profession is becoming increasingly concerned about these interactions. Governmental organizations and various professional bodies that oversee and regulate the accounting profession have applied more stringent controls over the most salient and damaging relationships that could give rise to the appearance of ethical impropriety.

The ethical domain for accountants and auditors usually involves four key constituent groups, which include the client organization that pays the practitioner for services rendered; the professional accounting firm that employs the practitioner, typically represented by the collective interests of the firm's management; the accounting profession, including various self-regulatory bodies; and the general public who rely on the attestations and representations of the professional accountant, including all key exchange partners with the client organization and the public accounting firm. In this regard, the role of an independent profession is defined in the context of the conflicting interests caused by the different and competing goals or objectives of various constituents.

Simultaneous responsiblility to the profession, the general public, the economic needs of the accounting firm, and the client organization is at the core of many ethical problems. To make matters worse, the fact that accountants and auditors are paid a fee directly by the client organization for *independent* services is a potential conflict of interest. This problem is especially salient when the client organization represents a significant source of revenues for the public accounting firm, or when the firm has a long-standing professional or social relationship with the organization and its management.

As recent cases of audit litigation suggest, nontraditional accounting or consulting services, coupled with unorthodox fee arrangements between the public accounting firm and the client organization, can cause the appearance of accounting shenanigans. Fortunately, firm profitability is not the only factor affecting ethical behavior. Variables such as firm reputation, legal liability, and the stringent enforcement of standards and rules over unethical acts offset the motivation to seek unbridled profits without regard to professional or societal consequences.

Sources of Ethical Problems

In the public accounting profession there exists negative or instigating factors that tend to discourage compliance with ethical practices or professional standards. Ponemon and Gabhart (1993) suggested that the most common factors—which can be situational or environmental in nature—that cause ethical conflict include the following:

1. Fees are paid by the client organization rather than by the direct beneficiary of the independent auditing services (e.g., the general public).
2. Management consulting work is provided for the benefit of client management at the same time that an independent audit is being conducted.
3. Status and career attainment within the firm is often predicated on one's ability to develop new business.
4. Affiliation with personnel within the client organization often diminishes the auditor's objectivity and skepticism.
5. Social discourse and peer pressure within the public accounting firm often exacerbate dysfunctional work-related behaviors.
6. Competition among firms for audit clients causes the low balling of audit fees, which often reduces the quality of audit services.
7. Job security for staff and partner-level personnel within the public accounting firm may mitigate the disclosure of sensitive information in the workplace.

It is important to note that these factors do not represent an exhaustive list of possible sources of ethical problems in the practice of accounting and auditing. Rather, it is maintained that these factors play a very instrumental role in the process by which the individual accountant forms his or her ethical judgment and chooses to take some course of action. Furthermore, these factors often work in tandem to create potential conflict areas for individuals working in accounting and auditing firms.

Mitigating Factors

In recognition of the potential for serious ethical conflicts, the profession has attempted to institute formal and informal control mechanisms to encourage the individual practitioner's ethical behavior in a way that is deemed to be consistent with the espoused rules and guidelines of the profession. These positive factors work in conjunction with an individual's ethical reasoning capacity and many other exogenous variables not discussed here. According to Ponemon and Gabhart (1993), mitigating factors that potentially lessen unethical acts in accounting and auditing practice include the following:

1. Professional standards, codes of conduct, and behavioral guidelines espoused by the public accounting firm.
2. Internal controls to audit work, such as adequate supervision and training of staff and the careful review of workpapers.
3. Team auditing, wherein a group of individuals are assigned to one client so that audit functions are properly segregated.

4. Peer reviews of auditing engagements by an independent group of expert auditors from another firm or from a regulatory body.
5. Affiliation, social discourse, and peer pressure within the public accounting firm.
6. The individual's personal integrity, ethical capacity and orientation toward professionalism.
7. Governmental laws, internal and external regulations, and congressional oversight.

In summary, the mitigating and instigating factors listed above affect the degree of ethical impropriety in the accounting and auditing profession. We also posit that the contribution of these factors to a practitioner's ethical choice is a function of many other intervening variables, including the individual's ethical capacity to reason in an ethical sense about problems in everyday practice.

Ethical Development

To show how the theory of ethical development as advanced by Kohlberg (1969) and Rest (1979a) can be used to understand ethical behavior in the accounting and auditing domain, consider a hypothetical case based on the conflict of interest caused, in part, by an auditing firm's management consulting (MAS) endeavors on active auditing clients, as follows:[2]

> Alice is a senior auditor for a national public accounting firm that provides auditing, tax, and consulting services. The firm has developed a package called the ACME ACCOUNTING SYSTEM that is sold to the general public as well as the firm's audit clients. Alice is the auditor-in-charge of the ABC Company, Inc. engagement. During the course of this project, Alice is asked to evaluate the control structure of the client's internal accounting system, which is based on the ACME package. In the course of her evaluation, Alice uncovers several significant control weaknesses in the system. Before rendering her conclusions to ABC management, however, Alice is told by her boss to modify the negative comments in the management letter regarding the ACME system problems. What should Alice do?

Preconventional Level. An individual at the preconventional level makes the decision to do what is right to avoid punishment or to serve one's own interest so Preconventional persons are not cognizant of differences among individuals. They view their actions in physical terms and are not conscious of the psychological interests of others. Using the hypothetical dilemma as a measure of moral reasoning, the independent accountant (Alice) at the preconventional level would make the judgement to inform ABC Company management, the bank, or her superior

---

[2]It is important to note that the following example of ethical reasoning at different developmental levels or stages is incomplete. For a more detailed discussion of ethical reasoning in accounting and auditing situations, see chapter 3 in Ponemon and Gabhart (1993).

6. ETHICAL REASONING RESEARCH—ACCOUNTING

partners only if it was deemed to be less harmful to her personally than if she concealed the facts. Conversely, if Alice could get away with not informing them, or if there is a low probability of getting caught, she would do so.

An independent accountant at Stage 1 (i.e., the first stage in the preconventional level) would decide to abide by the rules rather than seek personal gain, simply to avoid punishment or reprimand from a higher authority, such as the partners in the firm, the accountancy board, or the general business community. At Stage 2 of the preconventional level, the reasons to do right are not only dictated by the threat of punishment, but also by an overwhelming desire to serve one's own interest. Thus, if the accountant felt strongly enough about concealing the facts about the system, he or she would do so—even if the penalties were high.

The auditor at the preconventional level, might not pursue the ethical highroad in a number of circumstances, which includes the following: (a) if the risks of getting caught were relatively low, (b) if the punishment from authorities was deemed to be minor or insignificant, or (c) if the personal gains were substantially greater than any of the perceived risks. The preconventional accountant might go well beyond the selection decision; he or she might seek to profit (or make a commission) from the sale of the software, assuming that the penalties for such action were perceived to be trivial or harmless.

Conventional Level. An individual at the conventional level has a need to be a good person and desires to maintain rules and authority that support stereotypical good behavior. The individual feels obligated to keep the system of rules and conventions going, and seeks ways to avoid breakdown in the system. The conventional individual is aware of shared feelings, agreements, and expectations that take primacy over individual interests. At Stage 3 (i.e., the first stage of the conventional level), the accountant's need to be a good person in the eyes of fellow accountants, the client, and the profession as a whole, is the primary motivator of moral action. The Stage 4 accountant is also aware of the needs of others, but has learned to differentiate the societal point of view from personal motives. Thus, at Stage 4 the rules of the profession tend to be upheld, except when they conflict with other social contracts that are believed to be more pressing or important (such as family issues or the church).

If Alice were at Stage 3, she might be motivated to keep silent on the software problems in order to win the approval of her colleagues within the firm, as well as that of her boss. At Stage 4, however, because of a need to abide by the rules of the profession, Alice probably would feel morally obligated to share her findings with the client, as well as those individuals in the firm who were responsible for developing the ACME product. Alice would recognize that her own self-interest was at risk, but would conclude that the best interests of the client organization and the public accounting firm should always take precedence.

Postconventional Level. The postconventional individual follows self-chosen ethical principles, in which case particular laws or social agreements are usually valid because they rest on such principles. However, when laws or rules violate these principles, one acts in accordance with the principle rather than abiding by the rule. The individual's social perspective is that of a rational individual who is aware of values and rights prior to social attachments and contracts. At Stage 5 (i.e., the first stage in the postconventional level), the independent accountant believes that the rules and laws governing moral action in the accounting profession are based on some rational calculation of overall utility or benefit to society. Here, the individual recognizes that moral and legal points of view sometimes conflict—and often has difficulty integrating them. Stage 6 accountants have learned to balance moral principles and the rules and expectations of their profession and society. At Stage 6, the auditor makes a choice to do right if it is consistent with his or her self-chosen ethical principles.

The postconventional practitioner also would recognize the client's interests; however, he or she might conclude that informing ABC Company management is more than abiding by a rule, is the morally sound position to take. Furthermore, the postconventional accountant or auditor might have first considered if it were appropriate to audit the ABC Company system, given the firm's involvement in the software selection project.

Postconventional auditors might continue to advise the client to purchase a particular software package if they felt that the recommendation were given in the best interest of the client—and even if it might compromise independence and objectivity. In summary, the postconventional individual knows the rules, understands the underlying principles, and makes a decision that is guided by the principles rather than by the rules. The objective of this hypothetical dilemma is to show that the behavior of the independent accountant is a function of moral reasoning capabilities. The way Alice perceives the problem and resolves the conflict will result in some action that is consistent with her developmental stage or level of morality.

Benefits From This Kind of Analysis

As can be seen from this simple analysis of a very complex process of ethical reasoning, notions such as independence, objectivity, and professionalism are all grounded in the individual's reasoning ability (see Jones & Ponemon, 1993). Taking this one step further, assuming that an individual's ethical reasoning is a primary determinant of ethical judgment and behavior in the accounting or auditing environment, then what value does this area of research provide? One way to answer this important question is to discuss the potential use of such information, which can be divided into three general areas as advanced by Arnold and Ponemon (1987, p. 25).

1. Gaining an insight into the underlying reasoning levels of practicing accountants or auditors in their resolution of ethical conflicts.
2. Recognizing the problems caused by differences in ethical judgment among professional accountants and auditors and their effect on practice.

3. Identifying the means necessary to effect ethical propriety in the accounting and auditing professions.

Perhaps an integral understanding of the ethical reasoning process of accountants and auditors should be a prerequisite to the legislation of rules and regulations promoting desirable behavior. Rules or guidelines that attempt to mitigate a Stage 1 or Stage 2 mode of ethical reasoning will do little to affect the actions of individuals whose reasoning is at higher levels. For example, the primary motivator of ethical behavior for an individual at the lowest ethical reasoning level in the Kohlberg (1969) stage model is to avoid punishment. In this case, rules that are not backed by punishment will normally not be adhered to by the individual at a lower stage of ethical cognition. Thus, behavioral norms that are consistent with the ethical framework of the intended population should certainly improve compliance. It is important to note, however, that rules in accounting may be seen as an institution for avoiding punishment. In this case, preconventional auditors may follow the rules only to defend themselves against allegations of wrongdoing or audit failure.

The theory of ethical development provides a framework that can be used to gauge those conflict areas that would have the most severe and damaging consequences to the profession. For example, if an overwhelming majority of partners are at a level where it is very likely that the quality and integrity of their firm's work product will come before marketing and promotion activities, then stringent rules limiting practice development would be unnecessary or perhaps dysfunctional to the desired behavior. On the other hand, if most partners are at a level where profitability and personal economic gain are of primary concern, then rules on marketing activities that are not backed by authority would do little in mitigating behavioral impropriety.

Although this theory places an individual at a ethical reasoning stage, it is possible for individuals to move to higher stages. Thus, although the preceding issues deal with fitting the rules of the profession to the stages at which we currently find the accountant, another possibility is to raise the level of the accounting practitioner such that he or she can better function in a dilemma-prone world. Here an understanding of the theory of ethical development is a necessary condition for effective training and education. The following section describes the results of several recently published research studies in the area of public accounting, auditing, and accounting education.

STUDIES IN ACCOUNTING AND AUDITING

Recent empirical studies have explored the underlying ethical reasoning processes of accountants and auditors in practice. Findings in this relatively new area of research were threefold. First, studies suggested that members of the public accounting profession are not reaching their potential for higher levels of ethical reasoning by virtue of selection-socialization in education (Ponemon & Glazer, 1990) and within public accounting firms (Ponemon, 1990, 1992a; Shaub, 1994). Second, findings showed that ethical reasoning may be an important determinant of professional judgment, such as the disclosure of sensitive information (Arnold Ponemon 1991), and auditor independence (Ponemon & Gabhart, 1990). Third, results suggested that unethical and dysfunctional audit behavior, such as the underreporting of time on an audit time budget, may be systematically related to the auditor's level of ethical reasoning (Ponemon, 1992b). In general, these works implied that ethical reasoning may be an important cognitive characteristic that may affect individual judgment and behavior under a wide array of conditions and events in extant professional practice. To show how the present work extends earlier research, brief synopses of recent studies in this area are provided. Table 6.1 summarizes this literature.

Descriptive Studies

Armstrong (1984, 1987) studied accountants' ethical reasoning and moral development employing the Defining Issues Test (DIT) for a sample of CPAs and accounting students in southern California. Based on a mailed survey instrument, she found that CPAs and accounting students tended to be at lower levels of ethical reasoning than comparable groups of college-educated adults or college-aged students, as published in Rest (1979a). Drawing from Rest's (1986) findings that a significant rate of ethical development can occur for many adults during their college years, she advanced the notion that accounting education may inhibit development to higher stages of ethical reasoning.

Ponemon (1988, 1990) examined the ethical reasoning and ethical judgments of accounting practitioners in public firms. Fifty-two practicing public accountants from large and small CPA firms in the northeast region of the United States agreed to participate in a field study that required them to resolve the standardized Moral Judgment Interview (MJI) and an auditor role conflict based on a real-life case study. Their stated responses were analyzed using a protocol analysis technique, resulting in an MJI stage score measure of ethical reasoning. Variables pertaining to the practice environment were also collected and examined to determine possible interactions with MJI scores. Findings revealed differences in subjects' ethical choices and stated resolutions to the auditor-role conflict according to their social position in the public accounting firm. That is, junior- and senior- level CPAs tended to acknowledge rules of conduct, whereas managers and partners tended to view profitability and litigation concerns, as the most important antecedents to the resolution to the auditor-role conflict.

Ponemon (1990) also found a significant curvilinear association between MJI scores and years of public accounting experience, where ethical stage increased from the staff to supervisory levels and then sharply decreased in the manager and partner ranks. Although findings are based on cross-sectional evidence from a relatively small, nonrandom sample of CPAs, Ponemon argued that findings may have been brought about by socialization processes within accounting firms, thus causing individuals with too high or too low a level of ethical reasoning to leave the firm or profession.

Shaub (1989, 1994) extended the work of Armstrong (1987) by attempting to measure the ethical sensitivity of CPA practitioners at all position levels from several offices of a Big-Six accounting firm (located in the Midwest) and then related these ethical sensitivity measures to DIT p-score results. Although Shaub (1989) did not find a significant association between ethical reasoning (DIT p scores) and measured ethical sensitivity, his studies did provide three interesting findings. First, similar to Ponemon's (1990) MJI results, in this study CPAs' DIT p scores also decreased in the manager and partner ranks. Second, Shaub found significant differences between men and women, wherein both female accounting students and female CPAs tended to have higher DIT p scores than men at the same level or rank within the firm. Third, Shaub (1993) found a significant association between self-reported GPA and DIT P scores for both accounting students and practitioners, thus suggesting that ethical reasoning may be inextricably linked to other intellectual capacities as well as school achievement.

Lampe and Finn (1992) also conducted a study of accounting students and CPAs in public firms (not including partners) using the DIT. This work built upon and extended Shaub's (1989) research by comparing subjects' DIT results to responses on a questionnaire containing seven short ethical scenarios. Their findings showed that both accounting students and practitioners tend to have lower DIT p scores than college-aged students, college-educated adults, and other professions groups such as law and medicine. They also found that DIT stage measures (e.g., rather than p scores) were better predictors of ethical choice on the ethical scenarios. They also found that while DIT p scores were relatively low for most subjects, their percentage Stage 4 scores tended to be higher than those reported by Rest (1986). Accordingly, Lampe and Finn concluded that this finding may indicate that, by virtue of the rule-oriented nature of accounting and auditing practice, the development of a Stage 4 moral orientation rather than principled reasoning (e.g., Stages 5 and 6) may be more important for professional accountants and auditors.

Ponemon (1992a) also studied the influence of accounting firm socialization upon the individual CPA's level of ethical reasoning. Using the DIT, the selection-socialization phenomenon was explored using a triangulated research design based on a random cross-sectional sample of 180 CPAs, a longitudinal sample of 221 auditors in one national firm over a 2-year period, and an experimental study of 23 audit managers' promotion assessments of 54 senior level auditors located in one large practice office. Findings of all three studies corroborate the existence of ethical socialization whereby those progressing to manager and partner positions within the firm tended to possess lower and more homogeneous DIT p scores. Experimental findings also suggested that firm managers' promotion decisions are biased in favor of individuals possessing ethical reasoning that is closer to their own capacity. According to Ponemon, these findings implied that the ethical

TABLE 6.1
Review of Ethical Reasoning Studies in Accounting and Auditing

Author(s)	Description of the Studies	Major Research Findings
Armstrong (1984, 1987)	DIT and ethical sensitivity survey completed by CPAs and accounting students from the West Coast.	CPAs and accounting students have relatively low DIT P scores in comparison to other populations studied.
Ponemon (1988, 1990)	MJI and audit case completed by CPAs at various position levels in public firms in the Northeast.	MJI scores decrease for CPAs at higher positions in public accounting firms.
Ponemon & Gabhart (1990)	DIT survey and between-subject experiment on auditor independence completed by senior-level auditors while attending a national firm's training program.	Auditor independence judgment and DIT P scores are related, wherein low DIT auditors were more sensitive to penalty than affiliation when framing judgment.
Ponemon & Glazer (1990)	DIT survey and comparative analysis of accounting students and alumni in public accounting practice from one state university and one liberal arts college, both in the East.	Students and CPAs from liberal arts college have higher DIT P scores than those from the conventional university program.
St. Pierre, Nelson, & Gabbin (1990)	DIT survey and comparative analysis of accounting and nonaccounting students in large university located in the Southeast.	Accounting students have lower DITs than other nonbusiness students, and female accounting majors have higher DITs than males.
Arnold & Ponemon (1991)	DIT survey and between-subject experiment on internal auditors from public (State Government) and private companies located in the Northeast.	Auditors with higher DITs are more likely to disclose sensitive audit findings, even under conditions of retaliation by management.
Icerman, Karcher, & Kennelley (1991)	DIT survey and comparative analysis of accounting, business, and nonbusiness students at a large university in the Southeast.	Although all students, on average, had relatively low DIT P scores, accounting students tended to have higher DITs than other business majors.
Bernardi (1991)	DIT survey and complex experimental study requiring the identification of fraudulent financial information for a large sample of auditors at different experience levels in several large CPA firms throughout the Northeast.	Findings revealed that experienced auditors with a relatively high DIT P score were best able to detect a material financial statement error and fraud.
Lampe & Finn (1992)	DIT survey, ethics questionnaire, and comparative analysis of CPAs and accounting students from the Midwest.	Accounting students and CPAs have relatively low DIT P scores and relatively high DIT Stage 4 measures.
Ponemon (1992a)	DIT survey of CPAs in nationwide cross-sectional sample of a 2-year longitudinal study of auditors from one large public accounting firm in a large city in the Northeast.	DIT P scores increase from staff to senior levels and decrease, becoming more homogeneous, in the manager and partner ranks in two separate studies.
Ponemon (1992b)	DIT survey and experimental-lab study of underreporting on a simulated audit exercise for a sample of staff auditors from various practice offices in the United States who were attending a national training program.	Auditors with low DIT P scores are more likely to underreport time, under conditions of peer or time budget pressure, than auditors with high DITs.
Jeffrey (1993)	DIT survey of accounting, business, and liberal arts students from one large university in the Midwest.	Accounting students have higher DITs than students in the other programs at the same university.

TABLE 6.1
(Continued)

Author(s)	Description of the Studies	Major Research Findings
Ponemon (1993a)	DIT survey and experimental study of auditor sensitivity to the ethical characteristic of client management within the context of audit risk and the assessment of fraudulent financial information.	Auditors with high DIT P scores are configural in the processing of competence and integrity cues regarding client management, whereas low DIT auditors are not.
Armstrong (1993)	Pre- and post-DIT survey of ethical development for students who elected to take a one semester course on ethics and professionalism in accounting.	Students who elected to take the one semester course had higher DITs than the average student population. They also developed higher DIT P scores by the end for the semester.
Ponemon (1993b)	Pre- and post-DIT survey of ethical development and an economic choice experiment of undergraduate and graduate accounting students in one state university located in the Northeast.	Students did not experience DIT P-score increases over a one semester auditing course, even if they participated in a 10-week ethics program. A U-shaped relationship between students' DITs and free-riding behavior was found.
Shaub (1993)	DIT survey of CPAs from the midwestern offices of one large public accounting firm and accounting students from one large university in the Midwest.	Students and CPAs have lower DITs than the population of college educated adults, and DITs are inversely related to CPAs' position level.
Ponemon & Gabhart (1993)	DIT survey and multiple experimental studies of auditing professionals in U.S. and Canadian accounting firms.	Canadian auditors had higher and less homogeneous DIT P scores than U.S. auditors at comparable position levels.

culture of the accounting firm stymies an individual's development to higher levels of ethical reasoning.

Ponemon and Gabhart (1993) studied auditing professionals from the two large accounting firms with practices in the United States and Canada, using the DIT and other experimental instruments. The primary objective of this research was to assess the impact of cross-national differences upon the ethical judgments of individual auditing practitioners. Results provided clear evidence of wide differences between Canadian and U.S. accounting professionals in terms of average DIT p scores. Canadian auditors at all position levels possessed markedly higher and less homogeneous DIT p scores than did U.S. auditors. In other words, the process of selection-socialization, alluded to in earlier works of U.S. CPAs, may not exist in large Canadian firms.

Results of the above mentioned studies indicate the importance of ethical reasoning as a determinant of ethical choice and professional behavior in a wide array of decisions, including the assessment of client competence and integrity, audit materiality, and audit risk. These findings should be of consequence to auditing researchers and practitioners alike because they suggest that the examination of task performance in accounting and auditing would be incomplete without first considering the ethical reasoning of the individual practitioner. Thus, the present collection of work may explain salient performance differences, heretofore not explained by experience or expertise alone, on tasks requiring the accountant or auditor to exercise professional judgment when evaluating the client organization and its management.

Ethical Judgment and Behavior

Five recent studies have sought to determine the existence of a relationship between ethical reasoning and ethical judgment or behavior in the context of accounting and auditing. The first study, conducted by Ponemon and Gabhart (1990), was an experimental investigation of auditor independence judgments and employed 119 partners and managers in one national public accounting firm.[3] Using the DIT p score to measure ethical reasoning, a hypothetical case study dealing with an independence dilemma framed in the third person to avoid potential self-reporting bias, and two between-subject manipulations, three significant findings were reported. First, the authors found a systematic relationship between auditors' ethical reasoning and their resolution of the independence conflict, where auditors with relatively low DIT p scores were more likely to violate independence rules than those with higher DIT scores. Second, they found that the existence of penalty, or the likelihood of losing a job, has a much stronger effect on the independence judgment than the existence of affiliation, defined as the likelihood of hurting others. Furthermore, interaction effects suggested that penalty is most salient for low DIT auditors. Third, findings showed that DIT p scores explain a priority ranking of independence attributes, wherein auditors with lower DITs assign greater importance to economic factors, such as client profitability and litigation, than auditors with higher DIT results.

In a related study, Arnold and Ponemon (1991) investigated the internal auditor's perceptions of whistle-blowing within the context of his or her level of ethical reasoning as measured by the DIT. Their experiment required 106 internal auditors to predict whether another person would engage in a whistle-blowing act under two different sets of conditions. The first set of conditions concerned the position of the individual discovering a fraud, and the second dealt with the nature of the retaliation posed against the whistle-blower. Similar to Ponemon and Gabhart (1990), the task was presented in the third-person to minimize potential self-reporting bias that often accompanies studies of ethical issues. Findings revealed that internal auditors with relatively low levels of ethical reasoning are unlikely to predict whistle-blowing as a means for disclosing wrongdoing. This result was especially prominent when the probable retaliation meant job termination for the whistle-blower. Findings also indicated that the organizational position of the individual contemplating the whistle-blowing act influences internal auditors' predictions, with external auditors considered most likely to act, internal auditors next, and marketing analysts least likely to act.

Bernardi (1991) studied the relationship between ethical reasoning and the auditor's ability to detect fraudulent financial statement information. In this

---

[3] Audit independence is defined in Rule 101 witin the Code of Professional Conduct of the American Institute of Certified Public Accountants (AICPA, 1988). In short, it simply means that the auditor, as well as the auditing firm, cannot have a financial interest in the organization that is being audited.

doctoral dissertation, 494 experienced auditors participated in an experimental study that required them to review a fairly complex and somewhat realistic set of contextual and financial cues regarding the quality of financial statement information for a hypothetical client company. In addition, one of the cues received by all individuals contained a seeded error that unambiguously indicated the existence of material error and the real possibility of fraud. Experimental findings showed that experience, ethical reasoning, and the configuration of experience and ethical reasoning, all influence the individual's ability to detect and frame the questionable accounting entry. In particular, high DIT (postconventional) auditors with relatively high levels of domain-specific experience were substantially better in detecting fraud than low DIT (conventional and preconventional) auditors.

Ponemon (1992b) examined the relationship between auditors' ethical reasoning and their underreporting tendencies by employing an experimental lab design for a sample of 88 staff level auditors from a national public accounting firm. The design of this experiment permitted the author to observe actual underreporting on a simulated audit task exercise during a firm training program. In summary, findings revealed that underreporting was systematically related to the auditor's level of ethical reasoning—as measured by the (DIT)—where those with relatively low DIT scores were shown to underreport most severely. Results also showed that although an unattainable time budget affected behavior, peer pressure had the most significant impact upon underreporting. In summary, this study makes three contributions to the auditing and psychology literatures. That is, it is the first study to establish the significance of peer pressure as an antecedent to underreporting. Furthermore, it suggests that an auditor's ethical reasoning may be an important determinant of underreporting behavior under conditions of work-related pressure. Finally, and perhaps most importantly, it indicates that ethical reasoning is, in fact, related to ethical behavior in auditing practice.

Most recently, Ponemon (1993a) and Ponemon and Gabhart (1993) studied the influence of ethical reasoning on auditors' sensitivity to the normative characteristics of client management. Both works found that auditors with relatively high DIT p scores were more sensitive to client characteristics, such as integrity and competence, when framing audit risk and materiality judgments for client organizations. In particular, auditors with higher DIT p scores were found to more effectively frame competence and integrity characteristics of client management than auditors with lower DIT p scores, especially when management were believed to possess low integrity and high competence. This finding is especially important in auditing because effective practice means that the individual auditor is always sensitive to the possibility of the clever concealment of fraud, distorted financial records, and/or illegal acts in the client organization.

Ethics Education

Several studies have attempted to investigate the role of college education on accounting students' ethical development. For example, Ponemon and Glazer (1990) examined accounting students and alumni from a small liberal arts college and a large state university. Using the DIT, they found that only accounting seniors and alumni of the liberal arts college progressed to levels of ethical reasoning comparable to the DIT norms published by Rest (1986). They concluded that differences in students' moral development, "may be caused, in part, by an educational process that inhibits students' abilities to develop an increasing sense of ethics, integrity or moral beliefs during the college years. These findings suggest that liberal learning in college may be an important factor in the development of students' and accounting practitioners' moral reasoning (p. 204)."

Other studies confirm Ponemon and Glazer's (1990) findings, showing that students of traditional accounting programs may not be developing to higher levels of ethical reasoning (see, e.g., Armstrong, 1987; Lampe & Finn, 1992; Shaub, 1993). Icerman, Karcher, and Kennelly (1991) and Jeffrey (1993), however, found that accounting students from large state universities tended to have higher DIT scores than nonaccounting students from the same schools. Jeffrey's study also revealed that students who choose accounting as their major have higher DITs than students choosing other business and nonbusiness disciplines. Despite generally positive findings for accounting majors, however, the results of both studies showed that accounting majors, on average, have DIT p scores that are well below the norms for college students published by Rest (1986) and others.

Although most accounting academics and practitioners readily agree that ethics should become a more significant part of the accounting curriculum, only four studies have attempted to assess the effectiveness of ethics education in accounting. Using the DIT, St. Pierre, Nelson, and Gabbin (1990) and Shaub (1993) studied the influence of ethics courses on accounting students' ethical reasoning. Although findings were mixed, neither study found that participation in a college ethics course consistently influenced students' ethical development as measured by the DIT.

Armstrong (1993) studied the influence of a dedicated accounting ethics course to the ethical development of accounting majors. Her findings showed that accounting students who elected to take the ethics course had higher DIT p scores than those who did not, and developed significantly higher DIT p scores by the end of the semester. In a similar study, Ponemon (1993b) studied the influence of ethics interventions—integrated into a one semester introductory auditing course at both the undergraduate and graduate level—on the ethical development and ethical behavior of accounting students. In this work, ethics interventions were based on the review and discussion of ethics cases following a well-known pedagogical framework over the first 10 weeks of one academic semester. The effectiveness of these interventions was tested two ways. First, using the DIT in a pretest/posttest research design, the ethical development of accounting seniors and graduate students in four separate auditing classes was assessed. Second, students' unethical behavior, defined as excessive free-riding on an economic choice experiment based on the Prisoners' Dilemma, was observed by the researcher. Results of his study revealed that ethics interventions did not cause accounting students' level of ethical reasoning to develop (increase) and did not curtail students' free-riding behavior. Findings also provided evidence of an association between ethical reasoning and students' economic choices, where students with pre- and postconventional levels of ethical reasoning were most likely to engage in free-riding. In summary, empirical differences among accounting education studies may indicate that only certain types of ethics interventions or programs will effect ethical development.

RESEARCH IMPLICATIONS

Table 6.2 provides descriptive statistics for the DIT p score (means and standard deviations) for the aforementioned studies. It is our belief that these works provide collective evidence that the psychology of ethical reasoning is of consequence to the study of behavior in accounting and auditing because many professional judgments are conditioned upon the beliefs and values of the individual practitioner. It is important to note, however, that the findings of this research do not necessarily mean that the ethical motivation or action of audit firm management in the United States should be seriously questioned, because, according to Rest (1986), ethical reasoning is only part of an individual's overall capacity to frame and resolve ethical issues. Many other variables also may play an equally important role in ethical behavior. What these findings do suggest, however, is that partners in U.S. firms tend to think at the conventional level of ethical reasoning. This means that the ethical reasoning of partners in U.S. firms is primarily influenced by their need to affiliate with peers or a referent group (e.g., the client, office colleagues, or the accounting firm) when judging or attempting to resolve ethical conflict. Assuming that the referent group is the accounting firm, adherence to the rules of the profession will result as long as such rules are consistent with the norms of the firm. If, on the other hand, rules of the profession are not consistent with the norms of the firm, then the norms of the firm will take precedence.

By virtue of higher DIT p scores, partners in Canadian CPA firms may be better able to independently frame ethical judgments in a manner separate and apart from the values and needs of clients, colleagues within the firm, or the accounting firm as a whole. In addition, in comparison to U.S. partners, these individuals may have a greater sensitivity to ethical conflict not well defined by the firm or the profession. Because the practice of accounting is dynamic, many conflicts are not resolved by simply adhering to codes of conduct or professional standards (Gaa, 1992). This is especially true for partners who, by virtue of their position, are typically exposed to the most difficult and pressing problems within the organization. Although those at higher ethical reasoning levels would be expected to be better able to resolve difficult ethical conflicts, this research, as well as earlier studies by Ponemon (1990, 1992a) and Shaub (1993), suggest that relatively few of these individuals rise to upper management positions in U.S. firms. If this is true, then CPAs making it to the top of the auditing firm hierarchy may be ill-equipped to deal with and resolve ethical conflicts that require postconventional reasoning.

There are at least two remedies available. First, management of firms in the United States can adopt new and detailed rules of conduct that attempt to specify

TABLE 6.2
DIT P Score Means from Studies of Accounting Practitioners and Students

DIT P Score	Accountant Group Studied	Location	Author(s)
Panel A: Accountants in Public Accounting Firms			
49.6	Senior-level female accountants	Midwest	Shaub (1993)
47.7	Accountants with liberal arts education	Northeast	Ponemon & Glazer (1990)
46.8	Supervisory-level accountants	Nationwide	Ponemon (1992a)
44.7	Accountants at the staff level	Nationwide	Ponemon (1992a)
44.2	Canadian auditors	Ontario	Ponemon & Gabhart (1993)
43.6	Third-year staff accountants	Midwest	Shaub (1993)
43.0	Second-year staff accountants	Midwest	Shaub (1993)
42.4	Accounting seniors	Nationwide	Ponemon (1992a)
41.9	Accounting managers	Northeast	Ponemon (1992a)
41.4	Accounting seniors	Midwest	Shaub (1993)
41.4	Senior-level male accountants	Midwest	Shaub (1993)
41.0	First-year staff accountants	Midwest	Shaub (1993)
40.0	American auditors	Northeast	Ponemon & Gabhart (1993)
39.8	Accountants at the staff level	Southwest	Lampe & Finn (1992)
38.6	Internal and governmental auditors	Northeast	Arnold & Ponemon (1991)
38.5	Manager-level accountants	Midwest	Shaub (1993)
38.1	Accountants (general sample)	West	Armstrong (1987)
38.1	Accountants with business education	Northeast	Ponemon & Glazer (1990)
38.1	Senior manager-level accountants	Midwest	Shaub (1993)
37.1	Partner-level accountants	Midwest	Shaub (1993)
35.7	Manager-level accountants	Nationwide	Ponemon (1992a)
35.6	Senior-level male accountants	Midwest	Shaub (1993)
32.2	Partner-level accountants	Nationwide	Ponemon (1992a)
Panel B: Students in Educational Institutions			
47.4	Liberal arts accounting seniors	Northeast	Ponemon & Glazer (1990)
45.8	Female accounting major	Midwest	Shaub (1993)
45.1	Accounting majors in ethics course	West	Armstrong (1993)
41.8	Graduate-level accounting majors	Southeast	Icerman et al. (1991)
38.6	Graduate-level accounting major	Northeast	Ponemon (1993)
37.4	Business school accounting seniors	Northeast	Ponemon & Glazer (1990)
37.1	Business school accounting majors	Midwest	Jeffrey (1993)
36.3	Male accounting majors	Midwest	Shaub (1993)
35.5	Business school accounting majors	Southeast	Icerman et al. (1991)
34.5	Undergraduate accounting majors	Southwest	Lampe & Finn (1992)

in concise and clear language a single, correct ethical strategy to any particular ethical conflict. It is important to note, however, that the rule makers themselves should possess high ethical reasoning, since they must deal with many new and uncharted conflicts that are likely to arise. Second, those in management positions in U.S. firms can develop to higher levels of ethical reasoning. As a result of their ethical development, partners also will develop greater tolerance for subordinates with differing ethical capacities. This, of course, would discourage selection-socialization as evidenced by Ponemon (1990, 1992a) in his research.

Effective pedagogical interventions at both the university and the firm level may foster the moral development of individual accountants and auditors. Furthermore,

Rest (1988) suggested that development to higher levels of ethical reasoning can occur at all ages and in all learning environments. This may indicate that education in Canada may be more conducive for developing the ethical reasoning skills of students choosing to pursue a career in public accounting than that in the United States. As a starting point, perhaps accounting educators in the United States should seriously consider the effectiveness of traditional ethics interventions in accounting and, when necessary, replace these with formal courses and programs that are designed to foster the highest order of ethical reasoning (Ponemon & Glazer, 1990).

Some might doubt the need for change on the grounds that the market for public accounting services dictates the level and value of ethical standards within the accounting profession (Noreen, 1988). Thus, as long as firms in the United States are profitable, ethical standards must be acceptable to the public at large. However, this justification is inappropriate for two reasons. First, if selection-socialization in U.S. firms effectively weeds out those individuals with high ethical reasoning, it will be difficult to attract and retain such employees. That is, many of the best and brightest accounting students will choose alternative career paths. The lack of diversity among those progressing to partnerships will cause the ethical culture or moral atmosphere of U.S. public accounting firms to become stagnant. Perhaps stagnation and an inability to adapt to new cultures will cause accounting firms in the United States to find it increasingly difficult to compete and survive in the global business community. This may not be the case for Canadian firms, where the ethical reasoning of public accounting professionals may not diminish at higher position levels.

Second, the savings and loan debacle and downward economic trends in the United States may have caused the public to view the public accounting profession in a more negative light. As a consequence of negative perceptions, client organizations and financial statement users in the future may depend less on the attestations provided by independent auditors, thus reducing the demand for public accounting services. Such declines might prompt governmental authorities such as the Securities and Exchange Commission (SEC), General Accounting Office (GAO) and Congress to become more actively involved in the regulation of the profession. This, in turn, may cause firms in the United States to lose their professional autonomy and incentive to provide high quality auditing services. In the end, this would be most detrimental to the general public, who are the beneficiaries of accounting and audit quality.

It is precisely these problems and concerns that have generated much interest in ethics within the public accounting profession in the United States, including revised codes of conduct, an independent public accounting oversight board, proposed governmental regulatory action, and a continuing stream of academic research in the applied professional ethics area. Assuming that this research can be extended to the general population of practicing auditors in the United States and Canada, then these findings may have significant implications to auditing practitioners and auditing researchers alike, because they show that the auditor's ethical reasoning is inextricably linked to his or her capacity to form both ethical and technical judgments in the professional domain. Furthermore, and perhaps more importantly, the trend of decreasing DIT p scores brought about by firm socialization may not extend to audit firms operating in other countries. Hence, the management of U.S. public accounting firms should look to practice offices in other countries (such as Canada) to model a firm wide moral atmosphere than permits an individual's development to the highest levels of ethical reasoning.

REFERENCES

American Institute of Certified Public Accountants. (1988). *Code of professional conduct.* New York: Author.
Armstrong, M. (1984). *Internalization of the professional ethic by certified public accountants: A multidimensional scaling approach.* Unpublished doctoral dissertation, University of Southern California, Los Angeles.
Armstrong, M. (1987, Spring). Moral development and accounting education. *Journal of Accounting Education,* 27–43.
Armstrong, M. (1993, Spring). Ethics and professionalism in accounting education. *Journal of Accounting Education,* 1–14.
Arnold, D., & Ponemon, L. (1987, April). Moral judgment perspective for the various auditing judgment issues. *Proceedings of the British Accounting Association,* pp. 47–57.
Arnold, D., & Ponemon, L. (1991, Fall). Internal auditors' perceptions of whistle-blowing and the influence of moral reasoning: An experiment. *Auditing: A Journal of Practice and Theory,* 1–15.
Bernardi, R. (1991). *Fraud detection: An experiment testing differences in perceived client integrity and competence, individual auditor cognitive style and experience, and accounting firms.* Unpublished doctoral dissertation, Union College, Schenectady, NY.
Gaa, J. (1992). The philosophy and psychology of auditor independence and objectivity. In R. Srivastava (Ed.), *The 1992 Deloitte & Touche University of Kansas Symposium of Auditing Problems* (pp. 7–43). Lawrence, KS: University of Kansas.
Icerman, R., Karcher, J., & Kennelley, M. (1991, Winter). A baseline assessment of moral development: Accounting, other business and nonbusiness students. *Accounting Educator's Journal,* 46–62.
Jeffrey, C. (1993, Spring). Ethical development of accounting students, business students, and liberal arts students. *Issues in Accounting Education,* 26–40.
Jones, S., & Ponemon, L. (1993, April). A comment on a multidimensional analysis of selected ethical issues in accounting. *The Accounting Review,* April, 411–416.
Kohlberg, L. (1969). Stages and sequences: The cognitive developmental approach to socialization. In D. Goslin (Ed.), *Handbook of socialization theory and research.* Chicago: Rand McNally.
Lampe, J., & Finn, D. (1992). A model of auditors' ethical decision process, *Auditing: A Journal of Practice and Theory.* Supplement, 1–21.
Noreen, E. (1980). The economics of ethics: A new perspective on agency theory. *Accounting, Organizations, and Society,* pp. 231–244.
Ponemon, L. (1988). *A cognitive-developmental approach to the analysis of certified public accountants' ethical judgments.* Unpublished doctoral dissertation, Union College, Schenectady, NY.
Ponemon, L. (1990). Ethical judgments in accounting: A cognitive-developmental perspective. *Critical Perspectives on Accounting,* 191–215.
Ponemon, L. (1992a, April/May). Ethical reasoning and selection-socialization in accounting. *Accounting, Organizations and Society,* 239–258.
Ponemon, L. (1992b). Auditor underreporting of time and moral reasoning: An experimental-lab study. *Contemporary Accounting Research,* 171–189.
Ponemon, L. (1993a). The influence of ethical reasoning on auditors' perceptions of management's competence and integrity. *Advances in Accounting,* 1–29.

Ponemon, L. (1993b, Fall). Can ethics be taught in accounting? *Journal of Accounting Education*, pp. 1–29.

Ponemon, L., & Gabhart, D. (1990). Auditor independence judgments: A cognitive developmental model and experimental evidence. *Contemporary Accounting Research*, 227–251.

Ponemon, L., & Gabhart, D. (1993). *Ethical reasoning in accounting and auditing*. Vancouver, Canada: Canadian General Accountants' Research Foundation.

Ponemon, L., & Glazer, A. (1990). Accounting education and ethical development: The influence of liberal learning on students and alumni in accounting practice. *Issues in Accounting Education*, 21–34.

Rest, J., (1979a). *Development in judging moral issues*. Minneapolis, MN: University of Minnesota Press.

Rest, J. (1979b). *Revised Manual for the Defining Issues Test*. (MMRP Technical Report). University of Minnesota, Minneapolis.

Rest, J. (1986). *Moral development: Advances in research and theory*. New York: Praeger.

Rest, J. (1988, Winter). Can ethics be taught in professional schools? The psychological research. *Ethics Easier Said Than Done*, 22–26.

Shaub, M. (1989). *An empirical examination of the determinants of auditors' ethical sensitivity*. Unpublished doctoral dissertation, Texas Technological University, Lubbock.

Shaub, M. (1994, Spring). An analysis of factors affecting the cognitive moral development of auditors and auditing students. *Journal of Accounting Education*, pp. 1–24.

St. Pierre, K., Nelson E., & Gabbin, A. (1990, Summer). A study of the ethical development of accounting majors in relation to other business and nonbusiness disciplines. *Accounting Educators Journal*, 23–35.

Chapter 7

Influencing the Moral Dimensions of Dental Practice

Muriel J. Bebeau
University of Minnesota

My purpose in this chapter is to present an overview of what we have learned about each of the four component processes (see chap. 1) from our studies of the moral development of dental professionals. I begin by pointing out some of the features of the instructional programs. Then, I take up each process in turn, addressing the research questions that motivated our inquiry, describing the assessment methods we developed or used, and summarizing the evidence to date on program effectiveness. Evidence is drawn from students enrolled in the dental ethics curriculum since its inception, and from 20 practicing dentists and auxiliaries who were referred for ethics instruction by the Minnesota Board of Dentistry.[1]

FEATURES OF THE DENTAL ETHICS CURRICULUM

Our program began in 1981, with a $63,000 grant from the American Fund for Dental Health. Rather than argue in the abstract for the worthiness of an ethics program, we showed to faculty examples of advanced students' and residents' responses to common professional problems. When we revealed that the responses, which faculty judged to be inadequate, were developed by our best students and

---

[1]The referrals came about because some of the board members have been involved in development of the undergraduate dental ethics curriculum, and came to believe that, at least in some cases, violations of the Dental Practice Act reflected ethical deficiencies that could be remediated by the kinds of experiences provided for students.

residents, the faculty were galvanized to action. They authorized the inclusion of small group seminars and even volunteered to lead discussions. Over the next 2 years, they participated in faculty seminars in which we reviewed student performance and designed cases and criteria for evaluation. As the need for performance assessment and personalized feedback became apparent, they helped recruit high-status practicing professionals from the American College of Dentists[2] to serve as external assessors (Bebeau, 1983), and to participate in case and criteria development. As I have worked with faculty to incorporate ethics instruction in other institutions, I have come to realize that showing examples of performance helps to bypass the widespread beliefs that ethics could not, or should not, be taught, or that faculty are not equipped to teach ethics.

In keeping with the process we initiated, the curriculum is subjected to regular review[3] and is constantly being refined. It is among the most documented and intensively studied programs and has been widely disseminated.[4] Most dental schools have incorporated some parts of it, and the American Dental Association often points to it as an example of what can be done in an institution. The local chapter of the American College of Dentists has not only supported the program financially, but practically all members have participated at one time or another in the ongoing research and program development projects, and each year, at least 20 members participate as external assessors. At the national level, the American College has often showcased the program, using it as a model for the way other chapters might become involved with their local schools to promote the teaching of ethics. The program has also served as a model for development of videotapes and case material[5] that serve as a basis for a seminar series for practicing dentists.

The undergraduate curriculum (see Table 7.1) consists of 43 contact hours distributed over 4 years. Attendance is required and small group instructional techniques (Bebeau, 1985) ensure participation. As shown in Table 7.1, each course activity is keyed to one or more of the four components. There is a heavy emphasis on student performance, self-assessment, and personalized feedback, using validated assessment methods. Involvement of many faculty and practitioners insures that the program isn't the isolated theme of one instructor. Scoring manuals and facilitator notes for each of the cases promote instructional consistency.

Remedial courses for practicing professionals use many of the methods and materials developed for the undergraduate program. However, courses are individually designed, based on an assessment of each practitioner's ethical sensitivity, moral reasoning, and role concept using the Dental Ethical Sensitivity Test (DEST),

---

[2]The American College of Dentists is an honor society that is committed to promoting the ethical values of the profession. Membership is awarded based on demonstrated professionalism and outstanding community service.

[3] A review of the ethics curriculum is included in the University of Minnesota School of Dentistry Dental Program Self-Study for 1992 Accreditation, Vol. II, Standard 8, pp. 1–26.

[4]The curriculum materials (Bebeau, 1990) have been disseminated since 1982.

[5]The materials, designed by Bebeau, Born, & Ozar (1993) to promote the development of ethics workshops for practicing dentists, are available from The American College of Dentists, 839 Quince Orchard Blvd., Suite J, Gaithersburg, MD 20878–1603.

the Defining Issues Test (DIT), and the Role Concept Essay, described in the next sections. Results of the initial assessment and a plan of study are discussed with participants, then submitted to the Board of Dentistry for approval. A typical course consists of 20 to 25 hours of instruction spread over several months and may involve four or five participants. As with the undergraduate curriculum, there is heavy emphasis on performance and personalized feedback. Following instruction, participants develop an ethical analysis of the act that resulted in disciplinary action and retake the initial assessment measures, or an alternate form. A final report, documenting change in performance, is submitted to the Board of Dentistry for approval. Reinstatement of the license is conditioned on the Board's satisfaction with the outcome. The effectiveness of the remedial courses and the undergraduate courses are described in the following sections.

ETHICAL SENSITIVITY

Research Questions

When Rest proposed his Four Component Model in 1979 (see chap. 1), much progress had already been made on the measurement of moral judgment, and although there was some empirical support for his notion that moral sensitivity was distinct from moral reasoning, there were no measures or methods to study Component I processes. In 1980, we began a program of research to address these questions: Can ethical sensitivity be reliably assessed? Do students differ in ethical sensitivity? Can sensitivity be enhanced? And, is ethical sensitivity distinct from the ability to develop a well-reasoned argument?

Assessment Strategies

We deliberately chose to construct methods of assessment for moral sensitivity in a well-established health-care profession. To develop a valid measure of sensitivity, we needed agreement[6] that there were some basic obligations the professional owed to others. You will notice that we use the term *ethical sensitivity*, rather than *moral sensitivity*, because we are measuring the individual's ability to interpret factors in the care setting that relate directly to obligations stated in the profession's code of ethics. The DEST (Bebeau, Rest, & Yamoor, 1985) and a subsequent Geriatric Dental Sensitivity Test (GDEST; Ernest, 1990), placed students in real-life situations, where they witnessed an interaction on video or audiotape. The interaction replicated professional interactions and provided technical and psychosocial clues to a professional ethical dilemma. Distinct from cases used to assess moral reasoning, or those typically used in ethics courses, the stimulus case was not predigested or interpreted. At a point in the presentation, students took on the role of the professional in the drama and responded on audiotape as though they

---

[6]One factor that distinguishes among occupations (Hall, 1975) is the extent to which they have achieved consensus on their basic obligations and codified them in codes of ethics.

TABLE 7.1
Professional Ethics Curriculum, University of Minnesota, School of Dentistry

Year	Activity	Purpose	Assessment	Feedback	Contact Hours
1	Orientation/Pretest	To alert students to need for program	DIT, PROI	• Personalized letter detailing DIT results • Personal consults for students with DIT P scores less than 30	2.5
	Lecture: "Characteristics of a Profession"	To influence professional identity (Component III)	Role concept essay on midterm and final	Scores posted; Essays available for review; Misconceptions discussed in a review session; Rewrite on final	2
	Assignment: Read "ADA Code of Ethics"	To familiarize students with code	Multiple choice questions	Scores posted	
	Lecture: "Judging the Adequacy of Moral Argument"	To present the elements of a well-reasoned argument (Component II)	Essay		1
	Assignment: Read "Guidelines for Developing a Well-Reasoned Moral Argument" and "Principles of Biomedical Ethics"	To present principles of biomedical ethics (Component II)			
	Discussions: Preclinical ethical problems (issues defined) led by dental faculty	To improve ethical reasoning (Component II)	• Pre-and postessay for each case discussed • Checklists for each case keyed to instructor notes	Essays (with comments) scored by course coordinator and returned prior to next discussion	10
	Self-assessment of: • Participation in discussions • Learning	To encourage reflection on the goals of instruction	• Check list following each discussion • Four-item open-ended questionnaire	Personalized comments if requested, or if indicated	

(continued)

TABLE 7.1 (continued)

Year	Activity	Purpose	Assessment	Feedback	Contact Hours
3	Lecture/Discussion: "Patient Characteristics That Influence Informed Consent"	To enhance ethical sensitivity (Component I)	Case write-up	Written comments and group discussion of common errors	1
	Assignment/Discussion: Read "Getting to Yes," by Fischer and Ury (1981)	To enhance problem-solving and communication skills (Component IV)	• Quiz • Case write-up	Written comments on case write-up	1
	Case discussion and role play of clinical cases (issues undefined)	To enhance ethical sensitivity and implementation of action plans (Components I and IV)	Case write-up includes action plan and dialog	• Written comments on case write-up • Group discussion of common errors	7.5
	Case Discussion: Clinical ethical dilemmas (issues defined)	To improve ethical reasoning	Case write-up	Written comments addressing criteria for a well-reasoned argument	4
	Ethical Sensitivity Assessment	To alert students to strengths and weaknesses (Component I)	DEST cases	Transcripts prepared over summer and sent to students and dentists for evaluation	2

(continued)

125

TABLE 7.1 (*continued*)

Year	Activity	Purpose	Assessment	Feedback	Contact Hours
4	Self-assessment of DEST transcipts	To encourage reflection on professional development	DEST scoring manual		1.5
	Meeting with high status practicing dentist	To convey professional standards and commitment to professional values (Component III)	DEST scoring manual	• Comparison of student self-assessment with practitioner assessment • Personalized comments on implementation and communication (Component IV)	1.5
	Discussion of clinical cases (issues undefined) Assignments: case related readings	To enhance sensitivity and practice reasoning and implementation skills (Components I, II, IV)	Case write-up	• Written comments • Group discussion of common errors	7.5
	Self-assessment	To encourage reflection on goal attainment	Five-item open-ended questionnaire	If indicated	
	Final Assessment	• To encourage reflection on outcome attainment • To set goals for further professional development	DIT PROI Anonymous course evaluation	Personalized letter detailing results on DEST, DIT and PROI, and comparing performance to others	2

7. INFLUENCING THE MORAL DIMENSIONS OF DENTAL PRACTICE 127

were the professional involved. Following a response to the patient, students answered probe questions to ascertain why they said what they did, how they expected the patient to respond, what they thought should be done in like situations, and so on. We have experimented with various modes of response, and found that verbal responses gave the best estimate of what the student attended to. Using a scoring manual developed in collaboration with practicing dentists, transcribed responses were rated for the extent to which the student recognized the significant patient characteristics and professional responsibilities presented in the situation.

Appendix A provides a synopsis of one of the cases drawn from the GDEST and an excerpt from the GDEST scoring manual illustrating different levels of sensitivity to one of the patient characteristics assessed by the test. The sample case is of interest because many students believed this patient was cognitively impaired (although she wasn't), whereas they failed to recognize blatant symptoms of impairment in the other four GDEST cases.

Evidence of Effectiveness

The initial studies investigating the validity and reliability of measures of ethical sensitivity were summarized by Rest (1986). The most recent summary appears in the 1990 edition of the DEST manual (Bebeau & Rest, 1982). Validity and reliability are sufficiently established to support the following conclusions:

1. Ethical sensitivity can be reliably assessed. The following estimates were established over a series of studies. Calibrated raters were able to achieve item agreement ranging from 84.7% to 88%. Reliability estimates for the total score assigned to each individual case ranged from 0.83 to 0.92.

2. Students and practitioners (Table 7.2) vary greatly in their ability to recognize the ethical problems of their profession, and the DEST is sensitive to institutional differences (Baab & Bebeau, 1990), presumably accruing from differences in the effectiveness of clinical programs. Also, Harvan (1989) noted that students at different levels of education in medicine and dentistry differed significantly in sensitivity to the DEST, such that those with longer preparation for entry to a profession (physicians vs. technicians or dentists vs. hygienists) showed higher levels of sensitivity. She also noted that the DEST distinguished levels of sensitivity

TABLE 7.2
Change Scores for Five Remedial Ethics Courses*

Component	n	Pretest Mean	SD	Postest Mean	SD	p
Ethical Sensitivity (DEST Scores)	15	44.05	6.39	56.72	10.93	< .006
Moral Reasoning (DIT Scores)	16	39.38	12.36	49.96	12.48	< .0005
Role Concept (Essay Scores)	17	3.05	1.78	11.06	1.25	< .0001

*Scores are reported for participants ($n = 20$) who completed both pre- and posttests.

regardless of a student's technical knowledge of dentistry, suggesting that the measures may not be as profession-specific as previously thought.

3. Women appear to have a slight edge over men in recognizing ethical issues (Bebeau & Brabeck, 1987), but the differences were not attributed to differential recognition of the care and justice issues embedded in the test, nor to differences in moral judgments. In the aggregate, some women were as blind to ethical issues as their male colleagues, and all could benefit from ethical sensitivity training.

4. Ethical sensitivity can be enhanced through instruction (Baab & Bebeau, 1990; Bebeau & Brabeck, 1987). Table 7.2 shows the change in ethical sensitivity scores resulting from the special remedial course for practicing professionals.

5. Ethical sensitivity is distinct from moral reasoning abilities. In other words, professionals may be skilled at interpreting the ethical dimensions of a situation (ethically sensitive), but unskilled at working out a balanced view of a moral solution (moral judgment), and vice versa. One of the cases referred by the Board of Dentistry showed how a disparity between these two abilities can affect real-life decisions.

A group practice was referred for an ethics course because they had allowed auxiliaries to perform duties that exceeded the limits set by the Dental Practice Act. Results of the DEST pretest revealed that the senior dentist, who trained the auxiliaries to perform the prohibited duties, scored very high on our measure of ethical sensitivity, but very low on the moral reasoning test. In the intake interview, he confirmed that he knew the duties asked of auxiliaries were prohibited, but he offered these justifications for the action: others did it (including Board members, he thought); the rules were archaic (some states allowed the duties that Minnesota prohibited), and he was actively working to have them changed; no patients had been harmed; and so on. The associate, who joined the practice after the prohibited practices were instituted, scored very low on ethical sensitivity, but reasonably high on moral reasoning. He said he honestly didn't realize the duties were prohibited. In discussion, he was quick to see the fallacies in his colleague's argument. He was also much less angry about the disciplinary action the Board had taken. One of the benefits of the course was that they came to respect each other's strengths.

Because new ethical issues emerge on a regular basis in the professions, the development of stimulus cases, modeled after the DEST cases, is an ideal way for a profession to keep abreast of emerging concerns. The GDEST is such an example. Geriatric specialist Ernest (1990) developed his cases to assess general dentists' ability to recognize ethical issues involved in the care of medically and cognitively compromised elderly. As with the DEST, he observed striking individual differences in students' and professionals' ability to recognize technical as well as ethical issues that would impact on their ability to deliver competent care. Work on the GDEST enabled us to identify eight generic patient characteristics that can be varied in cases to assess sensitivity, and six generic responsibilities that may be implied by the circumstances presented in a case. Appendix B lists these characteristics and responsibilities that may be useful to others who wish to develop profession-specific cases for measuring ethical sensitivity in the health professions.

MORAL JUDGMENT

Research Questions

Despite the amount of research conducted on Component II processes, there were questions that arose when we planned the dental ethics educational program. We wondered:

1. How competent (in moral reasoning) are entering dental students? Do they need extensive training in moral reasoning development?
2. Is the dilemma discussion technique, which has been demonstrated to be effective with younger students, also effective with professional school students?
3. Can moral reasoning performance in courses be reliably assessed?
4. How does performance on course measures relate to DIT scores?
5. Do courses in ethics or the humanities prior to professional school predict moral judgment scores?

Assessment Strategies

We use two methods to assess Component II processes. The DIT is used as an outcome measure to assess the impact of the curriculum on moral judgment development over time. A classroom assessment strategy (Bebeau, 1990) was developed to monitor student progress, provide systematic feedback, and evaluate course effectiveness. The need for validated methods for assessing classroom performance was prompted by student reactions to learning their DIT pretest score and by their reactions to course grades. With respect to DIT scores, students often asked (usually in a challenging way): "Who says higher is better?" With respect to grades, these reactions were common: "This course should be pass/fail. Grading arguments is purely subjective. You are grading our values. You have no right!!!" or "This course is a mega-waste of time. There are many right answers to moral problems. Who's to say that one opinion is any better than another. We'd be better off spending our time in labs."

Although such views were not widespread, we felt the concerns expressed ways of thinking that required attention. Furthermore, although almost all the students said they enjoyed the discussions and thought they were worthwhile; the well thought out reasons expressed during discussion were not consistently reflected in the essays students wrote following the class discussion. Also, we tended not to see improvement in the quality of student essays as the course progressed. I see now that the instructional procedures probably contributed to the lack of improvement. During the initial years of the curriculum, essays were graded at the end of the course. Feedback on the quality of written responses was neither systematically given, nor was it tied to explicit criteria. Even though the graders had criteria in mind when they judged student essays, these criteria were not shared with students ahead of time.

To address the relativistic perspectives expressed by students and to improve performance, we looked to the literature for examples of the ways moral arguments are assessed in exemplary ethics courses. We noticed that, although course developers claimed to evaluate the adequacy of arguments, criteria for doing so were not explicitly stated, nor were data presented on course effectiveness. When evaluation data were presented, these data were limited to student perceptions of the value of instruction (Miles, Lane, Bickel, Walker, & Cassel, 1989). We found one exception. Howe (1982) illustrated that courses could bring about improvements in the quality of written essays. To establish the reliability of judgments, Howe used the same evaluator to rate pretest and posttest essays. He did not establish interrater reliability (i.e., that two philosophers would rank-order the essays similarly). Furthermore, although he published the criteria, he did not establish face validity (i.e., that philosophy colleagues would agree that these criteria were the criteria one should use to evaluate the quality of moral argument). It may be easy to establish agreement for Howe's criteria because they were expressed in rather general terms. But it was not clear, at least to me, that such criteria would be useful to students trying to learn how to develop a well-reasoned argument, or to persons with limited training in philosophy who might wish to apply them.

Our criteria checklist emerged from discussions between myself and a philosopher colleague who assisted me in evaluating students' arguments and assigning course grades.[7] Points were assigned to an essay as follows: identifies all pertinent ethical issues (5 points); identifies affected parties (3 points); describes several possible consequences of acting (4 points); describes duties derived from the application of moral principles (5 points); and demonstrates a willingness to reassess or change one's initial position (3 points). Initial efforts focused on establishing interrater reliability for the general criteria. My colleague and I were able to achieve consistency in rating and ranking student essays (Bebeau, 1990), provided that we had established agreement on the issues, affected parties, consequences and duties, embedded in each dilemma. To ensure consistency across essays and across years when the essays were graded, I developed a template for each case which listed the issues, affected parties, and so on, and provided rules for assigning points. Facilitator notes for each case were rewritten to provide instructors with a detailed discussion of each of the issues, affected parties, consequences, and so on. Appendix C presents a sample case for assessing ethical reasoning, two sample responses, and a template showing how a case is scored.

Evidence of Effectiveness

Our initial decision to engage students in ethical reasoning was based on three pieces of information. First, a cross-sectional comparison (Bebeau & Thoma, in press) of three classes of entering freshman ($N = 385$) with two classes of

---

[7]Course grades are based on the quality of five written responses to dilemmas presented for discussion, and on the faculty members rating of the quality of their participation in course discussions.

3rd-quarter juniors ($N = 265$) on the DIT was conducted prior to implementing the ethics curriculum. There were no significant differences between groups, suggesting that our technically oriented dental curriculum had little impact on moral reasoning development. Second, an examination of the range of DIT scores indicated considerable variability (an average SD of 13.25), with up to 20% of the students scoring below the norm for high school graduates. Third, written responses to dental ethical dilemmas (Bebeau, 1990) indicated that even advanced-level students were not equally able to develop defensible arguments for dilemmas commonly encountered in dental practice. Furthermore, many students believed that judgments about the adequacy of ethical arguments are arbitrary, and that ethics could not, and perhaps should not, be taught.

Table 7.3 shows the improvements in performance (averaged over 2 or more years) that resulted from the addition of feedback (given after each essay), and then from the addition of a lecture and distribution of a paper entitled "Guidelines for Developing a Well-Reasoned Argument" that preceded small group dilemma discussions. To date, we have not analyzed the influence of having criteria over not having criteria, the circumstance that existed prior to 1985. Our impressions were that presenting criteria helped reduce perceptions that ethical judgments are arbitrary, but it did not improve the quality of written arguments. In an analysis of the impact of feedback on performance across five essays (we compared 94 students that were not given feedback after each essay with 158 students who were), we noted that the most dramatic improvements occurred with written feedback given after the first essay; improvements thereafter were incremental, though not significantly so (Bebeau, 1990). The main effect of feedback seems to be the reduction of variance.

To assess the impact of the curriculum, Bebeau and Thoma (in press) compared pretest and posttest DIT scores for eight classes of students who participated in the dental ethics program. Unlike the cross-sectional data obtained prior to the ethics program's implementation, seniors scored significantly higher than freshman. Furthermore, the overall effect size ($d = .36$) compares favorably to the value obtained by Schlaefli, Rest, and Thoma (1985) in their meta-analysis of 23 intervention studies using dilemma discussion techniques. The findings suggest an increased use of principled arguments associated with implementation of the ethics

TABLE 7.3
Effects of Instructional Improvements

	Criteria 2 years	+ Feedback 3 years	+ Guidelines 3 years
Points*	1985–1986	1987–1989	1990–1993
85–100	4.5%	28%	52%
76–84	19.5%	41%	36%
66–75	24.5%	24%	10%
56–65	27.5%	5%	2%
46–55	18.5%	2%	
36–45	5.5%		

*Based on total score for five 20-point essays.

program. Change in DIT scores is also associated with the remedial program for practitioners (Table 7.2).

Based on our experiences so far, we have concluded the following:

1. Students need instruction in ethical reasoning.
2. Dilemma discussion technique is effective in enhancing reasoning of professional school students, but criteria and feedback are essential for overcoming student's relativistic perspectives and for bringing about performance improvements.
3. Performance in courses can be reliably assessed.
4. Further work is needed to more broadly establish validity, because performance on the essays students write in class is not highly correlated with pre- or post-DIT scores (Bebeau, 1990).
5. The popular view that academic preparation in philosophy and the humanities should be required for admission to the professions was not supported. Bebeau and Waithe (1988) classified prior coursework in philosophy and humanities for two classes of students ($N = 240$). Academic preparation did not predict moral judgment scores for beginning dental students. Furthermore, such undergraduate preparation did not moderate the change in moral judgment that occurred during professional school.
6. Students value instruction in moral reasoning. On the self-assessment following the first-year course, we have reduced the number of complaints about the grading and increased the frequency with which we receive comments such as, "It never occurred to me that there were criteria for evaluating the adequacy of moral argument. I'm now much better at evaluating my own reasoning and the arguments of others."

Although certainly no guarantee exists that improvements in reasoning brought about by courses in ethics will assure ethical behavior, there is mounting evidence of a relationship between moral judgment and clinical performance in the professions (see chap. 3). Using a well-validated measure of dental clinical performance (Meetz, Bebeau, & Thoma, 1988), we examined the relationship between moral reasoning and clinical performance for two classes of senior dental students. Although we did not show the same linear relationship observed by Sheehan, Candee, Cook, and Bargen (1980), one aspect of the relationship was similar: Low scores on reasoning virtually excluded the possibility of high scores on clinical performance.

MORAL MOTIVATION AND COMMITMENT

Research Questions

Blasi (1984), Damon (1984), and others have worked on the notion that self-concept has a lot to do with moral motivation. Most professional schools try to socialize students to a professional identity—an identity that goes beyond a vision of technical expertise or good business acumen,—an identity that includes the moral elements that distinguish a profession from an occupation or trade. It is expected that this sense of identity influences a wide range of professional decisions, from how one interacts with patients, to how one advertises professional services. Most professional school curricula include goals related to professional identity, but it is difficult to identify the specific methods for influencing professional identity or methods for assessing attainment of the desired identity. If one examines the variety of models of professionalism[8] that appear to guide a professional's ethical decisions, one is likely to conclude that there is a discrepancy between the intent of professional school education and the outcome. The lack of empirical validation guided our efforts to address these questions: (a) Do professionals hold different conceptions of their role? (b) Can professional identity be reliably assessed? (c) Can professional identity be influenced? (d) Is professional identity related to other components, and to moral behavior?

Assessment Strategies

We began to work on assessment of professional identity or role concept, as we have come to refer to it, by asking beginning dental students to write a short essay on the subject: "What Does it Mean to you to Become a Professional?" We reviewed these essays for the presence of six obligations derived from sociologists' (Hall, 1975) descriptions of the characteristics that distinguish occupations from professions. Briefly, these include: acquisition of specialized knowledge (K); lifelong learner (CE); service to society (S); an expressed statement of the ethic of the profession (E); an agreement to abide by the profession's code (C); and participation in the self-governance and monitoring of the profession (SG). Appendix D presents a sample essay, written after instruction, that incorporates each of the concepts.

One drawback of this assessment technique is that it could either underestimate or overestimate a student's knowledge of the concepts. Performance required the student to articulate six rather specific ideas. Uninstructed students were unlikely to spontaneously express these six ideas even if they had a grasp of them, and instructed students could memorize the six ideas and repeat them without having internalized them. We noticed that if we required that students write the essay as part of an examination, they expressed the ideas in their own words, and misperceptions were quite apparent.

Our most recent work is aimed at designing an objective measure of role concept that can be used in population studies and with instructed or uninstructed groups.

---

[8]Veatch (1972), May (1983), & Ozar (1985) described 11 different images or conceptions of professional identity that they believe guide professional practice.

The Professional Role Orientation Inventory (PROI) (Bebeau, Born, & Ozar, 1993) measures underlying concepts of authority and responsibility that are common to the various models of professionalism described by moral philosophers (May, 1983; Ozar, 1985; Veatch, 1972). We thought that professionals' conception of their responsibility to others would fall along a continuum from *little responsibility to others*, to *maximum responsibility for others*. For example: A high rating on the item, "My first professional obligation is to myself," places a person on the Ivan Bowsky end of the continuum, whereas a high rating on the item, "I feel I have an obligation to use my knowledge and skills to help those who cannot pay for my services," places a person on the Mother Teresa end of the continuum. Summing across responses to five negatively stated and five positively stated items yields a score on the responsibility dimension.

We thought that a professional's conception of where the authority for professional decisions should rest also would fall along a continuum from *High on Authority* (i.e., all professional decisions ought to rest with the profession and the professional) to *Low on Authority* (i.e., all decisions ought to rest with the patient or with society). For example, "a high rating on the item, "Once a patient decides to use my services, he or she should follow my advice without questioning my authority," places a person high on the authority dimension, whereas a high rating on the item, "Since a patient is the best judge of his or her needs and values, a dentist should provide whatever services the patient wants," places a person low on the authority dimension. Summing across responses to five negatively stated and five positively stated items yields a score on the responsibility dimension.

None of the models described in the literature neatly fit the operational definitions that emerged for the four possible combinations of these two dimensions: (1) *High on Authority, low on Responsibility* (a version of the commercial model); (2) *High on Authority; High on Responsibility* (a version of the guild model); (3) *Low on Authority, High on Responsibility* (a kind of service model); and (4) *Low on Authority, Low on Responsibility* (a kind of agent model—reminiscent of the "hired-gun" in law). Thus, we developed model descriptions that borrowed from existing models and were consistent with our operational definitions. See Bebeau et al. (1993) for a description of the four models.

Evidence of Effectiveness

In studying dental students' understanding of the role of the dental professional, that is, the role-concept essay students write as first year students, key concepts like service to society (S), or the priority of patient well-being (E), or the duty to self-regulate (SG) were not well understood, especially at the time of entry to professional school. But even after attending a 2-hour lecture in which the characteristics of a profession were presented and the obligations of professionalism discussed and presented on slides (which students were free to copy), students were not equally able to write an essay on the midterm exam that clearly expressed each of the concepts. We have noticed (Bebeau, 1990) that if you arrange the contingencies of instruction, students do put forth effort to learn the concepts and seldom miscommunicate concepts like "acquisition of knowledge" or "lifelong learner," though they sometimes omit them, but even after feedback and an opportunity to rewrite the essay on the final exam, as many as 20% of the students miscommunicate the "priority of patient well-being" ethic, "service to society," or the obligation for self-governance. Here are three common misperceptions:

1. A failure to see the limits of obligation (e.g., "I am obligated to aid the community in whatever it endeavors to do" or "I must serve all individuals who are in need of dental care, regardless of their ability to pay for these services").
2. A failure to attribute the obligation to oneself (e.g., "Dentistry must provide the educational background commensurate with that of a doctor," or "The American Dental Association and State Boards have the responsibility to monitor the profession," or "It is recommended that a professional be a continuous student").
3. A narrow interpretation of the obligation (e.g., "I am obligated to serve [only] those who can pay for my services," or "Because the profession is self-regulating, I will regulate myself").

Two lines of outcome-evidence provide indirect evidence of the effectiveness of role concept instruction. The first comes from a comparison of scores on the PROI of the graduating class of 1992 (all students had completed the ethics curriculum before taking the test) with scores of entering students and two groups of practicing dentists (Bebeau et al., 1993). The graduates expressed a significantly greater sense of responsibility to others than entering students and practicing dentists from the region. The graduates' mean score, although somewhat lower, was not significantly different from a group of 40 dentists who demonstrated special commitment to professionalism by volunteering to participate in a national seminar to train ethics seminar leaders.

A second indication of instructional effectiveness comes from responses to a 1991 national survey (75% response rate) of senior dental students' willingness to treat patients infected with Hepatitis B-Virus (HBV) or Human Immunodeficiency Virus (HIV; Bebeau, manuscript submitted). Seventy-five percent of Minnesota seniors (compared to 62% nationally) claimed to have treated patients known to be infected with blood borne diseases (HBV/HIV). Ninety percent (compared with 76% nationally) felt the profession had a responsibility to treat such patients, and 86% (compared to 62% nationally) stated a personal willingness to treat such patients in practice. These patterns of difference were consistent across questions related to knowledge and attitudes.

Based on our experience and the evidence gathered so far, it is quite clear that (a) both students and professionals (see also Table 7.2) hold different conceptions of their role, and that (b) students need explicit instruction in role concept. Acquisition of a clear sense of professional identity cannot be left to the "hidden curriculum." Preliminary analysis supports the test/retest reliability of the PROI. Work to establish the construct validity of the PROI is in progress.

MORAL IMPLEMENTATION

Research Questions

We conceptualize Component IV as keeping the goal clear despite distractions, fatigue, diversions—managing the self so as to maintain an overall executive control over the self and the situation. While self-control, ego strength, and perseverance are essential, these qualities alone will not resolve moral problems effectively. Component IV also involves competence in implementation skills that can be called up in service of the larger goal. Malpractice insurance carriers are well aware that the lack of interpersonal effectiveness and problem-solving know-how often precipitates a law suit. As a consequence, some carriers offer reduced rates to practitioners who develop competence in interpersonal communication. Students and practitioners tell us that they approach some professional problems with dread. Responding to an apprehensive or angry patient, discussing a quality-of-care issue with an offending peer, confronting a self-destructive or abusive patient, are just a few of the issues that professionals would rather avoid. We think that practice in resolving difficult and recurrent problems of the profession can change the expectations of efficacy that are likely to change behavior. If persons think of a task as fun or challenging, they are more likely to persist in their efforts to resolve the problem. Our efforts to influence Component IV processes are guided by these questions: (a) What personal characteristics and self-regulation skills are essential? (b) What subskills (e.g., interpersonal skills, problem-solving skills) are needed for effective implementation?

Assessment Strategies

In our dental curriculum, we involve students in exercises that build competence and confidence in resolving ethical problems. We do so through real-life enactments of actual situations that frequently occur in practice. Students are required to plan strategies to handle the cases, try out dialogue on their peers, then submit a case write-up that includes actual dialogue, a plan of action, and a list of key factors that influence the plan of action. These plans are evaluated by the course instructor, who provides written feedback to students. In the development of their plans, students are expected to apply principles of informed consent, and principles of effective communication presented in class, and the problem-solving strategies presented by Fisher and Ury (1981).

Although we have not made much progress in validating assessment strategies, we do provide practice in performance of this ensemble of responses or behaviors. In addition to case write-ups, students must engage in self-assessment of their learning. At the end of the series of seminars, they respond to open-ended questions such as: What do you think you learned? Which cases were most challenging for you? What would you tell other students about the experiences?

Evidence of Effectiveness

Although we give students feedback on the adequacy of their solutions, to date we have not studied how the ability to devise and implement strategies in role-play settings translates to clinical performance or how the implementation skills relate to the other component processes. We have, however, studied student perceptions (Bebeau, 1988) of the benefits of the curriculum. When the senior seminar was first implemented in 1980, 86% of the students were very positive about the value of the course, 9% were uncertain, and 5% were negative. By 1986, 95% expressed very positive views about their learning, views that have been maintained. By way of contrast, initially only 22% of the students thought the course was well designed. By 1986, suggestions for improvements dropped to 20%. Today, about 80% of the class think the course is well designed; suggestions for improvement are minor.

Following are some examples of students' responses to the senior seminar self-assessment question: What do you think you learned from these experiences?

It exposed me to ways of thinking that I would never have come to on my own.

My approach to resolving problems is greatly improved, and I learned new skills which will be useful in the future.

To see the issues that exist behind the curtain of details and circumstances. To rationally reason them out to a logical conclusion, being careful to consider the perspective of each party, the consequences of alternative actions, and the ethical principles that apply. Then, to apply predetermined problem strategies and communication skills.

These comments illustrate the importance students attach to the development of implementation skills, but do not contribute to our understanding of the relevance of personal characteristics to effective implementation. The need for this kind of study is illustrated by the following example.

One of the groups referred for an ethics course by the state board consisted of three auxiliaries and a dentist. The auxiliaries had been performing duties both outside their training and prohibited by the Dental Practice Act. During the assessment it became obvious that the dentist's ethical sensitivity was well developed. He had a reasonably clear view of his professional role, but his moral reasoning was not well developed. In the intake interview, he expressed embarrassment about being disciplined. He readily admitted his error, and was most cooperative. In contrast, the auxiliaries' sensitivity and reasoning skills were poorly developed, and they were angry about having to take the course, even though they did not have to pay for it. What became obvious during the problem-solving exercises was that the dentist lacked assertiveness. He would allow the auxiliaries to decide on the course of action they should take, even when he did not agree with it. Much of the course was devoted to helping the auxiliaries see the shortcomings in their thinking and build respect for the perspectives and judgment of the dentist.

SUMMARY AND FUTURE DIRECTIONS

In the last decade, we have concentrated on designing and validating outcome measures and classroom assessment strategies for evaluating three of Rest's four components of morality: ethical sensitivity, moral reasoning, and moral motivation and commitment. We have been able to show that we can reliably assess these processes, that there are striking individual differences among students and practicing professionals on the measures, that competence on one of the processes does not necessarily predict competence on another, and that strengths and weaknesses in these processes can and do influence professional ethical decisions. Our findings not only support Rest's contention that moral failings can result from deficiencies in any one of the processes, but support the importance of attending to each of these processes when designing curriculum. For example, the kinds of cases typically used in ethics courses might promote moral reasoning, but would not likely influence ethical sensitivity or other processes, even though we have been able to show that improvements in each of the processes can be brought about though carefully designed and validated instruction.

Our ongoing monitoring of student performance in the curriculum shows the crucial role that criteria and personalized feedback play in (a) improving the quality of moral argument, (b) helping students develop a clear sense of their professional identity, and (c) influencing their perception that instruction in ethics is worthwhile. Our ongoing outcome studies have done much to dispel the popular belief that ethics can't be taught and that faculty without formal ethics training are not equipped to teach. Our ongoing studies also demonstrate that a curriculum of rather modest duration can influence ethical development in measurable ways, provided that curriculum incorporates the elements of effective instruction.

We have three goals for the future: first, to develop methods for quantifying levels of performance for Component IV processes; second, to continue validation work on Component III assessments (PROI and Role Concept Essay) and to design PROI items to study professional identity across professions; and third, to extend our study of the relationship of each component to each other and to real-life professional performance.

APPENDIX A: SAMPLE CASE FROM THE GERIATRIC DENTAL ETHICAL SENSITIVITY TEST

The Luella Case

The student is presented with a dental chart for Luella, previously treated by Dr. Mary Fields. The medical history indicates that Luella suffered a past CVA (stroke). The dental chart indicates that Luella has almost all of her own teeth and chart entries reveals a history of preferences for using dental services. Luella is financially secure and resides in an assisted-living care setting. She arranged the appointment to have the dentist examine a lesion on her tongue. After reviewing the chart, the student is asked to assume he or she is the dentist interacting with Luella on the video. During the video, Luella makes numerous attempts to answer the dentist's questions. She manages to convey that she consistently brushes her teeth twice a day with her left hand (the stroke having limited use of right hand), but often chooses words which merely approximate what she wishes to express. For example: When asked if the dentist posing the questions has treated her before, she (correctly) says "No." But, when asked who did treat her last, she replies, "A girl." The chart indicates that the previous dentist was Dr. Mary Fields. The dentist on the video (apparently questioning her competence as a decision maker), begins to ask questions (from the Mini Mental State Exam). Luella appears frustrated, but manages to convey that she is hampered by expressive aphasia in this way: Asked what year it is, she responds, "I know it, but I can't remember to say it." In addition to suffering the side effects of the stroke, Luella has on her tongue a highly suspicious lesion which has not as yet been diagnosed definitely. The dentist suspects a squamous cell carcinoma, which potentially could threaten her life, and wishes to verify his suspicion with a biopsy. Luella refuses the biopsy and says "No!" when asked if the dentist may contact her family or other caregivers.

Excerpt From GDEST Scoring Manual

B. The patient's cognitive competence as a decision maker.

Score 1. Assumes Luella is not competent. Seems unaware that the CVA impacts her expressive abilities rather than her ability to comprehend.
  Example: "Obviously, she's not competent to make her own decision."
  Example: "She doesn't have that kind of intellect anymore to make informed consent."
Score 2. Some recognition. Sees her impairment as affecting her ability to make a clear decision.
  Example: "She would probably understand, but not be able to communicate her feelings, so she may or may not be competent."
Score 3. Clearly recognizes that she is not at a point of being unable to make a decision.
  Example: "The patient understands what I'm saying. With a CVA they're still very intelligent. It's just that they have a difficult time communicating with other people. Just because she can't get the words into her mouth what her brain is thinking ..."
  Example: "When you ask her questions, she won't speak, but I think if you gave her a pencil and paper, she could probably write the answer."

APPENDIX B: GENERIC PATIENT CHARACTERISTICS AND PROFESSIONAL RESPONSIBILITIES

I. *Special Patient Characteristics*
   A. The patient's medical and dental health status.
   B. The patient's cognitive competence as a decision maker.
   C. The patient's psychological status as a decision maker.
   D. The patient's financial resources and their impact upon treatment.
   E. The patient's health care habits and values.
   F. The patient's understanding of the cause and prevention of disease.
   G. The patient's knowledge or perception of his of her health status.
   H. The patient's perception of the role and level of trust in the profession.

II. *The Dentist's Responsibilities to the Patient, the Profession, and the Community*
   A. Respects patient autonomy. Treats the patient as the ultimate decision maker.
   B. Clearly indicates what the best dental care would be and advocates the patient's long-term interest.
   C. Cultivates an ongoing, positive, interpersonal relationship with the patient, regardless of whether the patient follows the health professional's advice.
   D. Recognizes responsibilities of the dentist to a fellow professional. (Recognizes limitations as a dentist and does not overstep what others can do better; interacts with other caregivers, as needed.)
   E. Recognizes responsibilities to other family members, guardian, conservator, or other established or long-standing friends or family caregivers.
   F. Recognizes responsibility to the larger community (to educate the community, challenge bad practice, report suspected abuse or neglect, etc.)

APPENDIX C: SAMPLE OF AN ETHICAL REASONING ASSESSMENT

The Martin Sladick Case

Martin Sladick graduated from dental school five years ago. He is an excellent dentist, but business has been poor due to the economy in the area. Several businesses have closed and many of his patients are out of work. Martin has always had an interest in orthodontics and, since he has a lot of free time, he has been reading a lot about various orthodontic treatments. His dental training, like most

7. INFLUENCING THE MORAL DIMENSIONS OF DENTAL PRACTICE 141

dental programs, included 50 hours of lecture and 20 hours of lab designed to teach dentists how to tell when dentition is erupting normally. This would enable a dentist to give reasonable advice as to when a patient should be referred for treatment, but not how to do treatment. He realizes that formal training in orthodontics involves a 2-year graduate program.

Several of the children in his practice need orthodontic treatment and he is thinking of suggesting to their parents that he could do some of the easier treatments at a reduced rate. It would be a way of increasing his business and it would be a service to families who might not otherwise be able to afford the care.

Should Martin expand his practice to include orthodontics? YES__ NO__
What reasons would you give to support your position?

Sample Student Response: George

Before Discussion (Students Take a Tentative Position). No. Martin is a member of the dental community and in being so should abide by the Code of Ethics. This code states that a person shall not practice in a specialized field in which one is not qualified. If he does do the orthodontic work, he must inform the patient of his underqualifications. He could be at extreme risk of doing malpractice to the patient. If he is in a group practice, his partners or company could also be held accountable for his actions. I would expect that the State Board must also be monitoring the type of care he is doing, and could possibly revoke his license for practicing in an area in which he is not qualified. The patients have a responsibility to themselves to make sure that they are given appropriate care. I don't think that the dental school has any responsibility in this case, due to the fact that he graduated five years ago.

After Discussion (Students are Asked to Reassess the Initial Position).
No. I don't think that he should do the work because it seems as though he wants to do it only for the money, which is extremely unethical. However, if he really is concerned about his patients' health, then I feel that there are many avenues that are open to him in which he can find the care for the patients. Martin can take continuing education courses. Maybe with enough coursework, he might be qualified to do some limited work. He can also seek consultation from an orthodontist. He and the orthodontist might agree on what work he might be qualified to perform. Martin could try and find an orthodontist who will come in and provide services at a reduced cost. I do feel Martin has the obligation to his patients to provide them with adequate care. This might include having his patients get a second opinion on the work he is about to do. The patients' parents should seek a second opinion as an obligation to their children. I changed my mind about the State Board, but the rest of page 1 still represents the way I feel.

Analysis of George's Response

In the first paragraph of George's initial response, he states that the dentist has a duty to abide by the Code of Ethics, but he seems to think the code prohibits specialty practice if one has not completed specialty training. (Actually, the code permits dentists to practice in specialty areas; it merely prohibits those who have not completed specialty training from advertising as a specialist.) His confusion about the dentist's responsibilities is apparent in the next paragraph, where he states the conditions under which Martin could give treatment, (e.g., if he informed the patient of his lack of qualifications). Although he implies a duty to provide competent care when he lays out possible consequences of action, consequences are stated as they relate to Martin and his presumed colleagues, rather than consequences to the patients and the patients' parents. In George's view, responsibility for monitoring the quality of care delivered seems to reside with external agencies, the Dental School (though they would no longer be responsible, in this case) and the State Board, rather than with the individual professional. Furthermore, he sees the patient, rather than the dentist, as responsible to see that appropriate care is delivered. He seems not to see the situation from the perspective of the patient, that patients can't judge what kind of risk they are assuming when consenting to care given by someone who lacks training and experience. Similarly, George doesn't seem to see that Martin cannot reasonably inform the patients of the risks they are taking because he lacks the insight that comes from training, experience, and supervised practice.

As indicated on the scoring template, George's initial response was credited with recognizing the *duties* to inform, though he doesn't clearly see the duty to provide competent care. He also was credited with recognition of consequences to Martin and potential harm to the patient. He named three of the affected parties, but his lack of perspective taking may have inhibited his recognition of the full range of issues presented in this dilemma. He showed some recognition of Martin's legal right to practice and his right to learn, but did not see the other issues.

Following the discussion, George expressed concern with Martin's motivation, arguing that expanding his practice would be wrong because his motives are self-serving—rather than because he has obligations to do no harm, or to respect the patient's right to competent care. He recognizes new *issues*: the community's right to competent care and Martin's right to learn. He considers specialists as *affected parties* and offers solutions that are concerned with insuring quality by involving a specialist. He states a *duty* to provide adequate care, but does not clearly articulate other duties listed on the scoring template or the ethical principles that undergird them.

Sample Student Response: Jim

Before Discussion (Students Take a Tentative Position). No. The Code of Ethics for dentistry states that a dentist cannot advertise a specialty unless he or she has had accredited graduate study in that particular field. Even though this dentist is not placing an ad in the paper advertising this, he is still breaking an ethical code by giving false knowledge to the community. His view is not so bad in that, I think, he is basically trying to do good for people who need help but can't afford it, but he going about it in a wrong way. A professional cannot jeopardize any patient by performing operations on that patient which he or she is not qualified to do. The result could bring pleasure to dentist and patient, but more importantly, it could bring *discomfort* to patient, possible removal of dentist's license, and a bad name for dentistry in general. All of society is affected by this case. Society puts its trust in the dental profession to produce competent dentists and specialists. This act would be breaking that trust and everyone would be affected; dentistry in general, plus public health, could be lessened because of less trust in the dental practice leading to less people going to dentists.

After Discussion (Students are Asked to Reassess the Initial Position)
No. My position hasn't changed, but my reasoning has. On page 1, I talked about breaking the Code of Ethics, but within the past two hours I've learned that a general dentist has a license to do any kind of practice. There is an implicit agreement between dentists and specialists in which specialists don't practice general dentistry, but general dentists can practice specialties if they feel competent to do so. In this situation, the dentist may be "out in the bush" and people don't have any other alternatives. It is this dentist's responsibility, however, to be fundamentally capable in both the technology and hands-on aspect of orthodontics before practicing this specialty. He could practice on patients with some form of supervision from a specialist. I think that the lack of knowledge, basically not knowing all of the principles involved in orthodontics, could seriously do damage to the patients. He could cause more than discomfort, as I said earlier. Even if his mistakes didn't cause permanent damage, they could cost a patient and the patient's family time and money to solve the problem. Not knowing what he was doing could hurt his name as a dentist, the dental profession, and society as a whole. The dentist has duties to perform in areas where he is competent and, in some cases where he might be lacking, he should be responsible enough to refer the patient. Specialists, in general, do better work in that specialty, especially in the long run, than a general dentist would. Another point is that I feel that this dentist is probably looking a little too much at the monetary aspect. This is not bad if he is competent to do the work, but if he doesn't really know what he is doing, is he really doing the patient a service? No. Finally, if the dentist thought about it, he might realize that orthodontic care is usually elective rather than necessary. If the community is economically depressed, it is unlikely that parents would be interested in orthodontics.

Analysis of Jim's Response

As noted on the scoring template, Jim's response addresses many of the issues, affected parties, consequences and duties listed.

Scoring Template: The Martin Sladick Case

		George	Jim
Issues 5 pts			
Patient's right to competent care			X
Martin's legal right to practice		X	X
Communities' right to care		X	X
Martin's right to learn		X	
Martin's competence to inform and to provide adequate treatment			X
		3	4
Parties 3 pts.			
Martin		X	X
Patients	5–6 = 3	X	X
Parents	3–4 = 2	X	X
Specialists	1–2 = 1		X
Profession			X
Community			*X*
		2	3
Consequences 4 pts			
Harm to patients	4–5 = 4	X	X
Harm to Martin		X	X
Costs to patients			X
Generalist/specialist relationship			X
Harm to the profession			X
		2	4
Duties 5 pts.			
Do no harm	5–6 = 5		X
Place patients' rights first			X
To refer			X
To know your limits			X
To inform		X	
To provide competent care			X
		2	5
Reassess position 3 pts.		2	3
Total		11	19

APPENDIX D: A SAMPLE ROLE CONCEPT ESSAY[9]

The first thing I must do on my journey to becoming a professional is to *acquire a base of knowledge* [k], not just to the best of my ability, but to the standards set by the profession. This foundational knowledge is what I am now receiving in dental school. Acquiring the knowledge is only half the requirement. I must *keep abreast of the continuing changes* [CE] that occur in scientific and technical areas that relate to dentistry. This need of mine for continuing education begins even now, prior to graduation, but is especially relevant after graduation, and will be a lifelong endeavor for me. As a dental practitioner, I am responsible for conducting myself in an ethical manner, *placing clients' dental health above my desire* [1/2E] to profit from the profession financially. During my time as a student, and particularly in my years of practice, I must familiarize and refamiliarize myself with the Code of Ethics. The Code is not static, but evolves as new realities (e.g., AIDS) confront society. I must therefore be receptive to alteration or expansion of the Code over time. It goes without saying that I should *adhere to the Code* [C], but not blindly. If, in some instance, following the Code would be inconsistent with the basic ethic of the profession, I am bound by the ethic. But, I am also obligated to work through the profession to accomplish change. My attitude must be that my title "dentist" is a privilege to be cherished, not a right. Because some of my education was funded through taxes paid by the people, I need to be an active and positive force in promoting the oral health of my community. My aim should be to *serve the community* [S] in which I live, not to just put in my time at the office and then retreat to my private life. I can fulfill this obligation by being involved in local school dental education programs, by providing my share of care for the underserved, and by working through my professional association to promote the oral health of the nation. Finally, as a dentist I must *regulate myself* [1/2SG]. The autonomy of my profession depends on me doing my part in this. I must also be active in dental societies and organizations that, through peer interaction, aid in self-regulation and the regulation of one another [1/2SG]. My duty in regulation is not only to myself and the dental profession, but to the larger society. I must do my part to *put the health care needs of society above the profession's self-interest* [1/2E].

It is hard to say exactly when one becomes a professional. When one is licensed? Or, does a dental student also have professional responsibilities? It seems to me that no matter at what stage one is in their pursuit of professionalism, the responsibilities I outlined must be realized and internalized.

REFERENCES

Baab, D. A., & Bebeau, M. J. (1990). The effect of instruction on ethical sensitivity. *Journal of Dental Education, 54*(1), 44.
Bebeau, M. J. (1983). Professional responsibility curriculum report: American College fellows serve as expert assessors. *The Journal of the American College of Dentists, 50*(2), 20–23.
Bebeau, M. J. (1985). Teaching ethics in dentistry. *Journal of Dental Education, 49*(4), 236–243.
Bebeau, M. J. (1988). The impact of a curriculum in dental ethics on moral reasoning and student attitudes. *Journal of Dental Education, 52*(1), 49.

---

[9]Italicized phrases convey the six essential responsibilities. This essay received full credit, 12 points. One point was assigned for accurately expressing each of the six italicized phrases; a second point for an accurate discussion of each concept.

Bebeau, M. J. (1990). *A professional responsibility curriculum for dental education* (2nd ed.). Center for the Study of Ethical Development, University of Minnesota, Minneapolis.

Bebeau, M. J. (1990). *Using classroom assessment to improve instruction in ethical decision making: Two data-based examples.* Paper presented at the annual meeting of the American Educational Research Association, Boston.

Bebeau, M. J. (1994). *Developing dental students' conceptions of professional obligation.* Manuscript submitted for publication.

Bebeau, M. J., Born, D. O., & Ozar, D. T. (1993). The development of a professional role orientation inventory. *The Journal of the American College of Dentists, 60* (2), 27–33.

Bebeau, M. J., & Brabeck, M. M. (1987). Integrating care and justice issues in professional moral education: A gender perspective. *Journal of Moral Education, 16*(3), 189–203.

Bebeau, M. J., & Rest, J. R., (1982). *The Dental Ethical Sensitivity Test.* Minneapolis Division of Health Ecology, School of Dentistry, University of Minnesota, Minneapolis.

Bebeau, M. J., Rest, J. R. & Yamoor, C. M. (1985). Measuring dental students' ethical sensitivity. *Journal of Dental Education, 49*(4), 225–235.

Bebeau, M. J. & Thoma, S. J. (in press). The impact of a curriculum in dental ethics on moral judgment and student attitudes. *Journal of Dental Education.*

Bebeau, M. J., & Waithe, M. E. (1988). Undergraduate preparation in philosophy, humanities, and social sciences as predictors of the ability to identify and reason about ethical issues in dentistry. *Journal of Dental Education, 52*(1), 49.

Blasi, A. (1984). Moral identity: Its role in moral functioning. In W. Kurtines & J. L. Gewirtz (Eds.), *Morality, moral behavior, and moral development* (pp. 128–139). New York: Wiley.

Damon, W. (1984). Self-understanding and moral development from childhood to adolescence. In W. Kurtines & J. L. Gewirtz (Eds.), *Morality, moral behavior, and moral development* (pp. 109–127). New York: Wiley.

Ernest, M. (1990). *Developing and testing cases and scoring criteria for assessing geriatric dental ethical sensitivity.* Unpublished master's thesis, University of Minnesota, Minneapolis.

Fisher, R., & Ury, W. (1981). *Getting to yes: Negotiating agreements without giving in.* Boston: Houghton Mifflin.

Hall, R. H. (1975). *Occupations and the social structure* (2nd ed.). Englewood Cliffs, NJ: Prentice-Hall.

Harvan, R. A. (1989). *The relationship between technical competence and ethical sensitivity among health professionals.* Unpublished doctoral dissertation, Rutgers University, New Brunswick, NJ.

Howe, K. (1982). Evaluating philosophy teaching: Assessing student mastery of philosophical objectives in nursing ethics. *Teaching Philosophy, 5*(1), 11–22.

May, W. E. (1983). *The physician's covenant: Images of the healer in medical ethics.* Philadelphia: Westminster Press.

Meetz, H. K., Bebeau, M. J., & Thoma, S. J. (1988). The validity and reliability of a clinical performance rating scale. *Journal of Dental Education, 52*(6), 290–297.

Miles, S. H., Lane, L. W., Bickel, J., Walker, R. M., & Cassel, C. K. (1989). Medical ethics education: Coming of age. *Academic Medicine, 64*:705–714.

Ozar, D. T. (1985). Three models of professionalism and professional obligation in dentistry. *Journal of the American Dental Association, 110,* 173–177.

Rest, J. R. (1986). *Moral development: Advances in research and theory.* New York: Praeger.

Schlaefli, A., Rest, J. R., & Thoma, S. J. (1985). Does moral education improve moral judgment? A meta-analysis of intervention studies using the Defining Issues Test. *Review of Educational Research, 55*(3), 319–352.

Sheehan, T. J., Candee, D., Cook, C. D., & Bargen, M. (1980). Moral judgment as a predictor of clinical performance. *Evaluation and the Health Professions, 3*(4), 393–404.

Veatch, R. M. (1972). Models for ethical medicine in a revolutionary age. *The Hastings Center Report, 2,* 5–7.

Chapter 8

Moral Reasoning in Medicine

Donnie J. Self
Texas A & M University College of Medicine
DeWitt C. Baldwin, Jr.
American Medical Association

Highly moral conduct and adherence to a code of ethics that specifies expected norms of behavior and articulates a covenant with society have been the goal and the mark of the profession of medicine since the School of Kos. This is based on the belief and social expectation that the possession of special knowledge and skills carries with it the mandate for its moral and ethical use. The daily practice of medicine, however, complicates the issue in several important ways. First, the closeness and intimacy of the physician–patient relationship depends on trust and on a fiduciary responsibility that goes far beyond generalized, external standards. Second, each clinical encounter is different, indeed unique, based on the unlimited diversity of human life experience. Finally, the environment of medicine is in constant change, generating new problems not specified or anticipated by general codes. This requires that the individual physician exercise constant moral judgment in decision making, a task further complicated by the changing values and expectations of the patient and of society. Thus, it is imperative that the physician learn to make responsible decisions while living with predictable and ever present doubt and uncertainty. Helping the physician to do this is the responsibility of medical education, which must teach students to clarify and understand the ethical standards of the profession and of society; to seek and develop insight into one's personal values; to acquire a method of apprehending and appreciating the values and expectations of patients, families, and society; to maintain a constant attitude of vigilance toward this aspect of medicine; and to seek continued self-learning in personal and professional life.

The foregoing comments suggest the need for an emphasis or focus beyond that which is commonly taught or understood as medical education, or even bioethics. Bioethics is usually viewed as *external*, something that is objective, attached to, and inherent in the challenge of daily practice and medical progress, as well as in the technological imperative. What is being referred to here is different, although related. It is ethics viewed as *internal*, as more subjective, as the expectation placed upon the individual physician to reach privately generated and responsible moral decisions within the hectic and hurried environment of daily clinical practice. What is demanded of the physician is the ability and willingness to understand, develop, and exercise his or her own internal values and capacity for moral decision making.

Thus, it appears essential that medical educators and the curriculum instruct and model such knowledge, skills, and attitudes for entering students as part of the socialization and professionalization process. The unfortunate consequence of the overcrowded curriculum is that such material is usually taught in a structured lecture format and at a single, often inappropriate, point in the curriculum. Such learning cannot be left to chance, but must be carefully planned and taught at every level of medical education and training. As Sheehan, Sheehan, White, Leibowitz, and Baldwin (1990), as well as others have shown, students and residents in training frequently are exposed to examples of clinical and ethical misconduct, such as academic cheating, falsification of medical records, cheating on research, mistreatment of patients and cover-up of that mistreatment, as well as deliberate misdiagnosis or unnecessary treatment to achieve a financial end, whether it be for the patient, the doctor, or the institution. These experiences, along with many other medical decisions, offer the opportunity for frank, open discussion of their moral and ethical implications, giving students an opportunity to compare their beliefs and values to those of their peers and teachers.

Both Barnard (1992), and Hafferty and Franks (in press) support the position that ethics and values are deeply embedded in all aspects of medical education and practice and must be taught at all levels, including the supposedly values-free basic sciences. They present many examples of how such issues can be found and effectively discussed at all stages of the curriculum.

The importance of teaching values, integrity, and ethical decision making in the medical profession has been increasingly recognized over the past two decades. Since the 1970s, schools of medicine have gradually introduced courses in medical ethics, usually as a single course, often in a lecture format, but occasionally taught in the *ethical rounds* format as pioneered by Pellegrino and others (Bickel, 1986; McElhinney, 1981; Pellegrino & McElhinney, 1982). However, a formal review of the Association of the American Medical College (AAMC) Curriculum Directory in 1972–1973 did not reveal a single course with the word ethics or bioethics at any U.S. medical school. A decade later, in 1982–1983, however, the Directory indicated a majority of medical schools with such courses.

EMPIRICAL STUDIES IN MORAL REASONING

The First Wave

Interest in empirical studies of moral reasoning in medical students and residents is associated primarily with the work of two research groups, the first occurring from about 1977–1985 and the second from 1985 to the present. The earlier period, 1977–1985, features the work of Sheehan (1978) and a group of collaborators, whereas the latter, 1985 to the present, has been led by Self (1985a) and his associates. Many of the early reports were presented at the annual Research in Medical Education (RIME) conferences sponsored by the AAMC, or at the annual meeting of the American Educational Research Association (AERA) and, unfortunately, are not available in the published scientific literature.

Studies of moral reasoning in medicine have primarily featured the use of the Defining Issues Test (DIT) of Rest (1979), presumably because of cost and ease of administration, although several studies have utilized Kohlberg's (1984) original Moral Judgment Interview (MJI), as well as Gibbs' (Gibbs & Widaman, 1982) Sociomoral Reflection Measure (SRM). Because all of these measures are based on Kohlberg's cognitive moral development theory with the principle of justice as the highest moral good, discussion of the various studies has frequently included speculation on the possible gender effects on the measures, and on the need to consider the moral orientation of caring as proposed by Gilligan (1982) and Noddings (1984), among others. Self and Skeel (1992) developed a new instrument, combining part of Kohlberg's and part of Gilligan's interviews, which more clearly and efficiently document and delineate both of these orientations of justice and care, as well as assess stages of moral reasoning all in one interview of approximately 1 hour.

Perhaps the earliest study reporting use of a measure of principled moral reasoning in medical students appears in the *Journal of Medical Education* in 1977 under the section called "Briefs," and simply reports without detail that there was no significant difference in DIT scores between students who took an experimental class in human values in medicine and a comparison group (Blizek & Finkler, 1977).

In the proceedings of the 1978 RIME Conference, Husted (1978), from Sheehan's group at the University of Connecticut Health Center, reported on studies assessing moral reasoning in 488 medical students utilizing the DIT. The P scores of 50.2 and 50.8 for first- and third-year students respectively, are chiefly of note for their comparability to the scores of Bloom's (1976) graduate students and for their lack of progression from the first to third year. Husted also found that the students showed a preference for reasoning at stages 5A, 5B, and 6. In addition, she compared DIT results for U.S.-educated pediatric residents ($N = 46$) with those from graduates of foreign schools ($N = 58$) and found dramatic differences with the U.S. residents scoring higher (P scores = 57.2 vs. 32.3). This same report contained the intriguing finding that pediatric faculty affiliated with programs at high prestige institutions scored higher (P score = 54.2), as compared with faculty from less prestigious programs (P score = 47.6).

In these same 1978 RIME proceedings, Cook (1978), working with Sheehan's group and testing the same residents, found a significant correlation ($r = .32, p \leq .001$) between P scores and attitudes toward aggressive treatment of the critically ill. Those with higher P scores tended to be more sensitive to negative family attitudes and treat less actively than those with lower P scores.

The first report of findings with regard to moral reasoning and clinical performance (Sheehan, 1978), later published by Sheehan, Husted, Candee, Cook, and Bargen (1980), also appeared in these proceedings. Data on 260 pediatric residents from two university hospitals and three community hospitals indicated that a canonical correlation between the six levels of moral reasoning on the DIT and 18 dimensions of clinical performance (Cook & Margolis, 1974) was statistically significant ($r = .82, p \leq .05$). This group also found a statistically significant correlation ($p \leq .001$) between the overall rating of performance and the moral reasoning score derived from the Kohlberg MJI ($N = 45$).

A year later, in the 1979 RIME Proceedings, Daniels and Baker (1979) reported on changes in moral development in 60 students (41 males and 19 females), as measured by the DIT over an 18-month period starting at entry into medical school. He also attempted to relate such changes to concomitant changes in interpersonal relationship style as measured by the Fundamental Interpersonal Relationship Orientation-Behavior (FIRO-B) scale, developed by Schutz (1966). Summarizing mean stage and index scores for three time periods, Daniels found that there was a significant decrease in the use of less mature, Stage 3 responses and a significant increase in more complex 5B responses, as well as in the P index. Thus, the Daniels study suggested continuing development of moral reasoning during the first three semesters of medical school, with a greater preference for more complex moral judgments. He also concluded that the manner in which students adapt to their social environment influences their moral development, suggesting that "people who are comfortable with sensitive interpersonal involvements demonstrate greater development on a variable that is rooted in social relationship, i.e., morality" (p. 91).

Members of Sheehan's group returned to the topic of moral reasoning in these same 1979 RIME proceedings, expanding on Cook's study (1978) of the relationship between moral reasoning and decisions concerning the treatment of critical illness. They reported on a survey of 452 physicians (256 residents and 186 practicing physicians), hypothesizing that higher stage moral reasoning would lead to limitations in the use of active treatment in situations where the patient or the family had requested such a limit and/or where the future quality of life was problematic after the proposed treatment. Using a questionnaire designed by Crane (1975) which employed six simulated cases involving infants born with severe defects, Candee, Sheehan, Cook, and Husted (1979) found a significant negative

8. MORAL REASONING IN MEDICINE 151

correlation ($r = -.41$ for Form A and $r = -.23$ for Form B) between degree of activism with regard to treatment of such infants and moral reasoning in residents; among practitioners it was either unrelated or positively related to moral reasoning. In other words, among residents, but to a lesser extent among practitioners, "those subjects who were shown to reason in terms of universal ethical principles were most likely in particular cases to tailor their treatment of critical illness to both the explicit and implicit rights of patients. This was shown by correlations between DIT scores and the family attitude factor (explicit rights) and the salvageability factor (implicit rights)" (Candee et al., 1979, p. 98).

Meanwhile, Goldman and Arbuthnot (1979) reported an increase in moral reasoning skills in premedical undergraduate students who were exposed to moral dilemma discussions. A year later, Sheehan's group (1980) published the final version of their studies of the relationship between moral reasoning and clinical performance among 244 pediatric residents, utilizing a measure of clinical performance based on earlier work by Cook and Margolis (1974) and two measures of moral reasoning, the Kohlberg (1984) MJI and the Rest (1979) DIT. Results showed that the correlation between the 18 performance characteristics and the DIT scores was statistically significant at $p \leq .0001$, indicating nonchance differences in performance according to the predominant stage of moral judgment, together with a trend of improved performance with higher stage scores. Dividing the P scores and overall performance judgments into three levels produced an even more intriguing finding—that a high level of moral reasoning virtually excludes the possibility of being a poor performer, and, conversely, that a low level of moral reasoning virtually excludes the possibility of performing well. Also reported were significant differences between U.S.- and foreign-educated resident physicians on P scores and performance.

Sheehan, Husted, and Candee (1981) presented data at the annual meeting of the AERA, suggesting that there was no significant increase in the moral reasoning of 52 medical students from the beginning of their first year to the end of their third year. They also reported a narrowing of the range of scores over time, with higher scores generally decreasing and lower scores increasing. Unfortunately, this report was never published.

Between 1980 and 1982, there is no record of published work in the area of moral reasoning in medicine. Then Givner and Hynes (1983) conducted a study of first-year medical students who took a course in medical humanities. The DIT was used to assess moral reasoning. Fifty-one of 108 students fulfilled a commitment to complete the pretests and posttests and were compared with the 57 other students who failed to do so, the hypothesis being that students with higher levels of moral reasoning would be more likely to live up to their commitments. Results revealed that the mean principled reasoning score of the *fulfillers* was significantly higher (50.25) than that of the *nonfulfillers*, (45.75) on the pretest. The authors also observed that the principled reasoning scores of the fulfillers increased significantly ($p \leq .05$) from 50.75 to 54.75 from pretest to posttest. Stage 5B scores increased significantly ($p \leq .01$), whereas Stage 3 scores decreased significantly ($p \leq .01$). Thus, the study confirmed their hypothesis that principled persons would be more likely to live up to their commitments, while also demonstrating that a course on medical humanities that discussed moral dilemmas and ethical issues in medicine would enhance moral reasoning.

In the following year, Sheehan participated as coauthor in another project that assessed moral reasoning as a criterion for admission to medical school in Israel (Benor, Notzer, Sheehan, & Norman, 1984). Once again, the DIT was used in research involving two schools, one of which selected its students in a traditional manner based on competitive cognitive performance criteria, whereas the other, an innovative, community-based school, selected its students based on a complex process where personal interviews considering a number of noncognitive criteria determined the final choice after a basic screening for academic performance. Two hundred and forty out of 319 finalists at the community-based school agreed to take the DIT, while 216 of the 316 finalists at the traditional school participated. Both of these groups were further subdivided into *accepted* and *rejected* students. Results indicated that the overall P score for the entire studied population of applicants was 41 ± 13.8. The subgroup admitted by interview to the community-based school scored significantly higher (50.08 ± 17.0) than the other subgroups: namely, applicants rejected at the community-based school ($p \leq .001$), applicants admitted to the traditional school ($p \leq .005$) and applicants rejected at the traditional school ($p \leq .001$). There was a moderate, though significant correlation ($r = 0.19, p \leq .05$) between P scores and interview scores, suggesting that the interview process did indeed result in the selection of students with higher principled thinking. The authors close with a recommendation for replication of the study, as well as long-term follow-up of selectees.

Sheehan, Candee, Willms, Donnelly, and Husted (1985) were involved in a study of moral reasoning and physician performance at the University of Connecticut, this time with 39 family medicine residents as they interacted with each of two simulated patients. Two measures were used, the Kohlberg MJI and the Role Concept Inventory, a measure developed by Candee (1978) to probe the residents' concept of the physician's role in an ideal physician–patient relationship. Results indicated that there was a correlation of 0.38 between measures of moral reasoning and faculty ratings of resident performance, thus replicating their earlier findings. Since this work, Sheehan has continued to be interested in the process of how one enhances humanism and improves physicians' skills in managing morally problematic cases (Sheehan et al., 1987, 1989).

The Second Wave

The second wave of interest and research started in the mid-1980s and continued to the present. Although his first paper on moral reasoning in medicine did not appear until then, Self (1985a, 1985b) and his associates and collaborators at Texas A&M University have been extremely active since that time with a number of presentations at national meetings and publications in the medical and veterinary medical literature. It is also apparent that Self's interest and data collection started much earlier, and included all three of the commonly accepted measures of moral reasoning, the MJI, SRM, and DIT.

A significant body of work by Self and his associates consisted of introducing empirical assessment of moral reasoning in the evaluation of teaching medical ethics, demonstrating convincingly that such teaching can enhance the moral reasoning skills of medical students. The first published study (Self, Wolinsky & Baldwin, 1989) in this area used Gibbs' (1982) SRM and employed a natural experiment design to assess the value of incorporating medical ethics into the medical education curriculum, as well as the relative effects of two alternate methods of implementing that curriculum, namely, lecture and case-study discussion. The results showed a statistically significant increase ($p \leq .0001$) in the level of moral reasoning of students exposed to the medical ethics course, regardless of format. The unadjusted posttest scores indicated that the case-study method was significantly ($p \leq .03$) more effective than the lecture method at increasing students' levels of moral reasoning. When adjustments of the posttest scores were made by subtracting the pretest scores, however, this difference failed to achieve statistical significance. Regression analysis revealed that age, gender, undergraduate GPA, and Medical College Admission Test scores were unrelated to the changes in moral reasoning scores. All of the variance that could be explained was due to the students' being in one of the two experimental groups. The change associated with the lecture format, when compared to the control group, was statistically significant ($p \leq .004$), as was the change associated with the case study format ($p \leq .0001$).

Another study (Self, Baldwin, & Wolinsky, 1992) used the DIT to assess the hypothesis that the formal teaching of medical ethics promotes a significant increase in the growth and development of moral reasoning in medical students. A statistically significant increase ($p \leq .0005$) was found with unadjusted scores in the level of moral reasoning of students exposed to a course in medical ethics. Adjustment of the posttest scores by subtracting the pretest scores revealed that the differences between the control group and the experimental group were even more significant ($p \leq .0002$). Brief discussion was given of the fundamental premise that the appropriate function of teaching medical ethics in our modern pluralistic society is to improve students' moral reasoning about value issues, regardless of what their particular set of moral values happens to be.

Yet another study by Self, Baldwin and Olivarez (1993) used the DIT for evaluation of a project using film discussions for teaching medical humanities. The study involved three groups:

1. A control group of first-year medical students with no exposure to the film discussion.
2. A group of first-year medical students who participated in weekly 1-hour film discussions during the fall quarter.
3. A group of first-year medical students who participated in weekly 1-hour film discussions during both the fall and winter quarters.

Pre- and posttest measurements of moral reasoning skills showed statistically significant increases in moral reasoning scores of course registrants for both one quarter of exposure ($p \leq .002$) and two quarters of exposure ($p \leq .007$), as compared to the control group with no exposure ($p \leq .109$) to the film discussions. Several issues regarding these findings were addressed, including a potential for self-selecting bias and the design of the curriculum.

Another body of literature by Self and his associates involved longitudinal empirical research on the possible effect of medical education on moral development, using all three methods of assessment: the MJI, the SRM, and the DIT. Most of the studies involved use of the last measure because of cost and ease of administration. Nearly all of these studies demonstrated the lack of increase in moral reasoning and moral development generally expected in this age group, suggesting a possible inhibiting effect of this educational experience.

In their first longitudinal study Self, Schrader, Baldwin, and Wolinsky (1993) assessed the moral reasoning of 20 medical students (42% of the members of the class) in their first and last years of medical school, using the MJI. It was found that the students' normally expected increases in moral reasoning did not occur over the 4 years of medical education, suggesting that their educational experience served to inhibit their moral reasoning ability, rather than facilitating it. The weighted average scores (WAS) of the medical students ranged from 315 to 482 during the first year, and from 341 to 454 during the fourth year. The mean increase from the first year to the fourth year of the study of 18.5 WAS points was not statistically significant at the $p \leq .05$ level, thus confirming the hypothesis of no significant increase in the moral reasoning skills during medical education. Of additional interest was the finding that the range of moral reasoning WAS scores narrowed between the first and fourth years, indicating a strong socializing factor of the medical experience. During the first year, the students' WAS spread was 167, which corresponds to approximately one and a half moral development stages. During the fourth year, the WAS spread was 113 points, or approximately one stage. Taken together, these represent a theoretical difference between Years 1 and 4 of approximately three-fourths of a global stage—a significant reduction in moral reasoning variance.

There were no significant correlations at the $p \leq .05$ level between the change in moral reasoning WAS or global stage scores and either age, gender, Medical College Admission Test scores, or GPA scores. Therefore, it is unlikely that any sampling biases related to these factors attended the study outcome. Overall, the subjects scored in Kohlberg's conventional level of moral reasoning but there was no significant change—either in growth or regression—in the student's moral reasoning during their 4 years of medical education. Both the men and the women scored similarly on the pretest and posttest, thus failing to support the argument by Gilligan (1982) that Kohlberg's justice-oriented moral reasoning theory is genderbiased.

Similar longitudinal findings were reported in a paper presented by Galaz-Fontes et al., (1989) at the Fourth Adult Development Symposium held in Cambridge, Massachusetts, which presented data from a Mexican medical school.

Using a written form, which included dilemmas III-A and III-B from the Standard MJI, these authors studied 113 undergraduate medical students during the first ($N = 49$), third ($N = 24$), eighth ($N = 24$), and tenth ($N = 16$) semesters of medical school. Using the WAS, the moral reasoning of the students did not show any significant effect of semester ($p \leq .2099$), gender ($p \leq .1572$), or their interaction ($p \leq .3559$). For all the semester groups, subjects responded most frequently with developmental Stage 3 and Stage 3/4 level arguments (88%, 80%, 67%, and 94% for first, third, eighth, and tenth semesters, respectively). Likewise, there was no significant variation by gender; 83% of females and 82% of males responded at Stages 3 and 3/4.

In another study (Self, Baldwin, & Wolinsky 1994), Gibbs' (1982) SRM was used to assess the moral reasoning of 30 medical students (62.5% of the students in that class) at the beginning and again at the end of their medical education. Scores on the SRM ranged between 220 and 400. There was a mean increase from first year to fourth year of 10.67 points, which was not statistically significant at the $p \leq .05$ level. Data collection in an additional longitudinal study by Self, Olivarez and Baldwin, (1993) using the DIT and a larger number of students has been completed and is in the process of data analysis.

Together with results obtained by Self's group (see chap. 9) on students in veterinary medicine, these studies are consistent with the finding of students' failure to progress in their moral reasoning and moral development over the four years of medical and veterinary education. While they have the advantage of longitudinal, subject-to-subject testing, the numbers are small and it seems clear that further work must be done with much larger studies. This is especially important in view of another study (Baldwin, Daugherty, & Self, 1991). In this latter work, a longitudinal cross-sectional design was used to assess changes in moral reasoning among students in each of the 4 years of a medical school located in the Midwest. A total of 249 students completed DIT protocols. Due to problems with optical scanning, readouts and reliability indices, 43 protocols (17.3%) were lost for analysis, a figure in the expected range for DIT studies. The remaining population of 206 subjects included 82 women and 124 men distributed across the 4 years of medical school. When the average P score and number of participating students from each of the classes was broken down by gender, the results showed significant main effects for both gender ($F = 18.45$, $p \leq .001$) and year in school ($F = 4.806$, $p \leq .01$). Consistently higher moral reasoning scores were found for women than for men in every year of medical school.

Concerns regarding the retention of moral reasoning skills have also been addressed by Self's group. Self and Olivarez, (1994) documented an increase in moral reasoning skills following exposure to a medical ethics course taught in the first part of the first year of medical education and then tracked the same group of students who were retested annually until their graduation 4 years later. The hypothesis of this study was that retention of the increased moral reasoning skills would be maintained over the course of medical education. This hypothesis is in keeping with the theory of cognitive moral development, which claims that there is no significant regression from once-attained higher levels of moral reasoning

(Colby & Kohlberg, 1987). Confirmation of this hypothesis would affirm the importance of teaching medical ethics early in the medical education curriculum and offering a large enough exposure to make a significant difference when it is taught. Additionally, it would support the argument for medical ethics being a required course of all medical students rather than an elective course, as is often the case in many medical schools.

A total of 97 first-year medical students participated in the study. Because the study involved taking the DIT five times over a period of 4 years, different percentages of the students provided data at various times. However, 25 students filled out the questionnaire all five times and nearly 80% of the students completed the instrument three or more times. As a result, the data were analyzed as two separate sets, with the 25 students completing all five administrations as one set, and the other set being all students together that provided any data. The results of both analyses were virtually identical.

Statistical analyses showed that there was a significant difference ($p \leq .00025$) in the mean P score on the pretest (44.57) and the posttest (55.29) of the first-year students. The mean P score at the end of their second year was 57.33, which was significantly ($p \leq .00001$) higher than the first-year pretest, but not significantly ($p \leq .35535$) higher than the first-year posttest. Similarly, the mean P score at the end of their third year (60.20) and at the end of their fourth year (59.43) was significantly ($p \leq .00001$) higher respectively, than the first-year pretest. The mean scores following the pretest were not significantly different from each other. This systematic maintenance of higher mean DIT scores than the pretest throughout the remainder of medical education confirms the retention hypothesis that the increased moral reasoning skills from taking a medical ethics course would be retained over the course of medical education.

This study demonstrated that both the issues of social justice and the allocation of limited resources can be successfully addressed and positively influenced in terms of justice reasoning by the teaching of medical ethics in the medical education curriculum, and that these positive changes in justice reasoning skills are maintained throughout the remainder of medical education. No longer do the areas of values and attitude have to be relegated to the "soft sciences" that cannot be rigorously measured and tested. One way medicine can address the increasing concern over its loss of esteem and status in society is to give more attention to issues of social justice and the role of values in the profession.

Many of the research studies previously described above have indicated consistently higher levels of moral reasoning for women than for men, calling into question the highly publicized contention of Gilligan (1982) and others that women generally score lower on Kohlberg's moral dilemmas because of their different moral orientation. Since the use of the DIT in this study did not appear to work to the disadvantage of the women subjects, it would seem that the DIT and other Kohlberg measures of moral development can be appropriately used in research on moral development, although it would be helpful if comparable data could be secured from women in other professions that traditionally have been male-dominated.

Despite the finding that women in medical school score higher on a justice oriented instrument, considerable interest remains in further exploring the dimension of the orientation of caring, as proposed by Gilligan (1982), Noddings (1984), and others (Bebeau & Brabeck, 1987). Self and Skeel (1992) developed an interview instrument for assessment of moral reasoning and moral orientation in a single interview (MROI), with which Self, Jecker and Baldwin (1993) and other colleagues have conducted several studies that attempted to determine the existence and preference of orientations toward both justice and care in medical students, physicians, and clinical medical ethicists trained in philosophy and theology (Self, Skeel, & Jecker, 1993a, 1993b).

Using the MRO Interview (Self & Skeel, 1992), a study was conducted to assess the influence of philosophical versus theological education on the moral development of clinical medical ethicists (Self et al., 1993a). Moral reasoning and moral orientation data were collected from 50 clinical ethicists (26 philosophers and 24 theologians) from all sections of the United States. Analyses revealed that the philosophers (mean WAS 429) and the theologians (mean WAS 433) were not significantly different ($p \leq .621$) in their moral reasoning skills. Similarly, the philosophers and theologians were found not to be significantly different in their moral orientations toward justice or care in terms of their recognition, predominance, or alignment with these concepts. No significant relationship was found between age or gender and moral reasoning or moral orientation.

A follow-up study (Self et al., 1993b) compared these philosophical and theological clinical medical ethicists with practicing physicians. Significant differences were found. Interviews were conducted with 39 physicians representing a broad spectrum of specialties from all sections of the United States. The physicians (mean WAS 403) consistently scored lower in moral reasoning than the clinical ethicists (mean WAS 431) for a statistically significant difference of $p \leq .00028$. However, the physicians were found not to be significantly different from the clinical ethicists in their moral orientations toward justice or care in terms of their recognition, predominance, or alignment with these concepts. No significant relationship was found between age and moral orientation, although one was found between age and moral reasoning, with older persons scoring higher. No significant relationship was found between gender and moral reasoning, although one was found between gender and moral orientation—with females more likely to recognize elements of care in moral dilemmas and males more likely to recognize elements of justice.

In another study (Self, Jecker, & Baldwin, 1993), in which the Gilligan Real Life Conflict and Choice Interview (Brown et al., 1988) was used, the moral orientation of 20 medical students was assessed. Analysis of the data revealed that although the presence of justice issues were recognized in 95% of the moral conflicts of the medical students, the predominance of justice as the organizing principle or framework for resolution of the conflict occurred in less than half (30%) of the medical students' responses. Alignment with justice as the preferred mode of resolution of the conflict occurred in 20% of the cases. Conversely, the presence of care issues were recognized in 90% of the moral conflicts, with the predominance of care as the organizing principle or framework for resolution of the conflict occurring in 55% of the medical students. Alignment with care as the preferred mode of resolution of the conflict occurred in 25% of the cases. The presence of both justice and care in the moral conflicts was recognized by a vast majority of the medical students, yet only 15% of them exhibited a balanced approach where neither justice nor care were predominant. Nevertheless, many of them gave evidence of a personal alignment with a combined approach of justice and care as their preferred mode of resolution of moral conflicts.

It is interesting to note that, although statistical analysis showed no significant correlations between gender and predominance in moral orientation, these limited data tend to support Gilligan's (1982) claim of males being predominately justice oriented and females being predominately care oriented. The data reveal that 66.7% of the time, the justice orientation was exhibited as predominant by males and only 33.3% of the time predominant by females. Conversely, the care orientation was exhibited as predominant 72.7% of the time by females and only 27.3% of the time by males.

One conclusion that could be drawn from this study is that there may be other moral aspects beside justice and care that form the structure of moral reasoning in medical students. This is supported by the fact that combining those who aligned with justice (20%) as the preferred mode of resolution for the conflict, and those who aligned with care (25%), accounts for less than one half of the preferred ways of resolution of moral conflicts. Over half (55%) of the participants apparently preferred another mode of resolution for the conflicts, which was not identified by the bipolar analysis for justice and care. Other possible moral ideals need to be explored, including those of benevolence, following authority, and adherence to religious teachings.

Self and Olivarez (1993) attempted to summarize all this work by re-examining the DIT measures previously obtained on 705 first-year medical and veterinary students. Data from 79 students were lost to the study for reasons of test internal consistency and reliability violations. Analysis of the remaining 626 subjects showed that there was a significant difference between men and women in their DIT scores ($p \leq .0001$). The mean DIT score for men was 41.77 and that for women was 47.18. In the same study turning to an examination of gender and moral orientation, these same authors again reported on combined data available on 139 subjects (86 men and 53 women), using the MROI (Self & Skeel, 1992). Ages ranged from 24 to 76 years, with a mean of 39.8 years. Analysis revealed that 43.2% of the subjects exhibited a justice orientation and 51.8% a care orientation, with 5% using both, but exhibiting no predominance for either. When analyzed by gender, a justice orientation was exhibited by 48.8% of the men, as compared with 34% of the women, while a care orientation was exhibited by 50% of the men and 54.7% of the women. Thus, although there was no difference in men between the use of the justice and care orientations ($p \leq .22$), there was a significant difference between the use of these two orientations on the part of women, with a significant preference for a care orientation over a justice orientation ($p \leq .0198$). In addition, women were much more likely than men to use both orientations.

Finally, Baldwin, Adamson, Self, and Sheehan (1994) have been involved in an intriguing follow-up of the Sheehan hypothesis that there is a relationship between moral reasoning and clinical performance by examining this relationship in cases of malpractice claims against orthopedic surgeons. Demographic and malpractice claims data on the surgeons were available through a regional interindemnity liability trust. DIT's were secured from 149 physicians, of whom 57 were orthopedic surgeons. Results indicated that orthopedic surgeons with few (less than .09) or no claims per year demonstrated higher levels of moral reasoning with P scores of 44, as compared with P scores of 38 for orthopedists with multiple claims. This relationship approached statistical significance ($p \leq .07$). When the scatter plot for all scores was examined, it was clear that when the DIT score was greater than 40, there were 25 orthopedists with less than 0.2, as compared with only 6 who had greater than 0.4 claims per year ($p \leq .04$).

Pursuing another of Sheehan's findings, this study also showed that for orthopedists with P scores over 50, the result is even more dramatic ($p \leq .02$), suggesting once more that there may be a *floor effect*, or protective element, provided by higher levels of moral reasoning. Application of stepwise multiple regression techniques to the data on 57 orthopedists who completed the DIT indicated a significant relationship of claims with age ($p \leq .04$) and having a religious orientation ($p \leq .02$) and a close to statistically significant relationship with moral reasoning ($p \leq .07$). Adding to the regression, 64 additional orthopedists in the study who did not take the DIT brought out two additional factors of importance in malpractice claims experience: holding a clinical teaching appointment ($p \leq .03$), and membership in a professional society ($p \leq .0004$). This suggests that physicians with higher levels of moral reasoning (and lower claims experience) may be more likely to open themselves to peer review and professional relationships. These studies are continuing with larger samples and broader categories of physicians.

CONCLUSION

As a result of the many studies described here, Self and Baldwin (1993) have proposed that large-scale longitudinal research be conducted on the stages of moral development of entering medical students and residents, with the goal of assisting the selection process. Although they believe it would be unethical to use such test results to eliminate candidates categorically for selection, the work of Self and colleagues, as well as Blatt and Kohlberg (1975), which was later reproduced by many others (Schlaefli, Rest & Thoma, 1985), suggests that educational interventions for improvement of moral reasoning are available and perhaps should be part of every medical and residency graduate medical curriculum.

In spite of the encouragement from all the previous work discussed here, there is still much work to be done. Although these studies demonstrate that moral reasoning skills can be taught and retained during the 4 years of medical education, further longitudinal studies need to be done to assess the status of moral reasoning skills during residency training and the years of medical practice. It is not clear what influence the stressful environment of residency training has on moral reasoning. Furthermore, additional studies are needed regarding the relationship of moral reasoning skills and behavioral manifestations flowing from those skills. As indicated by many studies (Blasi, 1980; Kohlberg & Candee, 1984), the relationship between moral reasoning and moral behavior is complex and not well understood.

Similarly, further studies are needed regarding both the quantity and quality of activities required for increasing one's moral reasoning skill. Is one year, one quarter, or one lecture sufficient to increase moral reasoning skill in medicine? And what kinds of activities best foster the increase in moral reasoning—lecture, roleplaying, case study discussion, films? Much work needs to be done, but at least a foundation has been established for assessing the work when it is done. Several additional studies by Self's group are currently underway.

REFERENCES

Baldwin, D. C., Jr., Adamson, E., Self, D. J. & Sheehan, T. J. (1994). *Moral reasoning and malpractice: A study of orthopedic surgeons.* Unpublished manuscript.

Baldwin, D. C., Jr., Daugherty, S. & Self, D. J. (1991) Changes in moral reasoning during medical school. *Academic Medicine 66*, 1–3.

Barnard, D. (1992). Relation of ethics and human values to the sciences of medical practice. In R. Q. Marston & R. M. Jones (Eds.), *Commission on Medical Education and the Sciences of Medical Practice: Medical education in transition.* (pp. 100–101). Princeton, NJ: The Robert Wood Johnston Foundation.

Bebeau, M., & Brabeck, M. (1987). Integrating care and justice issues in professional moral education: A gender perspective. *Journal of Moral Education, 16*, 189–203.

Benor, D. E., Notzer, N., Sheehan, T. J., & Norman, G. R., (1984). Moral reasoning as a criterion for admission to medical school. *Medical Education, 18*, 423–428.

Bickel, J. (1986). *Integrating human values teaching programs into medical students' clinical education.* Washington, DC: Association of Medical Colleges.

Blasi, A. (1980). Bridging moral cognition and moral action: A critical review of the literature. *Psychological Bulletin 88*, 1–45.

Blatt, M., & Kohlberg, L. (1975). The effects of classroom moral discussion upon children's level of moral judgment. *Journal of Moral Education, 4*, 129–161.

Blizek, W. L., & Finkler, D. (1977). Teaching human values in medicine. *Journal of Medical Education, 52*, 858–859.

Bloom, R. B. (1976). Morally speaking, who are today's teachers? *Phi Delta Kappan, 57*, 624–625.

Brown, L. M., Argyris, D., Attanucci, J., Bardiger, B., Gilligan, C., Johnston, K., Miller, B., Osborne, D., Word, J., Wiggins, G., &Wilcox, D. (1988). *A guide to reading narratives of moral conflict and choice for self and moral voice.* Cambridge, MA: Center for the Study of Gender, Education, and Human Development, Harvard Graduate School of Education.

Candee, D. (1978). *Role concepts as predictors of pediatric residents' performance.* Paper presented at the annual meeting of the American Pediatric Association, New York.

Candee, D., Sheehan, T. J., Cook, C. D., & Husted, S. D. (1979). Moral reasoning and physicians' decisions in cases of critical illness. *Proceedings of the 18th Annual Conference on Research in Medical Education, 18*, 93–98.

8. MORAL REASONING IN MEDICINE 161

Candee, D., Sheehan, T. J., Cook, C. D., Husted, S. D., & Bargen, M. (1982). Moral reasoning and decisions in dilemmas of neonatal care. *Pediatric Research, 16,* 846–850.

Colby, A., & Kohlberg, L. (1987). *The measurement of moral judgment: Vol. I. Theoretical foundation and research validation.* New York: Cambridge University Press.

Cook, C. D. (1978). Influence of moral reasoning on attitudes toward treatment of the critically ill. *Proceedings of the 17th Annual Conference on Research in Medical Education, 17,* 442–443.

Cook, C. D., & Margolis, C. Z. (1974). Rating pediatric house officer performance. *Pediatric Research, 8,* 472.

Crane, D. (1975). *The sanctity of social life: Physicians' treatment of critically ill Patients.* New York: Russell Sage Foundation.

Daniels, M. H., & Baker, G. L. (1979). Assessing the moral development of medical students: An empirical study. *Proceedings of the 18th Annual Conference on Research in Medical Education, 18,* 87–92.

Daugherty, S. R., Baldwin, Jr., D. C., & Rowley, B. D. (1991). *National survey of resident educational and working conditions.* Report submitted to the American Medical Association Education and Research Foundation.

Galaz-Fontes, J. F., Pacheco-Sanchez, M. E., Sierra-Morales, I., Commons, M. L., Gutheil, T. G., & Hausen, M. J. (1989). *Medical school training and moral reasoning in Mexico.* Paper presented at the Fourth Adult Development Symposium meeting, Cambridge, MA.

Gibbs, J. C., & Widaman, K. F. (1982). *Social intelligence: Measuring the development of sociomoral reflection.* Englewood Cliffs, NJ: Prentice-Hall.

Gilligan, C. (1982). *In a different voice: Psychological theory and women's development.* Cambridge, MA: Harvard University Press.

Givner, N., & Hynes, K. (1983). An investigation of change in medical students' thinking. *Medical Education, 17,* 3–7.

Goldman, S. A., & Arbuthnot, J. (1979). Teaching medical ethics: The cognitive-developmental approach. *Journal of Medical Ethics, 5,* 170–180.

Hafferty, F. W., & Franks, R. (in press). Medical culture, medical ethics, and the medical school curriculum. *Academic Medicine*

Husted, S. D. (1978). Assessment of moral reasoning in pediatric faculty, house officers and medical students. *Proceedings of the 17th Annual Conference on Research in Medical Education, 17,* 439–441.

Kennedy, D. A., Pattishall, Jr., E. G., & Baldwin, Jr., D. C. (1983). *Medical education and the behavioral sciences.* Boulder, CO: Westview Press.

Kohlberg, L. (Ed.). (1984). *Essays on moral development: Vol. II. The psychology of moral development.* San Francisco: Harper & Row.

Kohlberg, L., & Candee, D. (1984). The relationship of moral judgment to moral action. In L. Kohlberg (Ed.), *Essays on moral development: Vol. II. The psychology of moral development.* (pp. 498–581) San Francisco: Harper & Row.

McElhinney, T. K. (Ed.). (1981). *Human values teaching programs for health professionals.* Ardmore, PA: Whitmore Publishing Company.

Noddings, N. (1984). *Caring: A feminine approach to ethics and moral education.* Los Angeles: University of California Press.

Pellegrino, E. D., & McElhinney, T. K. (1982). *Teaching ethics, the humanities, and human values in medical schools: A ten-year overview.* Washington, DC: Society for Health and Human Values.

Rest, J. R. (1979). *Development in judging moral issues.* Minneapolis: University of Minnesota Press.

Rest, J. R. (1988). Can ethics be taught in professional schools: The psychological research. *Ethics: Easier Said than Done, 1,* 11–26.

Schlaefli, A., Rest, J. R., & Thoma, S. J. (1985). Does moral education improve moral judgment? A meta-analysis of intervention studies using the Defining Issues Test. *Review of Educational Research, 55* 319–320.

Schutz, W. C. (1966). *The interpersonal underworld.* Palo Also, CA: Science and Behavior Books.

Self, D. J. (1985a). Applying cognitive moral development theory to medical education. *Proceeding of the Southwest Philosophy of Education Society, 35*, 286–302.

Self, D. J. (1985b). *Moral reasoning as a criterion for resident selection*. Paper presented at the 18th annual spring conference of the Society of Teachers of Family Medicine, Nashville, TN.

Self, D. J., & Baldwin, Jr., D. C. (1993). Should moral reasoning serve as a criterion for medical student and resident selection? Unpublished manuscript.

Self, D. J., & Baldwin, D. C., Jr., & Olivarez, M. (1993). Teaching medical ethics to first-year students by using film discussion to develop their moral reasoning. *Academic Medicine, 68*(5), 383–385.

Self, D. J., Baldwin, D. C., Jr., & Wolinsky, F. D. (1992). Evaluation of teaching medical ethics by an assessment of moral reasoning. *Medical Education, 26*, 178–184.

Self, D. J., Baldwin, D. C., Jr., & Wolinsky, F. D. (1994). Further evidence of the relationship between medical education and moral development. *Social Science and Medicine*. Manuscript submitted for publication.

Self, D. J., & Jecker, N. S., & Baldwin, Jr., D. C. (1993). A preliminary study of the moral orientation of justice and care among graduating medical students. Unpublished manuscript.

Self, D. J., & Olivarez, M. (1993). The influence of gender on conflicts of interest in the allocation of limited critical care resources: Justice vs. care. *Journal of Critical I, 8*(1), 64–74.

Self, D. J., & Olivarez, M. (1994). Retention of moral reasoning skills over the four years of medical education. *Medical Education*. Manuscript submitted for publication.

Self, D. J., Olivarez, M., & Baldwin, D. C., Jr., (1993). *Clarification of the relationship of moral reasoning and medical education*. Unpublished manuscript.

Self, D. J., Schrader, D. E., Baldwin, D. C., Jr., & Wolinsky, F. D. (1993). The moral development of medical students: A pilot study of the possible influence of medical education. *Medical Education, 27*, 26–34.

Self, D. J., & Skeel, J. D. (1992). Facilitating healthcare ethics research: Assessment of moral reasoning and moral orientation from a single interview. *Cambridge Quarterly of Healthcare Ethics, 1*, 371–376.

Self, D. J., Skeel, J. D., & Jecker, N. S. (1993a). The influence of philosophical versus theological education on the moral development of clinical medical ethicists. *Academic Medicine, 68*(11), 848–852.

Self, D. J., Skeel, J. D., & Jecker, N. S. (1993b). A comparison of the moral reasoning of physicians and clinical medical ethicists. *Academic Medicine, 68*(11). 852–855.

Self, D. J., Wolinsky, F. D., & Baldwin, D. C., Jr., (1989). The effect of teaching medical ethics on medical students' moral reasoning. *Academic Medicine, 64*(12). 855–859.

Sheehan, K. H., Sheehan, D. V., White, K., Leibowitz, A., & Baldwin, D. C. Jr., (1990). A pilot study of medical student abuse: Student perceptions of mistreatment and misconduct in medical school. *Journal of the American Medical Association, 263*, 533–537.

Sheehan, T. J. (1978). The relationship between moral reasoning and clinical performance. *Proceedings of the 17th Annual Conference on Research in Medical Education, 17*, 444–445.

Sheehan, T. J., Candee, D., Willms, J., Donnelly, J., & Husted, S. D. (1985). Structural equation models of moral reasoning and physician performance. *Evaluation and the Health Professions, 8*, 379–400.

Sheehan, T. J., Husted, S. D., Candee, D., Cook, C. D., & Bargen, M. (1980). Moral judgment as a predictor of clinical performance. *Evaluation and the Health Professions, 3*, 393–404.

Sheehan, T. J., Husted, S. D., & Candee, D. (1981). *The development of moral judgment over three years in a group of medical students*. Paper presented at the annual meeting of the American Educational Research Association.

Sheehan, T. J., Thal, S., Krause, K., Candee, D., Cotton, J., & Geer, S. (1987). *Improving physician skill in managing morally problematic cases*. Final Report to the National Fund for Medical Education.

Sheehan, T. J., Thal, S., Krause, K., Candee, D., Cotton, J., & Geer, S. (1989). Teaching humanistic behavior. *Teaching and Learning in Medicine, 1*(2), 82–84.

Chapter 9

Moral Reasoning in Veterinary Medicine

Donnie J. Self
Texas A & M University College of Medicine
Margie Olivarez
Texas A & M University College of Medicine
DeWitt C. Baldwin, Jr.
American Medical Association

As with other professions, in recent years veterinary medicine has become much more concerned about issues of values, attitudes, and ethical standards within the profession. High standards and adherence to a moral code have historically been basic tenets of the veterinary profession. This cultural tradition has been passed from one generation to the next through transmission of the knowledge, skills, and the social and moral norms of the profession. It frequently has focused on the Veterinarian's Oath (Veterinary Code, 1986). But increased social demands for moral accountability in public life following highly publicized abuses of power and authority, such as Watergate, the Iran-Contra affair, the Savings and Loan scandal and others, have required all professions, including veterinary medicine, to become more concerned about their attention to professionalism and the role of values, attitudes, and standards.

Veterinary medicine is also undergoing many social changes because it has rapidly developed into a highly technical profession in the past two decades. Its demography has steadily changed to the point that over 60% of the students now in veterinary school are females training to enter a historically male-dominated profession (Hart & Melese-d'Hospital, 1989). At the same time, public concerns over animal welfare and the use of animals for research have put new and added pressures on the profession. And even though, as a helping profession, veterinary medicine has always been inherently a moral endeavor, it is now finding itself needing to pay more attention to the moral aspects of the profession, including the teaching of ethics in the curriculum.

TEACHING VETERINARY ETHICS

A survey of all 27 veterinary medical schools in the United States was conducted in the spring of 1993 to determine how and to what extent veterinary ethics was being taught (Self, Pierce, & Shadduck, 1994). The survey consisted of a one-page questionnaire followed by a telephone contact several weeks later. The initial response rate for the written questionnaire was 85.2%, and the telephone follow-up brought the response rate for data collection to 100%. It was found that required formal ethics courses exist in only 6 (22.2%) out of the 27 veterinary schools. The teaching of ethics was integrated into other courses such as jurisprudence, practice management or professional regulations in 22 (81.5%) of the 27 veterinary schools, although informal teaching of ethics during clinical rotations and so forth occurred in all 27 (100%) of the veterinary schools. The number of curriculum contact hours for ethics varied from 4 to 43 hours, with a median of 15 hours. Although scattered throughout all 4 years of the curriculum in various schools, veterinary ethics was taught predominately in the first year.

Until recently, persons interested in teaching veterinary ethics were pretty much left to their own devices for curriculum materials. Sometimes useful materials from other fields, such as philosophy, were available (Feinberg, 1974; Regan & Singer, 1976). During the past decade, however, the literature on veterinary ethics has grown considerably (Kay, Cohen, & Nieburg, 1988; Kitchen, 1983; Miller & Williams, 1983; Rollin, 1981; Tannenbaum, 1989). Articles addressing ethics are now more frequently found in the main journals of veterinary medicine, and a series of case studies and discussions by Bernard Rollin appears regularly in the *Canadian Veterinary Journal*. However, the development of curriculum materials in the field of veterinary ethics is far behind that in many of the other fields of applied ethics. Development of an extensive set of ethical dilemma case studies is currently being sponsored by the Texas Veterinary Medical Foundation.

There appears to be a very limited amount of audio-visual material available for addressing ethics in the veterinary curriculum. This seems to be an area of enormous need and potential for growth for anyone interested in developing and marketing such materials, given the steadily increasing interest in veterinary ethics in recent years and the increased degree to which young people have become so video oriented. A study in human medicine has demonstrated that moral reasoning skills can be increased by the use of films and discussion of the moral dilemmas in them (Self, Baldwin, & Olivarez, 1993). Most materials that are available in veterinary ethics seem to be primarily limited to the issues of animal welfare and the use of animals for research and experimentation. For example, *Animal Welfare* by the American Farm Bureau Federation and *Animal Research* by Michael Criley are sometimes used in teaching, as well as *Man's Best Friend* by WGBH for PBS Video.

VETERINARY EDUCATION AND MORAL REASONING

Several studies assessing the relationship of veterinary medical education and moral reasoning have been conducted, yielding mixed results. These studies used different subject populations, different sample sizes, and different instruments of assessment. The first study (Self et al., 1991) used Kohlberg's (1984) original MJI. They pretested and posttested 20 veterinary medical students at the beginning of their first year of professional education and again at the end of their fourth year, just before graduation from the professional curriculum, to determine whether their moral reasoning skills had increased to the same extent as other persons of comparable age and education. The sample of 20 students represented 16% of the student body for that cohort but was not randomly selected. The students were recruited as nonpaid volunteers with appropriate informed consent.

They obtained complete moral reasoning data from all students, along with demographic data, including age, gender, Medical College Admission Test (MCAT) scores, and GPA scores. For first-year students, the weighted average scores (WAS) on the MJI ranged from 313 to 436, narrowing to a range of 348 to 421 when they were fourth-year students, with all scores grouped in the conventional level of moral reasoning. The mean increase from first to fourth years of 12.5 WAS points was not statistically significant. Thus, the normally expected increase in moral reasoning did not occur over the 4 years of veterinary medical education for these students, suggesting that their veterinary medical education experience somehow inhibited their moral reasoning growth. The WAS range of 123 points for first-year students represents approximately one and a quarter moral development stages in Kohlberg's theory. The WAS range of 81 points for fourth-year students represents only approximately three-quarters of a moral development stage, indicating a substantial reduction in moral reasoning variance.

No significant correlations between change in moral reasoning WAS scores and age, gender, or MCAT scores were found. Changes in the global stage scores were not significantly correlated with age, gender, or GPA. However, there were statistically significant ($p \leq .05$) associations between changes in WAS scores in relationship to GPA scores ($r = .470$) and in global stage scores with MCAT scores ($r = .389$). The higher the GPA or MCAT score, the greater the observed increases in moral reasoning scores.

A second study (Self, Baldwin, Wolinsky, & Shadduck, 1993), sought further evidence of the relationship of veterinary medical education and moral reasoning, and used the Sociomoral Reflection Measure (SRM) (Gibbs & Widaman, 1982). Unlike the MJI, which involves an audiotaped interview that is expensive to score, the SRM, being group administrable and relatively inexpensive to score, enabled the study to incorporate a considerably larger sample size. This study pretested and posttested 57 veterinary medical students at the beginning and end of their 4 years of veterinary education to determine what, if any, changes occurred in their moral reasoning skills. The sample of 57 students represented 47.5% of the students in that class. Again, the students were not randomly selected and were recruited as nonpaid volunteers with appropriate informed consent.

The moral reasoning SRM scores ranged between 250 and 400; the mean scores in first- and fourth-year students were 340.86 and 358.40, respectively. The mean increase of 17.5 points in the SRM score from first- to fourth-year was statistically significant at the $p \leq .05$ level. Similarly, statistically significant increases were found for slightly different indices from the SRM, with the global stage scores ($p \leq .01$) and the modal stage scores ($p \leq .02$).

A third study (Self, Baldwin, Olivarez, & Shadduck, 1993) assessed the relationship of veterinary medical education and moral reasoning using Rest's (1979) DIT and a still larger sample size. This third study pretested and posttested 68 veterinary medical students before and after their professional education. This sample represented 56.7% of the students in that class. Again, the students were not randomly selected, but were recruited as nonpaid volunteers with informed consent. The moral reasoning DIT scores ranged from 10.7 to 69.2 . The mean scores of the first-year and fourth-year students were 45.13 and 45.29, respectively. The mean increase of +0.16 points from first-year to fourth-year was not statistically significant (p .867). Statistical analysis revealed no significant correlations at the $p \leq .05$ level between the moral reasoning scores and age or gender, but there were significant correlations between the moral reasoning scores and the MCAT scores and the GPA scores; the higher the MCAT and GPA scores, the greater the increases in moral reasoning scores.

The third study, with a larger sample and the DIT, agreed with the findings of the first study with the MJI, suggesting that the experience of veterinary medical education appears to inhibit the increase in moral reasoning of veterinary medical students. However, all three studies found a narrowing of the range of moral reasoning scores as students progressed from the first year to the fourth year of their education. This regression to the mean suggests a powerful socializing influence in professional education, which results in a homogenizing effect. Higher scores coming down and lower scores coming up suggest a suppression of uniqueness, creativity, and individuality that may not necessarily be bad but should at least give one pause in light of the current widespread emphasis on diversity. Because these studies were conducted at the same institution, similar studies need to be conducted in other settings. Clearly, additional research is needed to clarify fully the relationship of veterinary medical education and moral development.

AN INTERVENTION STUDY IN VETERINARY ETHICS

An intervention study was designed to assess whether a one semester course of 15 contact hours devoted exclusively to veterinary ethics would significantly improve the moral reasoning skills of veterinary students (Self, Pierce, & Shadduck, in press). The students were pretested and posttested with the DIT. The course was taught in the first semester of the first year of the veterinary curriculum as a required course. There were seven 1-hour didactic lecture sessions on moral theory, ethical decision making, The Veterinarian's Oath, and so forth. There also were four 2-hour sessions involving small group case study discussions, with approximately 10 students per group.

Complete data were gathered on 105 of the 128 first-year students. The pretest DIT scores ranged from 10.0 to 68.0 (mean 42.2). The sample consisted of 38 males with pretest DIT scores ranging from 10.0 to 68.0 (mean 39.4) and 67 females with pretest DIT scores ranging from 15.0 to 66.7 (mean 43.7). The posttest scores ranged from 13.3 to 75.0 (mean 42.7) for all 105 students combined. Posttest scores for the males ranged from 13.3 to 61.7 (mean 36.7) and for the females 20.0 to 75.0 (mean 46.1). The difference in mean scores between posttest and pretest for the total population was only +0.5 and not statistically significant ($p \leq .6220$).

Although the gender difference in pretest DIT scores of 4.3 was not statistically significant ($p \leq .0788$), the gender difference in posttest DIT scores of 9.4 was statistically significant ($p \leq .0005$). Males decreased from the baseline, and females increased from the baseline. There were no statistically significant findings between moral reasoning scores and age or MCAT scores.

These data suggest that a 1-semester course of 15 contact hours of this format is not sufficient for improving the moral reasoning skills of veterinary students and that females may be more amenable to change in a positive direction. Previous studies indicated that both length and format of an intervention are important in influencing change in moral reasoning skills. The literature in human medicine addressed these issues and indicated that medical students' moral reasoning skills improve significantly when exposed to a course in medical ethics consisting of 44 hours of contact time, compared to this course with 15 contact hours (Self, Wolinsky, & Baldwin, 1989). The literature also revealed that exposure to a small group case study format improves moral reasoning skills more than does a traditional lecture format. This corroborates the pioneering work of Blatt and Kohlberg (1975). Clearly, additional studies need to be done considering both course length and format for designing a veterinary ethics course that will have the desired effect, yet still be practical for an already overcrowded curriculum.

GENDER AND MORAL REASONING

The influence of gender has been a controversial issue in the moral development literature. Because the original sample from which Kohlberg developed the theory was an all male sample, Gilligan (1982) claimed that cognitive moral development theory has a built in male bias that systematically discriminates against females. Others (Walker, de Vries, & Trevethan 1987) have carried on a lively debate in the literature regarding this point. But studies in both human medicine and veterinary medicine frequently found the contrary to be true, that females score significantly higher than males in moral reasoning (Baldwin, Daugherty, and Self, 1991). A similar finding was reported for social workers (Dobrin, 1989). Nevertheless, several other studies of healthcare professionals did not find a significant relationship between gender and moral reasoning, although many of their sample sizes were small (Galaz-Fontes et al., 1989; Self et al., 1989; Self, Skeel, & Jecker, 1993).

A recent study of 705 medical and veterinary medical students convincingly demonstrated that females score statistically ($p \leq .0001$) higher than their male classmates (Self & Olivarez, 1993). The hypothesis of this study was that there is no significant difference in the moral reasoning skills of medical and veterinary students with regard to gender. This hypothesis is in keeping with the theory of cognitive moral development (Colby & Kohlberg, 1987). For this study the DIT was used to measure moral reasoning skills. Of the 705 students initially enrolled in the study, 79 were dropped when they failed the consistency and reliability check. The mean DIT score for the 312 males was 41.77 and for the 314 females, 47.18, highly statistically significant at the .0001 level.

This finding appears to be in conflict with the common critique of moral development theory. The DIT is derived from cognitive moral development theory, which, in turn, is based on the principle of justice as the foundation of moral reasoning. This study suggests that females are no less, and probably more, effective in the use of justice for resolving moral conflicts.

LARGE VERSUS SMALL ANIMAL VETERINARIANS

This study was designed to compare the moral reasoning skills of small animal (pet) veterinarians and large animal veterinarians because of the social stereotypically different conceptions of the two groups (Self, Safford, & Shelton, 1988). It is often thought that small animal veterinarians are more concerned with animal suffering, compassion, the rights of the animal and owner, grief management, interpersonal relationships, and communication skills than their large animal counterparts, who are thought to be more concerned with the economic factors of large animal husbandry than with the individual welfare of the animals. The study tested the hypothesis that small animal veterinarians use higher levels of moral reasoning than do large animal veterinarians.

The instrument used for the comparison was the DIT. Questionnaires were sent to 350 practicing veterinarians throughout the state of Texas. There were 131 questionnaires returned for a 37.4% response rate. Of these, 107 provided complete and consistent data. There were 93 males (86.9%) and 14 females (13.1%) in the surveyed population. The respondents ranged from 26 to 66 years of age ($M = 40.5$ years). There were 69 (64.5%) small animal veterinarians, and 33 (30.8%) large animal veterinarians with 5 (4.7%) not indicating type of practice. They represented all geographic areas of the state. The mean score for small animal veterinarians (M

= 33.8) was slightly lower than the mean score for large animal veterinarians ($M = 36.0$) but represented no statistically significant difference ($p \leq .369$) between the two groups. Based on these data, the hypothesis of a difference in the moral reasoning of small animal versus large animal veterinarians had to be rejected.

MORAL ORIENTATIONS: JUSTICE OR CARE

The moral orientations of justice and care exhibited by 20 graduating veterinary students were analyzed as they entered the practice of veterinary medicine (Self, Jecker, Baldwin, & Shadduck, 1991). The data were gathered by use of the Gilligan Real-Life Conflict and Choice Interview (Brown et al., 1988), involving an oral, audio-taped 30–45 minute interview with a standard set of probe questions designed to elucidate the degree to which the subject relies on the concepts of justice and care in resolving a real-life moral conflict experienced in the past. The interview was designed to enable subjects to reveal the structure of their moral orientation in terms of the presence, predominance, and alignment with justice and care. These concepts have been elaborated elsewhere in detail by Gilligan and her colleagues (Brown et al., 1988). Briefly defined, *presence* means that a person recognizes, takes into account, or uses the concepts of justice or care in describing a moral conflict. *Predominance* means that one of the concepts is used exclusively or to a substantially larger extent than the other concept. *Alignment* means that a person accepts, personally owns, endorses, and uses the concept as the preferred mode for resolution of a moral conflict.

The sample consisted of 10 males and 10 females ranging in age from 25 to 37 years ($M = 28$), with MCAT scores ranging from 28 to 67 ($M = 46$) and GPA scores ranging from 2.47 to 3.60 ($M = 3.11$). Statistical analysis revealed no significant correlations between any of these demographic characteristics and the components of moral orientation.

Further analysis of these data indicated that although these veterinarians recognized the presence of justice issues in 90% of the moral conflicts, the predominance of justice as the organizing principle for resolution of the conflict occurred in less than half (45%) of the veterinarians. The alignment with justice as the preferred mode of resolution of the conflict occurred in only 35% of the veterinarians. At the same time, the veterinarians recognized the presence of care issues in 65% of the conflicts, with the predominance of care as the organizing principle for resolution of the conflict in 45% of the veterinarians. Alignment with care was the preferred mode of resolution of conflict in only 30% of the veterinarians. Although statistical analysis revealed no significant correlations between gender and the components of moral orientation (perhaps because of the small sample sizes), these limited data tend to support Gilligan's claim that males are predominately justice oriented and females are predominately care oriented. Of these veterinarians, the justice orientation was exhibited 67% of the time by males and 33% of the time by females, while the care orientation was exhibited 56% of the time by females and 44% of the time by males.

CONCLUSION

The veterinary profession is a fertile field for study into various aspects of moral development. Much more research needs to be done. Some of this research is already under way but awaits completion. Data have already been collected in a study of the relationship of moral reasoning to empathy, as well as a study of the relationship of moral reasoning to self-esteem in veterinary medical students. Finally, analysis of the data is also under way in a study of the relationship of moral reasoning to the Myers-Briggs (1985) Personality Type indicators.

There clearly is a need for further studies to be done regarding various aspects of moral development in the veterinary profession. In particular, intervention studies need to be conducted to determine the best structure and format for teaching veterinary ethics to improve the moral reasoning skills of students entering the profession.

Plans are currently underway to conduct a study of the relationship of moral reasoning to clinical performance in veterinary students. Similarly, there is interest in the development of a profession-specific veterinary moral reasoning instrument of assessment which might be similar in format to the DIT, but would contain vignettes directly relevant to the content of veterinary ethics. Finally, there is considerable interest in the development of a convenient instrument for assessing moral orientation in veterinary medicine. With the continued development and emergence of the field of veterinary medical ethics, it appears that there will be enormous opportunity for further moral reasoning research in this relatively unstudied profession.

REFERENCES

Baldwin, Jr., D. C., Daugherty, S., & Self, D. J. (1991). Changes in moral reasoning during medical school. *Academic Medicine, 66,* (September Supp.), 1–3.

Blatt, M., & Kohlberg, L. (1975). The effects of classroom moral discussion upon children's level of moral judgment. *Journal of Moral Education, 4,* 129–61.

Brown, L. M., Argyris, D., Attanucci, J., Bardige, B., Gilligan, C., Johnston, K., Miller, B., Osborne, D., Ward, J., Wiggins, G., & Wilcox, D. (1988). *A guide to reading narratives of moral conflict and choice for self and moral voice.* Cambridge, MA: Center for the Study of Gender, Education, and Human Development Harvard Graduate School of Education.

Colby, A., & Kohlberg, L. (1987). T*he measurement of moral judgment: Vol. I, Theoretical foundations and research validation.* New York: Cambridge University Press.

Dobrin, A. (1989). Ethical judgments of male and female social workers. *Social Work, 34,* 451–455.

Feinberg, J. (1974). The rights of animals and future generations. In W. Blackstone (Ed.), *Philosophy and environmental crisis.* (pp. 43–68). Athens, GA: University of Georgia Press.

Galaz-Fontes, J. F., Pacheco-Sanchez, M. E., Sierra-Morales, I., Commons, M. L., Gutheil, T. G., & Hausen, M. J. (1989). *Medical school training and moral reasoning in Mexico.* Paper presented at the 4th Adult Development Symposium meeting, Cambridge, MA.

Gibbs, J. C., & Widaman, K. F. (1982). *Social intelligence: Measuring the development of sociomoral reflection.* Englewood Cliffs, NJ: Prentice-Hall.

Gilligan, C. (1982) *In a different voice: Psychological theory and women's development.* Cambridge, MA: Harvard University Press.

Hart, L. A., & Melese-d'Hospital, P. (1989). The gender shift in the veterinary profession and attitudes towards animals: A survey and overview. *Journal of Veterinary Medical Education, 16,* 27–30.

Kay, W. J., Cohen, S. P., & Nieburg, H. A. (1988). *Euthanasia of the companion animal.* Philadelphia, PA: The Charles Press.

Kitchen, H. (1983). Exploring ethical and value issues in veterinary medicine. Proceedings of the Eighth symposium on veterinary medical education. *Journal of Veterinary Medical Education, 9,* 70–143.

Kohlberg, L. (1984). *Essays on moral development: Vol. II, The psychology of moral development.* San Francisco, CA: Harper & Row.

Miller, H., & Williams, W. H. (1983). *Ethics and animals.* Clifton, NJ: Humana Press.

Myers, I. B., & McCaulley, M. H. (1985). *Manual: A Guide to the Development and use of the Myers-Briggs Type Indicator.* Palo Alto, CA: Consulting Psychologists Press.

Regan, T., & Singer, P. (Eds.). (1976). *Animal rights and human behavior.* Englewood Cliffs, NJ: Prentice-Hall.

Rest, J. R. (1979). *Development in judging moral issues.* Minneapolis: University of Minnesota Press.

Rollin, B. E. (1981). *Animal rights and human morality.* Buffalo, NY: Prometheus Books.

Self, D. J., Baldwin, D. C., Jr., & Olivarez, M. (1993). Teaching medical ethics to first-year students by using film discussion to develop their moral reasoning. *Academic Medicine, 68*(5), 383–385.

Self, D. J., Baldwin, Jr., D. C., Olivarez, M., & Shadduck, J. A. (1993). *Clarifying the relationship of veterinary medical education and moral development.* Unpublished manuscript.

Self, D. J., Baldwin, Jr., D. C., Wolinsky, F. D., & Shadduck, J. A. (1993). Further exploration of the relationship between veterinary medical education and moral development. *The Journal of Veterinary Medical Education, 20*(3), 140–147.

Self, D. J., & Olivarez, M. (1993). The influence of gender on conflicts of interest in the allocation of limited critical care resources: Justice vs. care. *Journal of Critical Care, 8*(1), 64–74.

Self, D. J., Jecker, N. S., Baldwin, Jr., D. C., & Shadduck, J. A. (1991). Moral orientations of justice and care among veterinarians entering veterinary practice. *Journal of the American Veterinary Medical Association, 199,* 569–573.

Self, D. J., Pierce, A., & Shadduck, J. A. (in press). *Description and evaluation of a course in veterinary ethics.*

Self, D. J., Pierce, A., & Shadduck, J. A. (1994). A survey of the teaching of ethics in veterinary education. *Journal of the American Veterinary Medical Association, 204*(6), 944–945.

Self, D. J., Safford, S. K., & Shelton, G. C. (1988). Comparison of the general moral reasoning of small animal veterinarians vs. large animal veterinarians. *The Journal of the American Veterinary Association, 193,* 1509–1512.

Self, D. J., Schrader, D. E., Baldwin, D. C., Jr., Root, S. K., Wolinsky, F. D., & Shadduck, J. A. (1991). Study of the influence of veterinary medical education on the moral development of veterinary students. *Journal of American Veterinary Medical Association, 198,* 782–787.

Self, D. J., Skeel, J. D., & Jecker, N. S. (1993). The influence of philosophical vs. theological education on the moral development of clinical medical ethicists. *Academic Medicine, 68,* 848–852.

Self, D. J., Wolinsky, F. D., & Baldwin, D. C. Jr., (1989). The effect of teaching medical ethics on medical students' moral reasoning. *Academic Medicine, 64,* 755–759.

Tannenbaum, J. (1989). *Veterinary Ethics.* Baltimore, MD: Williams & Oilkina.

Veterinary code of ethics. (1986). *Journal of American Veterinary Medical Association, 189*(4), 475.

Walker, L., de Vries, B., & Trevethan, S. (1987). Moral stages and moral orientations in real-life and hypothetical dilemmas. *Child Development, 58,* 842-858.

Chapter 10

Applied Ethics and Moral Reasoning in Sport

Brenda Jo Light Bredemeier
University of California at Berkeley
David Lyle Light Shields
University of California at Berkeley

Sport is a social practice brimming with moral dilemmas. As a rule-governed activity, many of the moral decisions that take place in sport concern the rules. Athletes must decide whether to use illegal, performance-enhancing drugs, whether to surreptitiously violate the rules of play, whether to commit a strategically advantageous intentional foul, and so on. And even if an athlete decides to observe the rules scrupulously, there are other moral decisions that need to be made. Should one play when injured? Should one use aggressive but legal tactics? Should one employ harassing techniques designed to disrupt the opponent's concentration? These are just a few examples of the kinds of dilemmas encountered by athletes. A similar list could be generated reflecting the moral decisions that need to be made by coaches, fans, sports writers, and others involved in the world of sport.

In this chapter we probe major sources of influence that contribute to how athletes make their moral decisions. Although we concentrate primarily on athletes, similar points could be made about others involved in sport. We first discuss the relationship between moral reasoning and moral action within sport. We then examine what we know about the moral reasoning of athletes and other physical activity participants. Next, we discuss the unique qualities of moral reasoning in the context of sport, and, finally, we summarize a 12-component model of moral action that we believe can provide an organizing framework for theory, research, and intervention in this important area.

RELATIONSHIP BETWEEN MORAL REASONING AND SPORT

Moral Action in Sport

The relationship between moral reasoning, assessed in terms of stages of moral reasoning development, and moral action is complex. Part of this complexity is a direct result of the theoretically based decision of structural developmentalists to describe moral competency in terms of abstract, structural stages. If reasoning is described in structural terms, then no direct connection between moral reasoning and action can be expected. Each reasoning stage can support quite divergent actions. Nonetheless, stages are not irrelevant in predicting action. There are probabilistic associations between a person's stage of reasoning and the moral content that is likely to be endorsed or enacted by that person (see Kohlberg, 1984, chap. 7).

To open our discussion of the moral reasoning–moral action relationship in the context of sport, let us summarize a study we conducted (Bredemeier & Shields, 1984b) using Rest's Defining Issues Test (DIT). The DIT provides a profile of the extent to which a respondent endorses reasoning at each of six levels: Stages 2, 3, 4, 5A, 5B, and 6. In addition, an overall P score reflects the percentage of reasoning at the postconventional level (5A, 5B, and 6 combined); the P score is the index of moral reasoning development. In this investigation, we used the DIT to investigate how the moral reasoning stages of female and male collegiate basketball players ($N = 46$) related to the athletes' aggressive behaviors.

We hypothesized that high usage of either Stage 2 or Stage 4 would correlate positively with an index of athletic aggression. We believed that the egocentric and instrumental reasoning characteristic of Stage 2 can readily be adapted to support the retaliatory or instrumental use of aggression, and the belief among many athletes that aggression is simply normative within the system of basketball can make aggression appear legitimate to some who reason with a Stage 4 perspective. Conversely, we hypothesized that high usage of either Stages 3 or the postconventional stages would be inversely related to aggression scores. The naively prosocial, other-oriented nature of Stage 3 reasoning is generally inconsistent with aggression, as is a principled orientation that demands fairness for all. Study results indicated that, as predicted, Stages 2 and 4 were positively associated with aggression scores, and Stages 3, 5B, and 6 were inversely related to athletic aggression, though the inverse relationships were not equally strong for males and females. The reasoning–aggression relationship for males was significant at Stage 3, and for females at Stages 5B and 6.

In other studies, we have used Haan's (1977a, 1978, 1983, 1985, 1986, 1991; Haan, Aerts, & Cooper, 1985) interactional model of morality to investigate moral behaviors in sport. Using this model, Bredemeier (1985) found that those collegiate athletes who used less adequate moral reasoning were more likely to condone high levels of athletic aggression. Similar findings also have been reported for elementary school children (Bredemeier, Weiss, Shields, & Cooper, 1986). We also have found that even with young children there is a relationship between moral reasoning maturity and assertive and aggressive action tendencies in both sports and everyday life (Bredemeier, 1994).

These studies provide some evidence of the importance of taking moral reasoning development into account when moral actions, such as athletic aggression, are the topic of investigation. Moral reasoning plays a critical role in the production of moral behavior. In fact, even if other factors influence moral choices to a similar (or even greater) degree, moral reasoning is critical because it produces the moral meaning that an intended action has for the individual.

Sport Involvement

If moral reasoning is vital to responsible, moral decision making, then it is important to know whether those persons heavily invested in sports differ in any systematic way from the general population in their moral reasoning. Of course, the line separating athletes from nonathletes is somewhat fictitious, since most people are involved in physical activities to one degree or another. But for those who are dedicated athletes, the sport experience can be emotionally intense, highly demanding of one's time and energy, and revelatory of one's skills and character. For many, participation in sport is central to self-definition. Thus, involvement in organized sports may be a potent influence on participants' moral development.

In our study employing the DIT (mentioned previously), we found that both male and female athletes were below reported college norms on their P score, though females scored significantly higher than males. Similarly, Hall (1986) found that intercollegiate basketball players scored lower than college norms on a Kohlbergian measure of moral development. In a more elaborate study using Haan's model of morality (Bredemeier & Shields, 1986c), we found once again that intercollegiate basketball players had less mature moral reasoning patterns than those who were not engaged in organized sport, but the same was not true at the high school level. Interscholastic basketball players did not differ from their high school peers on moral reasoning maturity. Furthermore, we found that intercollegiate swimmers did not differ from nonathletes in their moral reasoning maturity.

In another study, we examined the relationship between children's sport participation and interest, on the one hand, and their moral reasoning maturity and aggression tendencies, on the other (Bredemeier et al., 1986). Analyses revealed that boys' participation and interest in high contact sports and girls' participation in medium contact sports (the highest level of contact-sports experience girls reported) were associated with less mature moral reasoning and greater tendencies to aggress.

It must be emphasized that all the previously reported studies have been correlational in design. Therefore, no cause–effect links between sport involvement and moral reasoning maturity can be claimed.

It is clear from these results that sport experience is not uniform. Clearly, there is little intrinsic moral significance to whacking a ball with a stick, or tossing a ball through a hoop. What has moral significance in sport is the particular configuration of social relationships and interactions that characterize particular sport experiences. The nature and quality of the relationships and interactions that occur in sport settings will vary from sport to sport, from team to team, and so on. The coach's leadership style, the characteristics of the athletes, the historical precedents and traditions, as well as the particular dynamics built into the rule-structure of the specific sport (e.g., level of contact, individual or team, open or closed skill) all combine to establish the unique qualities of a given sport experience.

In addition to studies of athletes, two studies provided information about others involved in physical-activity contexts. A study by Henkel and Earls (1985) used the DIT to study the moral reasoning maturity of K-12 physical education (PE) teachers. The authors found that the PE teachers on average were less developed in their moral reasoning capacities than most others of a similar age and educational background. Similar results were obtained by Malloy (1991), who investigated the level of moral reasoning of postsecondary students enrolled in a physical education degree program.

Game Reasoning

In some of our research, we presented specially designed dilemmas that contain parallel moral problems in sport and nonsport settings to both nonathletes (i.e., those not involved in organized sport) and active athletes (Bredemeier & Shields, 1984a, 1986a, 1986b, 1986c). Beginning around the dawn of adolescence, both sport participants and nonparticipants begin to use divergent patterns of reasoning for the two types of dilemmas, though athletes tend to diverge significantly more than the nonathletes (Bredemeier, in press; Bredemeier & Shields, 1984a). Reasoning in response to sport-specific dilemmas appears, on average, less mature or adequate than corresponding reasoning about everyday life.

The discrepancy we have found between life and sport moral reasoning may be one aspect of a larger phenomena. Huizinga (1955) has described play as a "stepping out of ‹real life› into a temporary sphere of activity with a disposition all its own" (p. 8). Other philosophers, anthropologists, sociologists, and psychologists have also suggested that play and/or sport exists in a unique sphere, and that entry into that sphere involves cognitive, attitudinal, and value adjustments (see Bateson, 1955; Corsaro, 1981; Giffin, 1982; Schmitz, 1976; Sutton-Smith, 1971). Firth (1973), for example, discussed how rituals and conventions serve to mark temporal boundaries of sport, and symbolize the reconstitution of people into players and players back into people.

If entry into sport involves a transformation of cognition and affect, then it is reasonable to hypothesize that moral reasoning undergoes some change in its underlying organization when one moves from general life into the world of sport. The divergence in moral reasoning scores described earlier partially supports this hypothesis. We have labeled the *transformed* moral reasoning that occurs in sport *game reasoning*.

The transition in moral perspective from life to sport is attested to by numerous informal observations as well. Consider, for example, a comment by former heavyweight boxing champion Larry Holmes. Before he enters the ring, he said, "I have to change, I have to leave the goodness out and bring all the bad in, like Dr. Jekyll and Mr. Hyde" (quoted in Bredemeier & Shields, 1985, p. 23). Ron Rivera of the Chicago Bears described the personality transformation he undergoes when entering his sport. The off field Ron, he said, is soft-spoken, considerate, and friendly. When asked to describe the on field Ron, he replied, "He's totally opposite from me.... He's a madman.... No matter what happens, he hits people. He's a guy with no regard for the human body" (p. 24). This theme is echoed continually by sports commentators who frequently note a perceived discrepancy between the on-field athlete and the off-field athlete.

Unfortunately, at this point in time, we know little about the genesis, developmental course, and behavioral implications of game reasoning. It is clear that entry into the realm of sport stimulates, at least for many, a change in moral reasoning patterns, but the phenomenon is not yet well understood.

A 12-COMPONENT MODEL OF MORAL ACTION

Moral reasoning is an important influence on moral behavior. But as we have said before, it is not the only influence. Before adequate educational programs can be designed to enhance moral action, the various influences on moral behavior need to be systematically identified and organized into logical clusters. This will facilitate an investigation of the interrelationship among coherent sets of relevant variables, providing a much more adequate portrait of moral action than any univariate analysis could offer. To provide a more comprehensive model of the influences that feed into moral action, we have elaborated a 12-Component Model of Moral Behavior (Shields & Bredemeier, 1994).

The model begins with the four processes identified by Rest (1983, 1984, 1986). Briefly, before a moral action can take place, a person must interpret the situation and the action possibilities (Process I), form a moral judgment about what should be done (Process II), choose a value (moral or nonmoral) to seek through action (Process III), and carry out the intended act (Process IV). Each of the four processes is necessary for moral action to take place, and if there is a deficiency in any process, moral action will be deficient.

In addition to the four major processes, we have identified three main sources of influence that impact on each of the processes: (a) the nature of the context, (b) the person's competencies, and (c) the person's characteristic and situationally evoked ego processing. Obviously a substratum of genetic and biological competencies and predispositions are also relevant, but they are not elaborated here. By

TABLE 10.1
Twelve Component Model of Moral Action

Influences	Processes			
	Interpretation	Judgment	Choice	Implementation
A. Contextual	Goal structure, situational ambiguity	Moral atmosphere	Domain cues	Power structure
B. Pesonal competencies	Role-taking, perspective-taking	Moral reasoning	Self-structure	Autonomy & social problem-solving skills
C. Ego processing	Intraceptive processes	Cognitive ego processes	Affective impulse regulating processes	Attention-focusing processes

intersecting the four processes with the three major sources of influence, we arrive at a 12-Component Model of Moral Action. A model with exemplars of each component is presented in Table 10.1.

Although we have tried to place our exemplars at the appropriate intersection between process and influence, some exemplars may influence more than one process. The goal structure may influence choice (Process III) as well as interpretation (Process I), for example. Nonetheless, we believe we have ordered the exemplars in a coherent manner that can facilitate theory, research, and intervention. Also, unlike the four processes, we do not claim that an optimal condition need be present in each and every one of the 12 components before appropriate moral action can occur. However, we do maintain that every moral action will reflect the influence of all 12 components. For example, a moral atmosphere that is supportive of immoral behaviors can be resisted, and persons can act morally even in such a context, but their behavior will still take account of the moral atmosphere. Finally, we do not claim that the model is comprehensive in the sense of including every possible influence. What we have attempted to do is identify critical exemplars of each component.

In the remainder of this chapter, we elaborate on the 12-Component Model of Moral Action by elaborating the three sources of influence, beginning with contextual influences. Readers interested in a more elaborate description of the 12-Component Model and a more comprehensive literature review on morality and sport should consult *Character Development and Physical Activity* (Shields & Bredemeier, 1994).

Contextual Influences

The environment certainly plays a central role in eliciting and sustaining various forms of behavior, including moral behavior. But contexts are infinitely complex. In our model, we focus only on those aspects of the environment that consistently and significantly influence moral action in sport contexts.

Two contextual influences that we have identified as relevant to Process I—interpreting the situation—are the goal structure and the degree of ambiguity present. By goal structure, we are referring to the cooperative/competitive structuring of the environment. A number of studies have indicated that competitive goal structures, such as occur in sports, tend to discourage prosocial behavior and/or encourage antisocial behavior (Barnett & Bryan, 1974; Berkowitz, 1973; Berndt, 1981; Bryan, 1977; Deutsch, 1985; Gelfand & Hartman, 1978; Kleiber & Roberts, 1981; McGuire & Thomas, 1975; Raush, 1965; Staub & Noerenberg, 1981). Conversely, cooperative goal structures can facilitate prosocial behavior and decrease antisocial behavior (Aronson, Bridgeman, & Geffner, 1978; Debellefeuille, 1990; Sherif & Sherif, 1969).

We hypothesized that competition interferes with moral behavior and cooperation facilitates it through at least two mechanisms, both related to Process I. First, competition and cooperation differentially influence people's sensitivities to the needs and concerns of others. Under competitive arrangements, attention is focused on one's own goals and aspirations, or those of one's team, to the relative neglect of others' concerns. Conversely, cooperative arrangements tend to heighten one's awareness of the needs and interests of others. Additionally, the action alternatives that are likely to be considered as feasible options will be determined in part by the goal structure. If, for example, one is competing in basketball and an opponent becomes upset after missing a basket, it is unlikely that one will consider giving the ball to that person. If one were playing a cooperative game, however, that action choice might be considered.

Process II involves arriving at a judgment about the moral thing to do. We suggest that the *moral atmosphere* is a significant contextual influence on this process. The moral atmosphere refers to the prevailing moral norms that are recognized in a group (see Power, Higgins, & Kohlberg, 1989). If the moral atmosphere supports prosocial moral behavior, such behavior is much more likely to occur. Stephens (1993), for example, found that when young female soccer players thought that other team members were likely to engage in unfair sport practices, they felt more tempted to do so as well. We believe that the moral atmosphere tends to make some moral issues salient, thereby influencing the moral content about which participants reason. The moral atmosphere is also likely to influence the next process—choice.

Selecting among competing values is at the heart of Process III. Related to the issues of value choice are what we call the *domain cues* present in the context (see Turiel, 1983). Environments are not uniform in terms of the competencies and motives they activate. Some contexts may tend to activate only a person's moral capacities and motives, but these are rare. More often, the environment will activate simultaneously a person's moral, social–conventional, and prudential reasoning, to name three domains of reasoning. Understanding how sport contexts provide cues that elicit different forms of processing and activate different motives is crucial for investigating Process III. When moral domain cues are salient, moral behavior is more likely.

Contexts also vary widely in how interpersonal power is distributed and exercised. Such variations clearly impact on the facilitators or impediments that may be encountered in carrying out one's decision to act in a particular manner, the process central to Process IV. Power structures play a major role in determining, for example, how one's gender, ethnicity, class, and social status influence one's ability, perceived and real, to carry out one's intended action. When the power structure is supportive of one's prosocial behavioral intentions, then one is more likely to actually engage in that behavior.

Personal Competency Influences

We adhere to the main tenets of the structural developmental approach to psychology and believe that an articulation of the cognitive and affective competencies that make moral action possible is essential to a full understanding of morality. Contexts can facilitate or impede various forms of behavior, but contexts are interpreted and their influence can be resisted or augmented. A description of a person's relevant competencies provides a window into how that person might behave when he or she live up to full potential. Sometimes these competencies can be described in structural terms. Structural competencies, however, are theoretical abstractions that can be studied and understood only through an analysis of specific contents. For example, knowing a person's moral stage is useful in understanding moral action only as that stage is manifest through particular moral beliefs, attitudes, and values (aspects of moral *content*).

Role-taking and perspective-taking abilities (see Selman, 1976, 1980) are important structural competencies that underlie Process I, interpreting the context. The associated content pertains to whose perspective is taken and what information is gleaned. The relationship between sport participation and role taking or perspective-taking is relatively unexplored. On a theoretical level, we might anticipate that sport experiences promote social perspective taking ability (see Cackle, 1983, 1984; Martens, 1976; Mead, 1934). Sport interactions, particularly in team sports, are predicated on an ability to coordinate actions and such coordinations, in turn, require an ability to comprehend the game through multiple frames of reference. For example, in order to play shortstop effectively, one must be able to anticipate what each teammate is likely to do in any number of fielding situations. That involves complex coordinations of different perspectives on the game. In addition, most sports involve a strategy component that pulls on the participants' abilities to anticipate the behavior of the opponent. Successful employment of game strategy quickly spirals up the perspective-taking ladder.

Despite the potential that sports may have for promoting social perspective-taking skills, it also appears that competition generally impedes role and perspective taking (see Johnson & Johnson, 1983). For example, Tjosvold, Johnson, and Johnson (1984) placed undergraduate students in dyads and assigned them a negotiation task. Some dyads were structured cooperatively, some competitively.

In the competitively structured dyads, participants were less accurate in understanding each other's perspectives.

Moral reasoning stage (see Haan, 1985; Kohlberg, 1984) is the primary structural competence underlying the second process. The content of moral reasoning consists of such things as the person's specific moral beliefs, attitudes, and values. The processing of moral contents through a person's moral stage yields two types of judgments that influence the production of moral action: *deontic judgments* and *responsibility judgments*. Deontic judgments reflect a person's belief about what is right in the given context, while responsibility judgments reflect whether a person believes that he or she has an obligation to act on that belief. A summary of the research on sport and moral reasoning maturity was presented earlier, and, consequently, we do not offer it here.

The self-structure is a dynamic psychological organization that underlies Process III. The self-structure refers to the person's organized perceptions and evaluations of the self. Two dimensions of the self-structure particularly important to the theme of moral motivation—the dominant theme of Process III—are *motivational orientation* (see Nicholls, 1983, 1989, 1992) and the moral self (see Blasi, 1984, 1989; Damon, 1984). Motivational orientation refers to whether one is oriented in achievement contexts to demonstrating competence relative to others (called an *ego orientation*) or relative to one's own performance (called a *task orientation*). The *moral self* refers to the saliency of moral concerns in one's core identity and the specific moral qualities that one uses to define oneself. Motivational orientation and the moral self influence the hierarchy of values that a person has and, hence, influence moral motivation. Stephens (1993) and Duda, Olson, and Templin (1991) provided some evidence that sport participants who are relatively task oriented are significantly more likely to choose moral values over nonmoral ones when the two conflict. We hypothesize that the same would be true of athletes who define their core identity in largely moral terms.

People with an ability to anticipate problems, creatively design solutions, negotiate differences, and rectify interpersonal errors are more likely to succeed in carrying out their moral intentions than others who are weak in these skills (Haan et al., 1985). The social–cognitive capacities that most clearly underlie these diverse skills are psychological autonomy and social problem-solving skills. A host of psychological skills—such as the ability to delay gratification, persevere at a challenging task, and risk peer censure when necessary to act on one's convictions—are relevant to this component of the model, although the distinction between these and corresponding ego processes is often blurred.

Ego-Processing Influences

We used Haan's (1977b) model of ego processing to articulate the third track of influences related to each process of moral action. According to this conceptualization, ego processes mediate and coordinate among intrapsychic structures and between the intrapsychic world and the environment. Psychological structures such as moral stages are theoretical abstractions, and in their actual psychological functioning they are dependent on the elicitation, use, and manipulation of various kinds of information. Ego processes are invoked for these tasks.

The distinction between personal competencies and ego processes is the distinction between what defines a person's optimal capacity for moral action and what mediates that capacity in actual performance. Stated differently, if moral action is less than optimal, it may be because of immaturity (i.e., a developmental deficiency in a relevant personal competency) or because the person situationally defaulted (i.e., a deficiency in ego processing). Ego processes help us understand why people sometimes fulfill their potential and at other times do not. In an elaborate series of moral investigations, Haan et al,. (1985, chap. 10) demonstrated convincingly that ego processes are significant mediators of moral action.

Haan's taxonomy of ego processes identified 10 generic ego functions, each reflecting a process or regulation that is required for constructive–integrative psychological activity. Thus, for example, the generic function of *discrimination* is involved when the individual must separate idea from feeling, idea from idea, or feeling from feeling. Haan organized the 10 generic functions into four categories, depending on the type of mental activity implicated. Thus, the generic functions are divided into *intraceptive*, *cognitive*, *affective-impulse regulating*, and *attention-focusing functions*.

Generic ego functions are theoretical abstractions. They are labels used for collections of concrete processes. When a psychological task is performed that requires the use of one of the generic functions, what is elicited is typically one of two modes of generic function expression—coping or defending. That is, a person will exhibit a coping or defending form of the generic function. Thus, each of the 10 generic functions can be further specified by distinguishing its two alternate modes of expression.

The modes of coping and defending are distinguished by a set of formal properties. Most importantly, coping processes are flexible, purposive, and responsive to reality. Coping processes involve accurate handling of information or affect. In contrast, defending processes are rigid, distorting, and pushed from the psychological past. Table 10.2 presents the complete taxonomy of coping and defending ego processes.

The coping and defending processes reflect a hierarchical order of utility. Coping processes are most useful in maintaining open, clear, and flexible interchange, both intrapsychically and in interaction with others and the environment. People will use coping processes when possible. When the sense of self is threatened, however, coping can be too painful or disturbing. Defending processes are used when necessary to maintain a positive, coherent sense of self. Stressful situations often result in the use of defensive ego processes. In actuality, people often use some combination of coping and defending processes in complex situations.

People have a repertoire of preferred coping and defending strategies. When faced with challenging situations, people tend to move up (or down) a hierarchy of preferred or situationally elicited processes to resolve the problem. With regard to

10. APPLIED ETHICS AND MORAL REASONING IN SPORT

TABLE 10.2
Taxonomy of Ego Processes

Generic Functions	Modes	
	Coping	Defending
Reflexive-Intraceptive Functions		
1. Delayed response	Tolerance of ambiguity	Doubt
2. Sensitivity	Empathy	Projection
3. Time reversion	Regression-ego	Regression
Cognitive Functions		
4. Discrimination	Objectivity	Isolation
5. Detachment	Intellectuality	Intellectualizing
6. Means-ends symbolization	Logical analysis	Rationalization
Affective-Impulse Regulations		
7. Diversion	Sublimation	Displacement
8. Transformation	Substitution	Reaction formation
9. Restraint	Suppression	Repression
Attention-Focusing Functions		
10. Selective awareness	Concentration	Denial

Note. Adapted from Haan (1977b, p. 35).

moral problems, people tend to function close to their optimal moral capacity if they remain coping, but moral defaults frequently accompany the slip into defensive processing.

In our model of moral action, we place the *intraceptive functions* under Process I. These processes reflect people's engagement with their own thoughts, feelings, and intuitions in response to what is happening both internally and in the environment. Two of the intraceptive coping processes are particularly relevant to moral action: empathy and the ability to tolerate ambiguity.

The *cognitive functions* are associated with Process II. Clearly, the coping processes of objectivity, intellectuality, and logical analysis are essential to the formation of moral judgments. Similarly, the defending processes of isolation, intellectualizing, and rationalization can derail moral action at this critical juncture of the moral action process.

The *affective impulse-regulating functions* are associated in our model with Process III. These ego functions are particularly useful when different motive forces need to be coordinated, as is the case with Process III. The coping processes of sublimation, substitution, and suppression are certainly vital if conflicting emotional needs are seeking expression. Similarly, the defending processes of displacement, reaction formation, and repression are likely to result in poor coordinations among activated motives.

Finally, the *attention-focusing function* of selective awareness is featured in Process IV. When people use the coping process of concentration, they are able to set aside disturbing or attractive feelings or thoughts in order to concentrate on the task at hand. Such ego regulation is needed to follow through on an action choice.

There is currently little empirical literature on sport and ego processing, although one study provided limited evidence that coping processes were more readily sustained in a sport context that was peer-centered rather than adult-dominated (Shields & Bredemeier, 1989).

SUMMARY

Athletes and others involved in physical activity contexts face many complex moral decisions. One of the main contributors to consistent, responsible moral action is a mature capacity for moral reasoning. There is no compelling evidence at this time that sustained sport involvement has any discernable effect on moral reasoning maturity, though some studies have indicated that collegiate basketball players score lower than their peers on moral reasoning tests. There is considerable evidence, however, that entry into sport often elicits a transformation in moral reasoning patterns. Reasoning about sport-specific dilemmas tends to be more egocentric than moral reasoning about parallel issues outside of sport. To what extent this is a nonserious, playful release from usual moral obligations, or a serious challenge to the moral integrity of the sports world, is not well understood. Finally, a complete model of moral action in sport must take account of numerous factors other than moral reasoning. To place moral reasoning in a broader and more encompassing framework, we have proposed a 12-Component Model of Moral Action. The model can serve as a guide to theory building as well as curricular intervention to improve the applied ethics of all those involved in or with sport.

REFERENCES

Aronson, E., Bridgeman, D. L., & Geffner, R. (1978). The effects of a cooperative classroom structure on student behavior and attitudes. In D. Bar-Tal & L. Saxe (Eds.), *Social psychology of education: Theory and research*. Washington, DC: Hemisphere.

Barnett, M. A., & Bryan, J. H. (1974). Effects of competition with outcome feedback on children's helping behavior. *Development Psychology, 10*, 838–842.

Bateson, G. (1955). A theory of play and fantasy. *Psychiatric Research Reports, 2*, 39–51.

Berkowitz, L. (1973). Sports, competition, and aggression. In I. Williams & L. Wankel (Eds.), *Fourth Canadian symposium on psychology of motor learning and sport* (pp. 59–61). Ottawa: University of Ottawa.

Berndt, T. J. (1981). The effects of friendship on prosocial intentions and behavior. *Child Development, 52*, 636–643.

Blasi, A. (1984). Moral identity: Its role in moral functioning. In W. Kurtines & J. Gewirtz (Eds.), *Morality, moral behavior, and moral development* (pp. 128–39). New York: Wiley.

Blasi, A. (1989). The integration of morality in personality. In I. E. Bilbao (ed.), *Perspectivas acerca de cambio moral: Posibles intervenciones educativas*. San Sebastian, Spain: Servicio Editorial Universidad del Pais Vasco.

Bredemeier, B. J. (1985). Moral reasoning and the perceived legitimacy of intentionally injurious sports acts. *Journal of Sport Psychology, 7,* 110–124.
Bredemeier, B. J. (1994). Children's moral reasoning and their assertive, aggressive, and submissive tendencies in sport and daily life. *Journal of Sport and Exercise Psychology, 16,* 1–14.
Bredemeier, B. J. (in press). Divergence in children's moral reasoning about issues in daily life and sport specific contexts. *International Journal of Sport Psychology.*
Bredemeier, B. J., & Shields, D. L. (1984a). Divergence in moral reasoning about sport and life. *Sociology of Sport Journal, 1,* 348–357.
Bredemeier, B. J., & Shields, D. L. (1984b). The utility of moral stage analysis in the investigation of athletic aggression. *Sociology of Sport Journal, 1,* 138–149.
Bredemeier, B. J., & Shields, D. L. (1985). Values and violence in sport. *Psychology Today, 19,* 22–32.
Bredemeier, B. J., & Shields, D. L. (1986a). Athletic aggression: An issue of contextual morality. *Sociology of Sport Journal, 3,* 15–28.
Bredemeier, B. J., & Shields, D. L. (1986b). Game reasoning and interactional morality. *Journal of Genetic Psychology, 147,* 257–275.
Bredemeier, B. J., & Shields, D. L. (1986c). Moral growth among athletes and nonathletes: A comparative analysis. *Journal of Genetic Psychology, 147,* 7–18.
Bredemeier, B. J., Weiss, M. R., Shields, D. L., & Cooper, B. (1986). The relationship of sport involvement with children's moral reasoning and aggression tendencies. *Journal of Sport Psychology, 8,* 304–318.
Bryan, J. H. (1977). Prosocial behavior. In H. L. Horn & P. A. Robinson (Eds.), *Psychological processes in early education* (pp. 233–259). New York: Academic Press.
Coakley, J. J. (1983). Play, games, and sport: Developmental implications for young people. In J. C. Harris & R. J. Park (Eds.), *Play, games and sports in cultural contexts* (pp. 431–450). Champaign, IL: Human Kinetics.
Coakley, J. J. (1984). *Mead's theory on the development of the self: Implications for organized youth sport programs.* Paper presented at the Olympic Scientific Congress, Eugene, OR.
Corsaro, W. A. (1981). Friendship in the nursery school: Social organization in a peer environment. In S. R. Asher, & J. M. Gottman (Eds.), *The development of children's friendships.* Cambridge: Cambridge University Press.
Damon, W. (1984). Self-understanding and moral development from childhood to adolescence. In W. M. Kurtines & J. Gewirtz (Eds.), *Morality, moral behavior, and moral development* (pp. 109–127). New York: Wiley.
Debellefeuille, B. (1990). *The influence of cooperative learning activities on the perspective-taking ability and prosocial behavior of kindergarten students.* Unpublished doctoral dissertation, McGill University, Montreal.
Deutsch, M. (1985). *Distributive justice: A social-psychological perspective.* New Haven: Yale University Press.
Duda, J. L., Olson, L. K., & Templin, T. J. (1991). The relationship of task and ego orientation to sportsmanship attitudes and the perceived legitimacy of injurious acts. *Research Quarterly for Exercise and Sport, 62,* 79–87.
Firth, R. (1973). *Symbols public and private.* New York: Cornell University Press.
Gelfand, D. M., & Hartman, D. P. (1978). Some detrimental effects of competitive sports on children's behavior. In R. A. Magill, M. J. Ash, & F. L. Smoll (Eds.), *Children in sport: A contemporary anthology,* (pp. 165–174). Champaign, IL: Human Kinetics.
Giffin, H. L. N. (1982). *The metacommunicative process in a collective make-believe play.* Unpublished doctoral dissertation, University of Colorado, Boulder.
Haan, N. (1977a). *A manual for interactional morality.* Unpublished manuscript, Institute of Human Development, University of California at Berkeley.
Haan, N. (1977b). *Coping and defending: Processes of self-environment organization.* New York: Academic Press.

Haan, N. (1978). Two moralities in action contexts: Relationship to thought, ego regulation, and development. *Journal of Personality and Social Psychology, 36,* 286–305.

Haan, N. (1983). An interactional morality of everyday life. In N. Haan, R. Bellah, P. Rabinow, & W. Sullivan (Eds.), *Social science as moral inquiry* (pp. 218–250). New York: Columbia University Press.

Haan, N. (1985). Processes of moral development: cognitive or social disequilibrium? *Developmental Psychology, 21,* 996–1006.

Haan, N. (1986). Systematic variability in the quality of moral action as defined by two formulations. *Journal of Personality and Social Psychology, 50,* 1271–1284.

Haan, N. (1991). Moral development and action from a social constructivist perspective. *In W. Kurtines & J. Gewirtz (Eds.), Handbook of moral behavior and development, Vol. 1: Theory* (pp. 251–273). Hillsdale, NJ: Lawrence Erlbaum Associates.

Haan, N., Aerts, E., & Cooper, B. B. (1985). *On moral grounds: The search for a practical morality.* New York: New York University.

Hall, E. R. (1986). Moral development levels of athletes in sport-specific and general social situations. In L. Vander Velden & J. H. Humphrey (Eds.), *Psychology and sociology of sport: Current selected research Vol. 1,* pp. 191–204. New York: AMS Press.

Henkel, S., & Earls, N. (1985). The moral judgment of physical education teachers. *Journal of Teaching in Physical Education, 4,* 178–189.

Huizinga, Johan. (1955). *Homo ludens: A study of the play element in culture.* Boston: Beacon Press.

Johnson, D. W., & Johnson, R. T. (1983). The socialization and achievement crisis: Are cooperative learning experiences the solution? In L. Bickman (Ed.), *Applied social psychology annual* (Vol. 4, pp.). Beverly Hills, CA: Sage.

Kleiber, D. A., & Roberts, G. C. (1981). The effects of sport experience in the development of social character: An exploratory investigation. *Journal of Sport Psychology, 3,* 114–122.

Kohlberg, L. (1984). *Essays on moral development: Vol. 2. The psychology of moral development.* San Francisco: Harper & Row.

Malloy, D. C. (1991). Stages of moral development: Implications for future leaders in sport. *International Journal of Physical Education, 28,* 21–27.

Martens, R. (1976). Kid sports: A den of iniquity or land of promise. In R. Magill, M. Ash, & F. Smoll (Eds.), *Children in sport: A contemporary anthology* (pp. 201–216). Champaign, IL: Human Kinetics.

McGuire, J. M., & Thomas, M. H. (1975). Effects of sex, competence, and competition on sharing behavior in children. *Journal of Personality and Social Psychology, 32,* 490–494.

Mead, G. H. (1934). *Mind, self, and society.* Chicago: University of Chicago Press.

Nicholls, J. G. (1983). Conceptions of ability and achievement motivation: A theory and its implications for education. In S. G. Paris, G. M. Olson, & H. W. Stevenson (Eds.), *Learning and motivation in the classroom.* (pp. 211–237). Hillsdale, NJ: Lawrence Erlbaum Associates.

Nicholls, J. G. (1989). *The competitive ethos and democratic education.* Cambridge, MA: Harvard University Press.

Nicholls, J. G. (1992). The general and the specific in the development and expression of achievement motivation. In G. C. Roberts (Ed.), *Motivation in sport and exercise* (pp. 31–56). Champaign, IL: Human Kinetics.

Power, F. C., Higgins, A., & Kohlberg, L. (1989). *Lawrence Kohlberg's approach to moral education.* New York: Columbia University Press.

Raush, H. (1965). Interaction sequences. *Journal of Personality and Social Psychology, 2,* 487–499.

Rest, J. R. (1983). Morality. In P. Mussen (Series Ed.) & J. Flavell & E. Markman (Vol. Eds.), *Manual of child psychology, Vol. 3. Cognitive development* (pp. 556–629). New York: Wiley.

Rest, J. R. (1984). The major components of morality. In W. Kurtines & J. Gewirtz (Eds.), *Morality, moral behavior, and moral development* (pp. 356–629). New York: Wiley.

Rest, J. R. (1986). *Moral development: Advances in research and theory.* New York: Praeger.

Schmitz, K. (1976). Sport and play: Suspension of the ordinary. In M. Hart (Ed.), *Sport in the sociocultural process.* Dubuque, IA: Brown.

Selman, R. L. (1976). Social-cognitive understanding: A guide to educational and clinical practice. In T. Lickona (Ed.), *Moral development and behavior* (pp. 299–316). New York: Holt, Rinehart & Winston.

Selman, R. L. (1980). *The growth of interpersonal understanding.* New York: Academic Press.

Sherif, M., & Sherif, C. (1969). *Social psychology.* New York: Harper & Row.

Shields, D. L., & Bredemeier, B. J. (1989). Moral reasoning, judgment, and action in sport. In J. Goldstein (Ed.), *Sports, games, and play: Social and psychological viewpoints* (pp. 59–81). Hillsdale, NJ: Lawrence Erlbaum Associates.

Shields, D., & Bredemeier, B. (1994). *Character development and physical activity.* Champaign, IL: Human Kinetics.

Staub, E., & Noerenberg, H. (1981). Property rights, deservingness, reciprocity, friendship: The transactional character of children's sharing behavior. *Journal of Personality and Social Psychology, 40,* 271–289.

Stephens, D. (1993). *Goal orientation and moral atmosphere in youth sport: An examination of lying, hurting, and cheating behaviors in girls' soccer.* Unpublished doctoral dissertation, University of California, Berkeley.

Sutton-Smith, B. (1971). Boundaries. In R. E. Herron & B. Sutton-Smith (Eds.), *Child's play* (pp. 103–109). New York: Wiley.

Tjosvold, D., Johnson, D., & Johnson, R. (1984). Influence strategy, perspective-taking, and relationships between high- and low-power individuals in cooperative and competitive contexts. *Journal of Psychology, 116,* 187–202.

Turiel, E. (1983). *The development of social knowledge: Morality and convention.* New York: Cambridge University Press.

Chapter 11

Tracking the Moral Development of Journalists: A Look at Them and Their Work

Tom Westbrook
University of Texas at Austin

THE FIELD

As members of an information society, we rely on the news to find our dilemmas, inequities, ills, and tragedies; and then to make us aware of them. The very manner in which the news people carry out that part of their job can help or hinder the social process of acknowledging and dealing with our problems. Therefore, as the first ones to encounter much of society's moral problems, journalists beg study.

The educational concerns for journalism are unlike other professions covered in this book, such as dentistry or nursing with their state established regulatory boards. Many journalists come to their jobs through circuitous routes, rather than as graduates of journalism schools. But the professionalization of the field in the last two decades has run more and more practitioners as journalism school graduates, and more of those schools offering ethics courses as part of the core curriculum (Johnstone, Slawski, & Bowman, 1971; Weaver & Wilhoit, 1991).

Like other fields in this volume, the news industry faces external forces that cause it to consider ethical and moral questions. The oldest force is that of the courts. The Supreme Court handles more First Amendment cases than any other type of case. The industry draws on past suits, appeals, and both majority and minority opinions of the Supreme Court in its legal codification of practices.

In *Associated Press v. Walker* (Teeter & LeDuc, 1992), the working out of what public officials or figures are, and what is legal coverage of them is complex, intricate, and a balance of many different concerns.[1] The phrase, *Public figure for public use* is a mere shadow of that discussion. It is the distillate of a decades-long legal discussion.

These answers, as written in both the Supreme Court majority and minority decisions for *Walker*, represent very advanced thinking. Some of those who would use the formulaic shorthand may have possibly worked out the aspects of the decision, or may have accepted their culture's answers. If merely accepting the culture's answers, they are relying on their syntheses, or the shorthand of others. In response to questions about the dilemmas, "Whatever legal says," was the answer heard often.

Two things, then, have arisen from the dialogue between the news industry and the courts. The first is a 200-year-long conversation balancing rights to privacy, the public's need to know, national security, treason, public figures' rights, and a plethora of other issues. The second product is a series of distillates from the involved, sometimes convoluted, legal decisions, briefs, and opinions. These distilled concepts and phrases have had to be translated back into practices which have been back through the courts in cycles to clarify imprecisions that did not serve as practical freedom, but as constrictive practices. In time, those distillates become bywords or catch phrases at the heart of newsroom routines for covering the news (Gans, 1979).

The challenge for the researcher in journalism ethics, then, is differentiating between what is principled thinking concerning tough ethical dilemmas, and what are rotely acquired distillates, or worse, little understood bywords. In a series of interviews over 6 years, the single most pronounced habit of journalists went something like this.[2] "Would you talk about ethics?" "Oh, sure! Do you think we should: allow advertorials, use of names of juveniles or rape victims, respond to obviously slanted candidate advertising, and so on?" The journalists would know the latest buzz topic in their news room and replay it.

For instance, after a race riot, the discussion in the news room included whether uses of color references for perpetrators perpetuated certain ethnic pictures and the resultant stereotypes. Reporters discussed whether the very coverage overplayed or downplayed the problem and thus perpetuated it. If the paper allowed the problem to go away without being addressed, would it be perpetuating the cycle of riots, or inciting another if it kept the "heat" on governmental authorities? Which

---

[1]Walker was the general in charge of federal troops to enforce the integration of the Little Rock, Arkansas schools. He also demonstrated as a private citizen against those supporting James Meredith, the first black to integrate the University of Mississippi. He brought a $23 million libel suit stemming from coverage of the Meredith story. The Supreme Court granted certiorari after the Texas Supreme Court upheld a trial court decision awarding Walker $500,000 saying that *Times v. Sullivan* rule was not applicable. The court ruled on Walker, *Associated Press v. Walker*, 393 S.W. 388 2d 671 (Texas Civil Appeals 1965), and Butts, *Curtis Publishing Co. v. Butts*, 388 .S. 130, 87 S. Ct 1975 (1967) at the same time. The ruling was clarified in the Gertz case, *Gertz v. Robert Welch, Inc.* 471 F 2d 801 (7th Cir. 1972) and *Gertz v. Welch, Inc.*, 680 F2d 527 (7th Cir. 1982), 8 Med. L. Reptr. 1769.

[2]These interviews are a part of each new research venture. They ranged in depth from 20 minutes to 16 hours in 1-hour blocks.

is to say, there are always a number of issues in an organization, region, or national setting that have captured the attention of the journalists in those settings. These issues become as much a part of the news room as slang, humor, uses of shorthand communications, and so on. As much as nursing, and more than dentistry, journalism is a day-to-day crush of socialization where journalists learn ethics in their news room. The news room educates and conforms most of its members.[3] What was obvious from oral interviews was that this socializing was appropriated at differing moral stages. Some clearly talked in preconventional terms; some in terms of the news organization, journalists, or society; and some in terms of principles.

THE FIELD: JOURNALISTS

I sought to know basic numbers in the field, so I first studied the available population of journalism majors at my university, the University of Texas at Austin. A journalism class, J360, was used as an intervention, with 8 weeks of class between the test and retest. Some subjects spoke of deconstructing their beliefs and paradigms because of the class use of dilemmas. Would this show up in lower Defining Issues Test (DIT) scores? Would students who were successful in reconstructing those beliefs and paradigms see their scores rise? Would students two-thirds of the way through a semester of dilemmas evidence either behavior?

The pre- and posttests were almost identical. The effect on the experimental group as a whole was low—0.02. This compared to a 0.09 effect level reported by Rest (1986), using only lectures. In the literature, that is considered to be a low effect. Controls were used for test sensitivity and none was demonstrated. Therefore, there was no evidence for the effects of moral interventions with journalism students.

Then, I moved on toward the more difficult issue of testing the general population of journalists. My first job was to use the available tool—the DIT. This met with interesting results. "I will not be a part of any quantification or mere inspection of journalists." "I suspect all of these little tests as being far too simplistic and silly." Time constraints, suspicious natures, and a host of other paranoias assailed this group concerning those who had an interest in them.[4]

Constructing the Journalist's Instrument

Writing Dilemmas. I started the process of writing a DIT-like instrument while conducting research and interviewing journalists who had written much of the copy for the Miami Race Riots. I was trying to focus on an issues-specific ethical

---

[3]The exceptions are themselves of note. There was a socialist as a reporter at the *Wall Street Journal.* The *Journal* denied he was that way, or that if he were, that it affected his stories!
[4]The tested population has a P of 48.29, SD 12.49, $N = 65$.

frame. While interviewing the journalists, I came to hear differing levels of how they treated their materials, subjects, and the dilemmas they had covered. Two quotes illustrate some of the varied responses I heard:

Any good journalist can react. It's instinct, stories. After the flames die down, then what? We believe we are smarter now than we were earlier. God knows, the truth has a lot more context, a lot more depth (than the White and Black portrayals.)[5] There is a change in racism. Back in the 60s, Whites didn't pay much attention to Blacks, and they continued within the guidelines laughing and scratching. Now there is a lot of the equal rights stuff, and they are self-righteous and all. Racism and riots are measurably more violent, intent on murdering and killing.[6]

The more I asked about the riots themselves (rather than ethics), the more I heard of empathy, assessment, abstractions, and analysis on the part of some writers, some of the time. I came to understand that an issue-specific dilemma could galvanize a journalist's thinking on that issue, allowing his or her cognitive moral thinking to manifest itself.

Developing the test instrument took 2 years. I spent 5 weeks in the summer of 1991 at the University of Minnesota studying with Jim Rest at the Center for the Study of Ethical Development. The two most important goals of the trip were to understand the nature of constructing dilemmas and writing stage-specific items.

For the 2 years I did the research into the issue-specific scenarios at the different newspapers, I would ask if any stories pointed up issues that the journalists were discussing. Often, there was a story that was recent or in progress to which they could refer. I copied a number of these down in hopes of using them in toto, or at least as bases for the dilemmas I would need to construct.

A part of the process was finding a master's student, Nadine Malo, who had attempted constructing some dilemmas. She had constructed some scenarios for use in oral interviews (American Society of Newspaper Editors Bulletin, 1984). At the same time, I was able to do a series of conversations with Don Coleman, the head of the Silha Center for Ethics in Media, and a journalism professor at the University of Minnesota who specializes in media law. I could run by him different scenarios with which I was working and gather his insights as to whether a legal issue overruled all other aspects of a scenario, quashing its ability to evoke conflicting possibilities in a practicing journalist.

Within those few weeks I had constructed some proto-dilemmas. I then spent hours walking through the dilemmas with journalists. To prepare for the interviews with journalists from the *Minneapolis Star Tribune*, I would read a few of their most recent pieces and interview them. I structured the interviews to allow them to read the dilemmas and then asked questions about the dilemmas to generate responses from them. I would then ask background and informational questions to see what the journalists thought bore on their decision-making processes. As I transcribed the interviews, I would frame responses that represented stage thinking and grade those responses. This was the beginning of developing items like the DIT

---

[5]Journalist 1, Miami.
[6]Journalist 2, Miami.

11. TRACKING THE MORAL DEVELOPMENT OF JOURNALISTS

format. I asked Jim Rest to see if he concurred with my assessments. I also compared my assessments with verbal and written responses that Nadine Malo had gathered in her interviews.

I put the interviews down for a few months and took another course in ethics. Kohlberg had drawn on an idea of universalizable principles which Aristotle, Mill and others asserted was the principle of utility, and that Kant and Sidgwick had purported was a sense of transcultural justice. Hegel was discussed on occasion, as the professor tried to prove that much of the Hegelian dialectic was grounded in the forms of Kantian, a priori arguments. Transferring these ideas to my own task of developing a test of journalists' moral thinking, I understood that the dilemmas must produce a dialectical frame within which journalists could work through their answers on at least as many levels as Kohlberg delineated stages, or at least as many as Rest tested: Stages 2 through 6. In going back through my notes of the interviews with the journalists, I found that the dilemmas that yielded the most responses, that caused the widest range of responses, had been those that tested two competing craft considerations, rather than exploring one consideration. The first dilemma to be constructed was the one involving a murder photo.

This and other dilemmas were presented to journalists at the *Star Tribune*. Their taped responses were then used in two manners. Some of their responses were used to rewrite and incorporate insights or probable considerations into the dilemma itself, and some were used as seminal wordings for responses that represented certain stage responses.

There were a series of events transpiring that summer in the news, which still hold a "news-peg," or instant series of two to five newspieces, in the news today. In Texas that summer, a federal lawsuit against the State of Texas had generated the furloughing of prisoners in order to get prison populations down to federally mandated levels. This would presumably return control of the Texas penal system to the state. The lawsuit had dragged on through the courts for 8 years at that point. There were stories of those repeat offenders who, having been furloughed, were already in trouble again.

The two dilemmas that follow originated in an American Society of Newspaper Editors Bulletin for discussion of ethical questions. The dilemmas were edited several times to the form shown here. The bold print indicates those variations of telling the dilemma that produced the most pointed or difficult reaction ratings from the journalists. The final instrument is currently called the Journalist's Instrument. It is used in conjunction with the DIT and survey materials:

JANET

Janet, a county commissioner, has been raped. The afternoon paper and evening TV news reported she was hospitalized following an assault, but does not indicate is was a sexual attack. **Your paper normally does not print the names of sexual assault victims.**

A conservative and antifeminist, she has blocked spending funds for a rape crisis center at the county hospital. This has been the center of a much-publicized controversy for the last 6 months. She now tells you she plans to rethink her position on the

crisis center. She also makes clear the deep personal trauma she is suffering because
of the assault and asks that you not say she was raped.

THE MURDER PHOTO

Derek Wilson is wanted for armed robbery. **He is Black and has a long list of prior
convictions for assault and robbery. He was recently furloughed from prison in
the governor's new plan to keep from building jails.**

After a tip following a crime-stopper segment, Derek is trapped by police at the
house of his former girlfriend. He takes the woman and her two children hostage,
forces them into his car and makes a dash for freedom.

Chased by police, **he is finally stopped at a roadblock.** Before he surrenders to
police, he shoots and kills the woman. Your photographer at the scene, is able to get
one photo **before being pushed out of range by police.**

In the photo, **Yolanda** is half slumped out of the car with her two children crying over
her, with Derek up against the car being handcuffed.

Item Construction. To these established and tested elements of the DIT, I
sought to add another element in testing. I came to call it the *craft element* and
differentiated it from true stage thinking in the ways described hereafter.

Craft elements are taught in class offerings such as J360, Media Law and Ethics
at the University of Texas. In such an ethics course, one expects to find the legal
history of decisions that mark the journalistic landscape in the United States. Many
of those, but not all of them, also cover day-to-day routines and the moral and
ethical challenges to journalists in those routines. Every major paper has a number
of these worked out through their legal counsels, city desk, and managing editor
choices in how to do story routines. But there are still a number of elements, such
as story construction, citing sources, relating to sources, and deciding what is a
conflict of interest, which are nebulous and are left up to individual reporters.

Items were written that introduced elements that are formulaic or shorthand,
within the journalistic culture for parts of the legal solutions of the dilemmas
encountered. For instance, in the case of Janet, the county commissioner who was
raped (see dilemmas presented earlier), one item states that Janet is a "public figure
for public use" as worked out in Walker v. Associated Press. Similarly, in the same
dilemma is a practice still widely used, but under consideration in a number of
newspapers. The dilemma reads "your paper normally does not print the name of
sexual assault victims." This idea is picked up in one of the items that follow.
Dilemmas and items are written to bring at least one legal/cultural answer and one
sociological/organizational answer to bear within the same dilemma.

These points of view, as written in both the majority and minority decisions for
Walker v. Associated Press, represent very advanced thinking. What might be
assumed is that the majority of those who would use the formulaic answer in the
dilemma have possibly worked out the aspects of that answer as it bears on the
dilemma, or have accepted their culture's answers to this dilemma. However, it
seems that subjects do not deal with the fact that the dilemma requires their

11. TRACKING THE MORAL DEVELOPMENT OF JOURNALISTS

TABLE 11.1
Studies Using the Journalist's Instrument

Age/Education Trends

Group	Mean	Number
9th grade	35.8	39
11th grade	36.7	27
College*	40.38	72
Seminary**	46.8	28
ANOVA $F = 13.8, p > .0001$		

Sex Differences

	Female	Male	t test	p
9th grade	37.6 ($n = 19$)	34.1 ($n = 20$)	.58	.57
11th grade	34.4 ($n = 14$)	38.8 ($n = 15$)	.56	.58

Resistance to Faking

Fake	No Fake	t test	p
41.5 ($n = 23$)	42.3 ($n = 35$)	.37	.72

Note. College students were randomly assigned to two treatment groups; one group took the Journalist's Instrument in the standard way; the other group took the instrument with instructions not to give their own best answers but to impress others as being morally mature.
*The college sample was taken from a journalism ethics class.
**This was a West Coast, conservative seminary philosophy class.

choosing between the two rote possibilities—they take the craft "rule" with no further analysis.

Validity Studies. As can be seen in Table 11.1, the Journalist's Instrument showed development with age/education. It showed scores from the low to mid-30s in high school to the low-40s in college, and the high 40s in one postgraduate sample. It showed no gender differences. It seemed to resist faking for the same reasons as the DIT. Subjects seemed to show that understanding precedes to preference, and higher understanding relegates lower stage answers as less desirable.

THE FIELD: COPY PRODUCED AND ANALYZED

The area in which journalism is very different from the other disciplines is in its product. Now, it is arguable that attitude and intent could significantly influence a lawyer's handling of a case, a doctor's surgery, or a dentist's handling of a patient. But none of these fields take it as a matter of course, that the doctor, lawyer, or dentist is to be relied on by a mass audience to help construct society's picture of reality. The product of journalists—journalism—is more prone to the journalists' ability to shape, color, and mold the picture than any of the other fields. In the European model of journalism, as many as four or five competing newspapers of differing ideological ilk will write of the same news, with their viewpoints inherent. The U.S. model's claims of fairness and balance (objectivity is used by almost no one now) is much more subtle, but all readers take it as self-evident that viewpoints are in the news, and those readers disagree with the viewpoint sometimes or often.

It is important to find how journalists' maturity might translate into their work. Three other factors in the Four Component Model (see chap. 1) that intervene between our understanding of where a journalist is in cognitive moral maturity, and what she or he may write. Still some attempt at finding out if these sorts of ideas are in the coverage of stories was important. Moreso than any other field under study, the product remains frozen in journalism: mistakes, false starts, brilliance, pathos, and mediocrity are all readable or viewable if the copy can be found.

Concurrently, a different approach to studying the ethical thinking of journalists is being pursued. This involves the use of content analysis of newspaper articles.

The approach defines key words as indicative of certain ethical themes (*sensationalism* [preconventional], *community restoring* [conventional], *principled*), then analyzes newspaper articles for frequency of occurrence. For instance, reportage changes over the days covering a race riot. Sensational coverage is high on the first day's accounts, and on Day 4. *Community restoring* [conventional] coverage starts strong and stays strong. Community restoring coverage seemingly anticipates "sensationalism" through Day 5 and remains strong after sensationalism trails. Principled coverage starts building from Day 2–Day 5, but never equals sensational or community restoring coverage.

THE FIELD: THE FUTURE

The questions from the education of journalists include whether the ethical training they now receive is sufficient, or if it prepares them for the burgeoning dilemmas in the field. Is training in legality sufficient preparation for the legal and ethical decisions journalists will have to make? Journalists, who work as the gatekeepers for the news flow, and the news industry's power to set agendas for an information society, create these critical questions. If the field continues, papers–radio–TV consortiums will become news and information brokers. The news rooms' protection from advertising and business concerns will continue to vanish, and the lines between news and entertainment will continue to blur. Is there any stratification of maturity in the field? Does whatever makes for excellent reporters also make for more principled thinkers? Do good journalists, recognized by their peers in awards of excellence, demonstrate a type of reportage that has as a hallmark principled concerns? Is the DIT and/or the Journalist's Instrument capable of finding such stratification?

Similarly, does good coverage, or at least, awarded coverage, show similar tendencies of higher principled concerns? Could current or computer content analyses find such a thing? Good possibilities for pursuing these points of interest will follow more theoretical work and better tracking methodologies.

REFERENCES

American Society of Newspaper Editors Bulletin. (1984). Oppe1, 10.

Gans, H. (1979). *Deciding what's news: A study of "CBS Evening News," "NBC Nightly News," Newsweek and Time.* New York: Random House.

Johnstone, W. C., Slawski, E. J., & Bowman, W. W. (1971). *The news people: A sociological portrait of American journalists and their work.* Chicago: Illinois Press.

Teeter, D. L., & LeDuc, D. R. (1992). Law of mass communications: Freedom and control of print and broadcast media (7th ed.). Westbury, NY: The Foundation Press, Inc.

Weaver, D. H., & Wilhoit, G. C. (1991). *The American Journalist* (2nd ed.) Bloomington: Indiana University Press.

Chapter 12

Moral Judgments and Moral Action

Stephen Thoma
University of Alabama

ESTABLISHING THE LINK BETWEEN JUDGMENT AND ACTION

One of the more common questions asked about moral judgment research revolves around the issue of how moral judgment development relates to behavior. This question is of concern because understanding moral actions has increasingly been identified as one of the chief goals for the field (e.g., Blasi, 1980; Rest, 1983). Indeed, for many, the degree to which we can understand moral action is the acid test for the whole research endeavor. A different but equally pointed interest in moral action is often expressed by consumers of moral judgment research. These practitioners note, for instance, that the implicit assumption of much of the applied work in the field is that efforts to develop moral judgments will translate into more justifiable actions. However, if it were shown that moral judgments offered little information on how and under what conditions people act in moral situations, then there would be much less motivation to continue investing in moral education and little interest in further exploring the developmental features of these judgments. In general, most researchers would agree that a failure to support the link between moral judgments and action would severely diminish the status of the field within developmental psychology and education.

Happily, this bleak picture of the field does not represent how most social scientists view the current evidence on the links between moral judgment and action, nor is it a probable future for moral psychology. However, it is also the case that much work remains in charting out how an individual's understanding and judgments about a particular situation relate to his or her actions. The purpose of this chapter, therefore, is to sketch out the current state of our knowledge about how moral judgments and actions are related, with a particular focus on Defining Issues Test (DIT) research.

HISTORY OF THE QUESTION

Traditionally, moral judgment researchers from the cognitive developmental tradition have made certain assumptions about how moral judgments relate to moral behavior. In general, these theorists have emphasized the role of moral cognitions in defining the situation. Specifically, moral cognitions are said to help the individual identify who is affected by the situation, the precedence of various claims, and finally, what one ought to do in the concrete situation. The main message from these writings is that moral cognitions exist in order for us to understand and solve problems within moral situations (e.g., Kohlberg, 1969).

In addition, cognitive developmentalists have further proposed that as the individual develops more sophisticated moral understandings, he or she is able to form a more adequate definition of the moral situation, and is thus able to more adequately construct a behavioral response. For instance, Kohlberg's theory suggests that a subject reasoning at the preconventional level would view a moral situation in terms of the potential threats and benefits to the self. Similarly, the products of this interpretation—such as moral action—would be constrained by this narrow and inadequate moral definition. Furthermore, it is assumed that with development, the behavioral choices become more optimal because they are constructed within the more broad and encompassing moral definitions offered by the higher moral levels. Thus, moral judgment and moral actions are linked insofar as the ability to more accurately define a moral situation leads to a more adequately constructed behavioral response.

This rather straightforward position on how moral judgments relate to actions is actually much more difficult to study than it seems. Particularly problematic is the choice of a moral situation within which the judgment and action link is assessed. As described previously, to adequately assess this relationship subjects must first recognize the situation as falling within the moral domain and then activate their moral judgment structures. Unfortunately, moral judgment theory does not help us define the domain of moral situations, nor do we know when subjects identify it as such. For the most part, researchers tend to gloss over this point and assume that subjects view the situation as the researchers describe it. Similarly, they assume that any behavior exhibited in the research situation is influenced in part by the moral reasoning strategies available to the subject. To emphasize this point, few of us would question behaviors that directly relate to the welfare of another as being within the moral domain. However, some researchers have defined moral behavior as a political choice, whether subjects smoke marijuana, whether one's lifestyle is considered traditional or nontraditional, among many others. This is not to suggest that political choice are outside of the moral domain. The point, however, is that situations vary in the degree to which we can assume that subjects view them as moral.

12. MORAL JUDGMENTS AND MORAL ACTION 201

The problem inherent in this tendency to expand the domain of moral behavior is that it increases the probability of misrepresenting the behavior of subjects. For instance, if we claim that Behavior X is a moral behavior, yet for many of our subjects moral judgments were never used in framing the situation and determining justifiable actions, then our study will most likely find that a measure of moral reasoning is unrelated to Behavior X. A practical implication of this problem is that current estimates of the strength of the link between judgments and behavior are most likely underestimates of the true values of this relationship because of the intermixing of studies that assess behavior within situations a majority of subjects view in moral terms with studies that do not.

CURRENT STATUS OF THE JUDGMENT AND ACTION LINK

Keeping in mind the difficulties in assessing the link between moral judgment and actions, there currently exists a large body of studies that relate a measure of moral judgment development (typically, the Moral Judgment Interview [MJI] or the DIT) to a specific action. In general, these studies can be viewed as providing an assessment of the singular contribution of moral judgments to moral action and therefore as a test of the traditional explanation of the judgment and action link.

Recently, a number of reviews published that summarize this literature (Arnold, 1989; Blasi 1980; Thoma & Rest, 1986). These reviews used a variety of methodologies to summarize studies ranging from Blasi's detailed narrative review to more statistical summary techniques (i.e., meta-analyses). Interestingly, the three reviews reached very similar conclusions. Overall, the authors agreed that various measures of moral judgment development are related to moral actions however, the magnitude of these relationships is not large. Specifically, the reviews that provide a statistical summary estimate of the strength of the association between judgments and actions put the estimate somewhere within a range of 10% to 15%. In addition, it also appears that the strength of the relationship varies across classes of behaviors. For instance, measures of altruism and delinquency were much more strongly related to moral judgment measures than were measures of social conformity and competence (e.g., Arnold, 1989). These relationship estimates may appear low but, by comparison, they are quite consistent with other estimates of judgment and action relationships in related fields (Ajzen, 1988).

IMPLICATIONS FROM THE FIRST GENERATION OF RESEARCH

Finding a reliable relationship between moral judgments and actions, the question becomes: How should research capitalize on these findings and further our understanding of this link? Unfortunately, the same reviews that supported further work on this question are limited in how much they can inform us beyond the original question. For the most part, the studies under review related a measure of moral judgment with an action, and the overall strength of the association was reported. Thus, these studies address the question of whether or not a relationship exists and little else. Unfortunately, the nature of the typical study rarely suggests the conditions under which the judgment and action links vary, nor does it help us understand the processes that actually describe how judgments inform actions. Thus, any review of this literature is similarly limited in going beyond this focus.

Without an empirical guide to suggest next steps, two possible routes seem most probable. One route would be to continue to frame our studies within the traditional model of the judgment and action link and minimize the methodological and conceptual problems that run through the current data set, in the hopes of developing a more detailed picture of the judgment and action link.

Although some researchers have followed this approach with success (e.g., Thoma, 1993), there are indications in the current database that question the utility of maintaining the traditional model. First, even the better studies suggest a more moderate relationship between judgments and action. This finding raises the possibility that moral judgments in isolation may have a more limited role in the formulation of behavior than was implied in the traditional model.

Second, there is a growing consensus in related areas that general interpretative systems such as moral judgments are insufficient predictors of specific behaviors in specific situations. In general, the concerns raised by these authors relate to the lack of a detailed explanation of the processes that link an understanding of a situation with the more subsidiary choices that are more closely linked to the situation and eventual action choice. Put another way, of growing interest to researchers is the interaction between interpretative systems and situational features in the production of individual actions. The traditional model of moral judgments and actions fails to clearly spell out these interactions.

The issues raised here suggest that the traditional model itself is inadequate and further advances in our understanding of moral action require a new theoretical model. Particularly important is a model that incorporates a number of additional factors beyond judgments that are reasonable descriptors of the process by which specific actions are constructed within a specific situation. Toward this goal, Rest's Four Component Model (described in chap. 1) was developed. Central to this model is the assumption that moral actions are the end result of conceptually distinct processes (i.e., Component I: moral sensitivity, Component II: moral judgments, Component III: moral motivation, and Component IV: moral character) operating together and in interaction. Although the model clearly retains the cognitive developmental emphasis on moral judgments, it regulates these processes to a more moderate role in the moral system (e.g., as one of four other processes). In general, however, Rest's model specifies other processes that may fill the gap between judgments and actions, and in so doing, provides a structure for a next generation of research on moral actions.

THE FOUR COMPONENT MODEL AS A GUIDE FOR RESEARCH

The Four Component Model has helped focus a second generation of research on the moral judgment and action relationship by suggesting additional processes and specific questions that may further our understanding of moral action. Although it is too early to evaluate the success of these research programs, there are some notable advances directly attributed to the model.

In general, the Four Component Model suggests two major directions for researchers interested in understanding moral actions. The first direction relates to the assessment of components and the development of empirical estimates of their contribution to moral functioning. Studies of this type include the work of Bebeau and others (see chap. 7 by Bebeau and also chaps. 3 and 10 by Duckett & Ryden, and Bredemier & Shields, respectively) on moral sensitivity (Component I). Briefly, Bebeau's program of research has shown that it is possible to assess moral sensitivity, that moral sensitivity can be influenced by direct instruction, and that this process is related to the clinical performance of dental students. Thus, moving forward in the description and assessment of the processes described by the four components is one direction for programmatic research on moral action. Because the specific features of this literature are described in other chapters in this book, they are not repeated here.

A second approach suggested by the model focuses our attention within the various components in order to identify the internal workings of each component. Examples of this research focus might include the following: Is it possible to identify social–cognitive subprocesses that may explain various patterns of moral sensitivity? Similarly, how do people arrive at a moral judgment (Component II)? Are there other systems that conflict with moral judgments as assessed by the DIT? These and many other possible intracomponent questions represent a second and complementary research focus suggested by the Four Component Model. Recently, prompted by the Four Component Model, a line of research that directly relates to the relationship between intracomponent issues leading to moral judgments (component II) and moral action was initiated. It is to this research that we now turn.

A NEW APPROACH

The Four Component Model describes moral judgments as the product of Component II. Component II, therefore, exists in order to help the individual identify a morally justifiable solution to a recognized moral problem. Traditionally, the primary description of an individual's moral judgment processes was Kohlberg's six-stage model of justice reasoning (Colby & Kohlberg, 1987). However, and in spite of the support for the Kohlbergian model, there are other systems that may inform a moral judgment. For instance, Turiel (1983) and his colleague showed that social conventions may influence social judgments that overlap with the moral domain. Similarly, Lawrence (1979) found that religious prescription can override a justice-based solution to a moral problem. Overall, these and other data suggest that individuals have at their disposal a set of interpretative systems that can inform a moral judgment. Thus, Component II processes should not be viewed as a direct reflection of Kohlberg's or DIT-defined judgment processes; other interpretive systems are contained within Component II as well.

The assumption that people arrive at a moral judgment through the use of various interpretative systems has important implications for the study of moral judgment and moral action relationships. With regard to the assessment of moral judgments, the description of Component II suggests that researchers cannot assume that the scores obtained on a measure of moral judgment development (such as the DIT or MJI) are equally meaningful across subjects. For some subjects, who prioritize other nonjustice-based interpretative systems, responses to measures such as the DIT will not be as representative of the processes leading to a moral judgment. Thus, by focusing on one type of Component II process, we may be measuring aspects of the reasoning process that are not very important to some subjects.

Similarly, if it is the case that some subjects do not prioritize justice reasoning, then we cannot assume that any products of their judgment process, such as actions and attitudes, are influenced by justice reasoning. This point underscores the difficulties in assessing the factors associated with moral action. Here, again, there is a clear indication that researchers cannot assume that moral action is, by definition, influenced by justice reasoning.

Recently, a research program was initiated that attempts to take into account the description of moral judgment provided by Component II and, therefore, better estimates the DIT and moral action relationship. The core questions of this research were predicated on the major assumption that the traditional DIT (or MJI) and action study lumped together individuals who use the interpretative system assessed by the DIT (i.e., justice reasoning) and those who utilize some other system. Thus, the main question addressed by this research was straightforward: If it is the case that individuals prioritize a variety of interpretative systems in forming a moral judgment, then can we identify those individuals who rely on justice reasoning? Further, if we can identify this subset of individuals who utilize justice reasoning, can we better predict the moral actions of these individuals in comparison to the group as a whole?

Using responses to the DIT, Thoma (1986), Thoma and Rest, (1986), and Thoma, Rest, and Davison (1991) described a method to objectively assess the degree to which subjects use justice reasoning. This method focused on subjects' responses to various sections of the DIT: the action choice (e.g., "Should Heinz steal the drug: yes or no?") and the item ratings (e.g., Isn't it only natural for a loving husband to care so much for his wife that he'd steal?). To understand this method, it may be helpful to consider the major assumptions of the procedure.

First, it is assumed that subjects may use different interpretative systems when filling out the various sections of the DIT. Specifically, the action choice is viewed as an unconstrained decision based on one of the Component II processes favored by the individual. We cannot presently claim to understand all of the interpretative systems that may inform such decisions, but we assume that one possible system employed is justice reasoning. In addition, ratings of the different DIT items are claimed to reflect the individual's judgments about justice-based consideration. Here, the position is that item ratings are solely representative of justice reasoning, whether or not justice reasoning is the preferred system for the individual providing the ratings.

A second assumption, which was later empirically supported, proposed that an implied action decision is embedded within the item ratings. For example, the item described previously seems to imply that Heinz should steal the drug. However, the item (whether a community's laws are going to be upheld) suggests the alternative action. Overall, it was shown that DIT items do support different action choices. Thus, it is possible to identify an implied action choice when the set of item ratings to a particular DIT story is summarized. It is important to note that this implied decision is determined when subjects are considering justice-based items. We conclude, therefore, that since the focus is on justice reasoning, the implied decision is plausibly the result of justice-based reasoning.

A third and final assumption of the method addresses the question of relations between action choices and the corresponding implied decisions based on item ratings. As described above, the action choice on a particular story is unconstrained by the DIT—a subject may arrive at this decision through the use of a number of interpretative systems—whereas the implied decision is based solely on justice reasoning. Following from these observations, the estimate of an individual's use of justice reasoning is very much tied to the degree of agreement between the actual and implied decision. Specifically, if the actual decision is consistent with the implied decision, then it is reasonable to assume that a single interpretative system—justice reasoning--is driving both decisions. If, on the other hand, there is a mismatch between the actual and implied decision, then it seems equally plausible that the subject used a nonjustice-based Component II system to arrive at the action choice.

In summary, the method proposed by Thoma et al. (1991) to identify those subjects who utilized justice reasoning is primarily defined by comparing an actual and implied decision based on DIT responses. When this method is applied to subject responses on the DIT, it yields a U- (or utilizer) score statistic. The U score, therefore, represents an empirical estimate of the agreement between the actual and implied action decisions which, in turn, is viewed as a measure of subjects' reliance on justice reasoning. As of 1988, U scores are routinely computed in the DIT scoring programs.

RESEARCH USING THE U SCORE

The first major study using U scores addressed whether or not the relationship between DIT scores and moral actions could be improved by considering U-score information (Thoma et al., 1991). As described earlier, this is the major area in which U scores and the underlying model were supposed to contribute. Indeed, there would be little further interest in this methodology if it were found that U scores offered little additional information regarding the links between Component II functioning and moral actions.

To adequately assess the contribution of U scores to the judgment and action relationship, Thoma et al. (1991) collected a set of five studies, each of which relate DIT scores to a variety of moral actions. Included in this set were delinquent behaviors, clinical performance of medical interns, laboratory-based assessments of cooperative behavior, political choices, and attitudes toward the law. Thus, in addition to the primary question, this study could also estimate whether U scores had a generalized effect or a more localized influence within a specific domain of actions.

To estimate the influence of U scores on the original DIT and action relationship, each data set was re-analyzed. First, the relationship between moral action and DIT scores was assessed (thereby duplicating the results of the original analyses). Second, the original results were compared to the findings of a reanalysis of the relationship, taking into account subject's U scores (see appendix at the end of this chap. for a more detailed description of an appropriate analysis strategy for moral judgment and action research using U scores). In each analysis, it was expected that the strength of the relationship between DIT scores and action would increase as U scores increased. That is, the relationship between a measure of moral judgment and action should be stronger for those individuals who prioritize justice reasoning.

Results of this study strongly supported the favored interpretation of U scores. As Fig. 12.1 suggests, the relationship between moral judgments and actions was stronger (i.e., accounted for more action variance) when U-score information was included in the analysis. The results also suggest that U scores are fairly generalizable across different types of actions. Thus, it appears that U scores do identify subjects for whom the judgment and action relationship is stronger.

Since this original study at least two additional researchers have included U-score information in their work. Morgan (1990) conducted a study that related DIT scores to dyadic communication behaviors in 64 adults (32 dyads). Morgan was interested in the relationship between moral judgment development and the adequacy of dyadic communication patterns of individuals involved in a significant relationship. In addition, subjects' perception of their communication patterns also was assessed. On both measures of dyadic communication, U score information singularly and in interaction with the traditional DIT scores, was a statistically significant correlate. Thus, using a procedure much like the one used in Thoma et al. (1991), Morgan found support for the U-score hypothesis.

Using a different approach, Hahn (1991), directly assessed the degree to which U scores were related to a justice-reasoning orientation. Using the domain distinction developed by Turiel (1983), Hahn, proposed that individuals make social judgments based on justice reasoning (i.e., the moral domain, involving concepts of welfare, justice, and rights), social–conventional reasoning (i.e., social norms,

12. MORAL JUDGMENTS AND MORAL ACTION

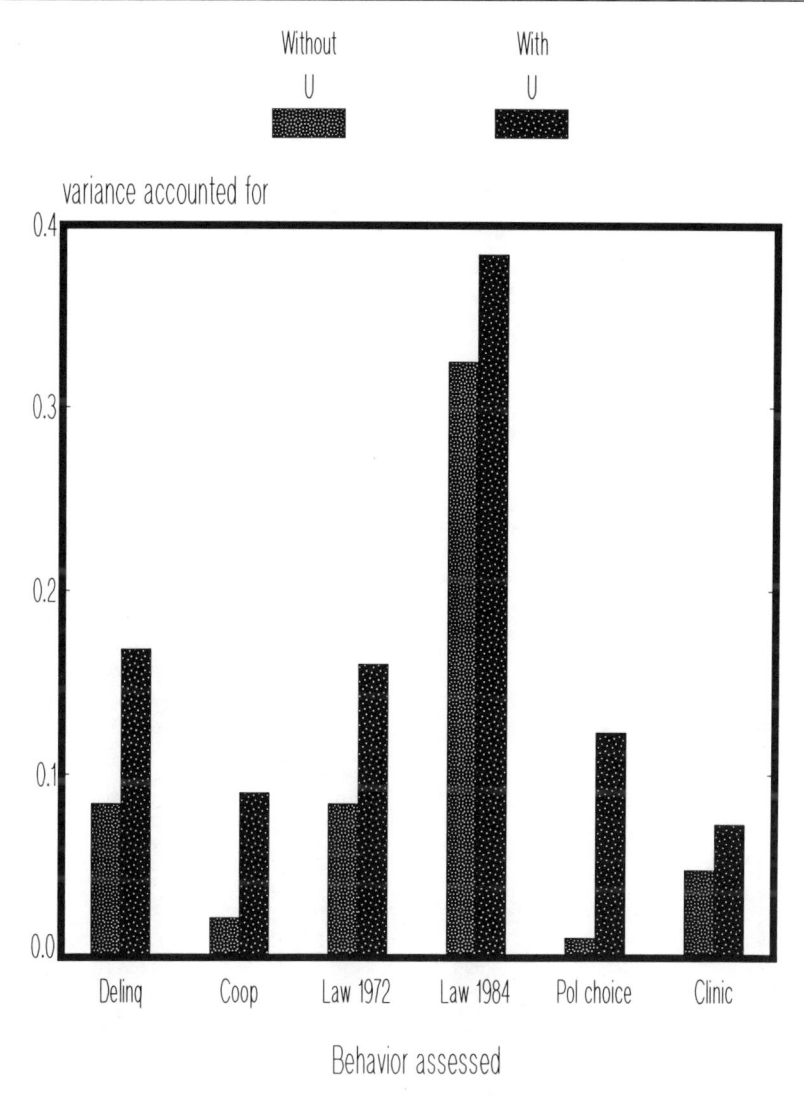

Without U

With U

FIG. 12.1. DIT scores and moral action: with and without U scores. *Delinq:* Delinquency status; *Coop:* Cooperative behavior in a laboratory setting; *Law 1972:* Law and order settings, 1972 testing; *Law 1984:* Law and order scores, 1984 testing; *Pol choice:* Political choices in the 1976 presidential election; *Clinic:* Clinical performance of medical interns.

involving culturally defined rules of conduct), or by personal choices (i.e., actions perceived as specific to the individual). Using a questionnaire, Hahn assessed domain preferences for 244 subjects of various socioeconomic levels and ages. As predicted, Hahn found higher U scores for subjects who prioritize the moral domain, regardless of moral judgment development and demographic characteristics.

Finally, Thoma (in preparation) assessed age trend and gender differences on *U* scores. Unlike the previous studies, the intent of this study was to provide descriptive data on *U* scores. Using a composite sample of over 950 subjects differing in age and education, Thoma found clear age/educational trends and the absence of gender differences (see Fig. 12.2). Further analyses, which attempted to assess the relative importance of general maturation and years of formal education, clearly indicated that education is a major correlate of *U* scores. Thus, it may be that educational environments may not only stimulate moral judgment development (e.g., Rest, 1986), but also may influence the reliance on justice reasoning in forming Component II decisions.

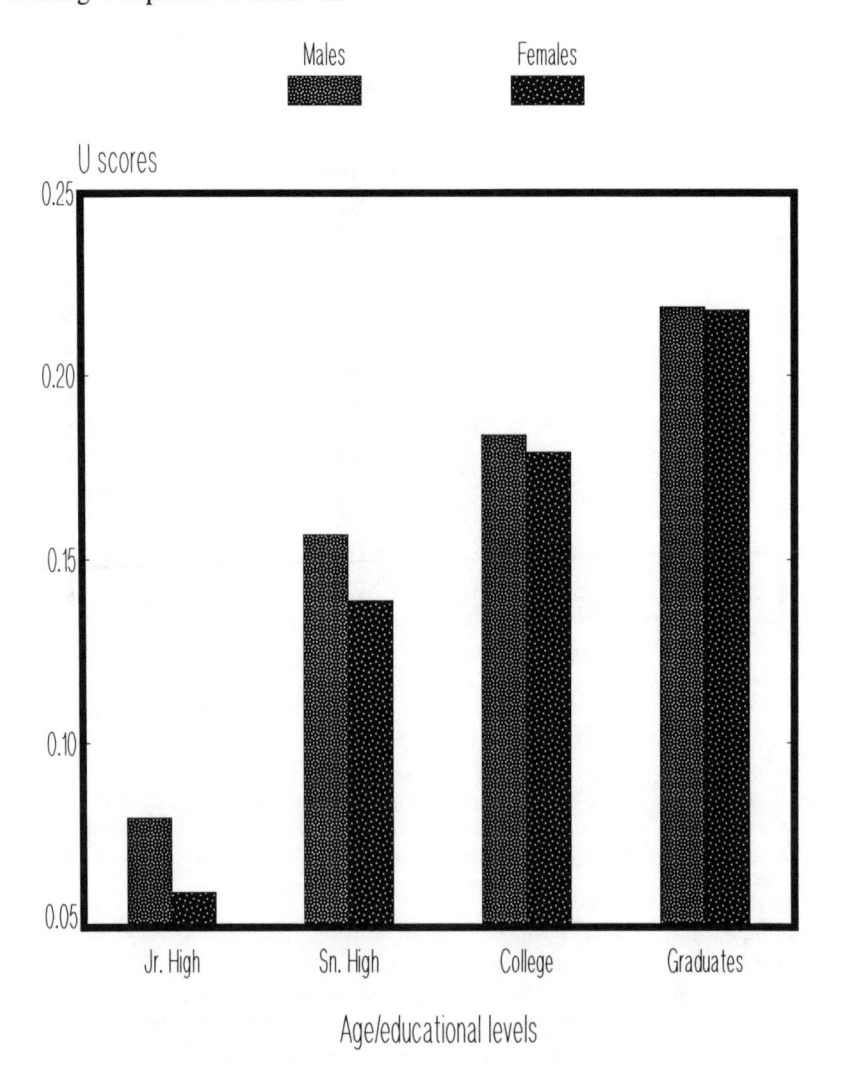

FIG. 12.2. *U* scores by age and education.

Also interesting was the fact that no statistically significant gender differences were found. One of the more persistent criticisms of a justice-based definition of morality is the gender bias claim (e.g., Gilligan, 1977). Briefly, Gilligan and others argued that women may not prioritize justice reasoning to the same degree as men. And therefore, when women are assessed on justice-based measures of moral judgment development, the resulting scores may not be as meaningful or accurate. Although most reviews of gender differences on justice-based measures failed to identify gender differences (e.g., Thoma, 1986; Walker 1984) it still may be that more subtle differences exist in the priority placed on various interpretative systems. The lack of gender difference on U scores speaks to this second possible type of gender difference and fails to provide support for a differential priority placed on justice reasoning by gender. As with measures of moral judgment development, similarities in U scores by gender are much more striking than differences.

Overall, the growing body of research on U scores supports the major assumptions of this methodology. It appears that people do differ in the degree to which justice reasoning informs moral judgments. Similarly, these results suggest that to adequately assess the relationship between moral judgments and action requires some assessment of a subjects' reliance on various interpretative systems.

CONCLUSIONS

This chapter has attempted to highlight the major trends in research on the moral judgment and action relationship. In particular, the emphasis has been on DIT research in general and more specifically, the influence of the Four Component Model on moral action research. The place of departure for this chapter was the well-established finding that moral judgments do relate to actions within a broad range of action categories. Thus, the question of interest is not whether or not a relationship exists but how do we improve our understanding of moral action? Toward this goal, it was argued that until recently, an adequate model to help guide this search was unavailable.

In many respects the Four Component Model has stepped in and helped to initiate a second generation of research on the moral judgment and action question. Unlike other expansions of traditional descriptions of moral judgment development, this model begins with a focus on moral action. Further, as a model that originated in Rest's attempt to summarize the field, it does not stray very far from the research literature. For these reasons, the Four Component Model offers very clear direction for research on moral actions. First, it suggests that justice reasoning is not everything; other processes need to be explored and linked to moral judgment in the service of understanding moral action. The model then specified the basic features of what these various component processes should provide a moral system, and in so doing helped to instate a new series of studies on the different components.

The U score research highlights a second focus of the model. Unlike previous models of the moral judgments, the Four Component Model proposes that justice reasoning is but one of many processes that can lead to a moral judgment. The acceptance of multiple processes suggests that there may be interesting and informative interactions between competing systems within the same component. Some of these intracomponent assessments may be modeled much like U scores and are described with the focus on a general preference for one system over others.

Overall, the success of recent research programs suggested by the Four Component Model highlights the key message of this chapter for future research on moral action. In brief, this message is that the existing literature strongly supports the position that advances in our understanding of moral action will be accompanied by a focus on the processes involved in the identification, construction, and implementation of an action within specific situations. Thus, only by broadening the focus of research on moral development will moral actions be more fully understood.

APPENDIX

There are a number of ways to use the U score in research studies. Perhaps the most straightforward approach is to use U scores as a variable in its own right and treat it much the same way other measures of moral judgment are used. If, however, U scores are to be used within the moral judgment and action relationship, then a specific analysis strategy is needed. As mentioned in the text, U scores help clarify the relationship between moral judgments and action by identifying subjects for which this relationship should be more pronounced. In statistical terms, this hypothesis suggests that U scores moderate the relationship between moral judgments and action. Assuming that the behavioral measure is expressed as a continuous variable, then the most common and acceptable way to assess moderator variables is through the use of a hierarchical regression analysis (see Thoma, Rest, & Davison, 1991). In this analysis, the behavioral measure is first regressed onto the DIT measure of moral judgment development (e.g., P scores), then onto U scores, and finally onto a cross-product term that is simply the product of U scores and the DIT measure. For example, if we call the cross-product term $P \xi U$ for "P by U" then $P \xi U = P$ Scores ξU Scores. This last term, when entered into the regression analysis after the individual scores have been entered, assesses the moderating effect of U scores on the judgment and action relationship. Therefore, if the interaction is shown to account for a statistically significant amount of action variance (usually assessed by an F test of the change in R for the cross-product term), then there is evidence for a moderating effect of U scores.

It should be noted that a significant moderating effect is only partial evidence for the utilizing hypotheses because the U-score model predicts a specific form for the moderating effect. The resulting regression model should indicate that the moderating effect is due to an increased moral judgment and action relationship as U scores *increase*. The statistical results mentioned above only suggest that the strength of the relationship varies by U scores but does not guarantee that the form of the relationship is as proposed. Thus, the researcher should carefully inspect the obtained regression equation to identify the direction of the effect. This is usually accomplished by attending to the signs of the regression weights (see Pedhazur, 1982, or other regression texts for a more complete description of this issue).

REFERENCES

Ajzen, I. (1988). *Attitudes, personality, and behavior.* Chicago: The Dorsey Press.
Arnold, M. (1989). *Moral cognition and conduct: A quantitative review of the literature.* Paper presented to the Society for Research in Child Development, Kansas City.
Blasi, A. (1980). Bridging moral cognition and moral action: A critical review of the literature. *Psychological Bulletin, 88,* 593–637.
Colby A., & Kohlberg, L. (1987). *The measurement of moral judgment.* Cambridge, MA: Cambridge University Press.
Gilligan, C. (1977). In a different voice: Women's conceptions of the self and morality. *Harvard Educational Review, 49,* 481–446.
Hahn, I. G. (1991). *The role of domain predominance and its relationship with utilization in moral decision-making.* Unpublished doctoral dissertation, University of Wisconsin, Madison.
Kohlberg, L. (1969). Stage and sequence. The cognitive-developmental approach to socialization. In D. Goslin (Ed.), *Handbook of socialization theory and research* (pp. 347–480). Chicago: Rand McNally.
Lawrence, J. A. (1979). The component procedure of moral judgment making (Doctoral dissertation, University of Minnesota, 1977). *Dissertation Abstracts International, 40,* 896B.
Morgan, E. J. (1990). *The relationship of moral development to dyadic communication behaviors.* Unpublished doctoral dissertation, Raleigh, North Carolina State University.
Pedhazur, E. J. (1982). *Multiple regression in behavioral research.* New York: Holt, Rinehart & Winston.
Rest, J. R. (1983) In P. Mussen (Series Ed.) & J. Flavell & E. Markman (Vol. Eds.), *Handbook of child psychology: Vol. 3. Cognitive Development* (pp. 24–40). New York: Wiley.
Rest, J. R. (1986). *Moral development: Advances in research and theory.* New York: Praeger.
Thoma, S. J. (1986). *On improving the relationship between moral judgment and external criteria: The utilizer and nonutilizer dimension.* Unpublished doctoral dissertation, The University of Minnesota, Minneapolis.
Thoma, S. J. (1993). The relationship between political preference and moral judgment development in late adolescence. *Merrill-Palmer Quarterly, 39,* 359–374.
Thoma, S. J. (in preparation). *Formal education and moral decision making.*
Thoma, S. J., & Rest, J. R. (1986). Moral judgment, behavior, decision making, and attitudes. In J. R. Rest (Ed.), *Moral development: Advances in theory and research* (pp. 133–175). New York: Praeger.
Thoma, S. J., Rest, J. R., & Davison, M. L. (1991). Describing and testing a moderator of the moral judgment and action relationship. *Journal of Personality and Social Psychology, 61,* 659–669.
Turiel, E. (1983). Domains and categories in social cognitive development. In W. Overton (Ed.), *The relationship between social and cognitive development.* Hillsdale, NJ: Lawrence Erlbaum Associates.
Walker, L. (1984). Sex differences in the development of moral reasoning: A critical review. *Child Development, 55,* 677–691.

Chapter 13

Summary: What's Possible?

James R. Rest
Darcia Narváez
University of Minnesota

The previous chapters describe many possibilities for research in applied ethics. Each chapter offers something different. If the various authors were to take each other's advice, what would a complete program of research look like? This chapter summarizes the possibilities.

Saying "complete program" does not imply that there is nothing else that can be done beyond what is suggested in this book. Rather, the chapters of this book suggest many kinds of studies that are technically possible at the current time. All of these suggestions, if applied to every profession, would comprise an ambitious program of research.

This chapter is organized around four themes: (a) describing moral reasoning with existing instruments; (b) discussing ideas for more effective educational interventions; (c) developing new measures for moral psychology; and (d) linking judgment to behavior.

DESCRIBING MORAL REASONING WITH EXISTING INSTRUMENTS

One of the first studies that researchers do is to administer one of the standard moral judgment instruments (e.g., Moral Judgment Interview (MJI), Defining Issues Test (DIT), Sociomoral Reflection test, Haan Moral Judgment test) to various groups.

The choice of instrument depends on many considerations.[1] In the previous chapters we have discussed various reasons for choosing one test or another.

But what difference does a moral judgment score make, anyway? Following the argument in chapter 1, moral judgment scores represent the basic interpretative framework that people naturally and spontaneously bring to moral problem solving (the *default schema*, the bedrock of conceptions for making sense of moral dilemmas). A DIT *P* score below 50 means that the person is predominantly not conceptualizing moral problems the way moral philosophers conceptualize the problem (i.e., by determining what is morally right from the perspective of a society that balances the interests of its participants, optimizes the stake of each participant in supporting that society, and eliminates arbitrary advantages or influence). It means that low scoring students do not appreciate the ethics professor's reading list of wonderfully insightful articles by moral philosophers. Low scoring students see just a lot of words in brilliant arguments that wend their way through thickets of complications. For low scoring students, discussions of intermediate-level concepts (e.g., *informed consent, paternalistic deception, privileged confidentiality*—see chap. 1) do not find lodging in a bedrock of basic cognitive structure, but rather seem like superfluous solutions for problems neither foreseen nor recognized. For students with low moral judgment scores, it means that the principled solutions to ethical problems must be learned one at a time (as special *overrides*), largely by rote, since their default schemas do not provide a general perspective for anticipating principled solutions. These students have trouble extending principles beyond the cases specifically taught. They are baffled when ideals conflict. In real life, it means that people with low moral judgment scores are likely to oversimplify life situations, and although they might have good technical skills and generally good intentions, they are vulnerable to finding themselves involved in ethical problems over their heads.

Three kinds of studies using existing moral judgment instruments to describe levels of moral judgment predominate in the literature: (a) studies that compare one subgroup of professionals with another; (b) studies that compare students beginning a professional program with students finishing the program; and (c) studies that use existing tests for pretest and posttest evaluation of specific courses or interventions in moral education.

Comparison of Subgroups of Professionals

Consider, first, comparison studies. In collecting moral judgment scores from, say, first year nurses or accountants or school teachers, often researchers compare the scores of these groups with other professional groups who have similar levels of

---

[1] The fact that the DIT is one of the easiest test to administer and score (being multiple-choice and computer-scored) should not be held against it. Despite its ease of use, there is no other program of research with other instruments that has produced clearer findings or more useful information about professional ethics. Although other instruments usually involve more pain, there is not inevitably more gain.

education. If the researcher finds that the target group scores lower than the comparison groups, then there is a concern that the target group is somehow deficient. This concern was raised by Ponemon and Gabhart for accounting students (chap. 6), by Chang for students going into public school teaching (chap. 4), by Self, Baldwin, and Olivarez for veterinary students (chap. 9), and by Bredemeier and Shields for athletes (chap. 10). On the other hand, in the nursing literature, Nokes (1989) mistakenly has stated that nurses have very low DIT scores (and she somehow concluded that nurses shouldn't be concerned with justice issues anyway); however, Duckett and Ryden (chap. 3; and Duckett et al. (1992) showed that nurses and nursing students are not deficient if the correct scores of the DIT are compared (Nokes confused raw scores with percentage scores—for instance, a raw score of 30 is a percentage score of 50).

Researchers have not only been interested in comparing one professional group with another, but also in comparisons within professions. For instance, Ponemon and Gabhart (chap. 6) found that senior members of accounting firms do not have higher scores than junior members, and that accountants from Canada have higher scores than those from the United States, McNeel (chap. 2) found that college seniors majoring in liberal arts have higher scores than seniors majoring in more vocational/careerist programs, Self and Baldwin (chap. 8) compared male and female medical students, and found that whenever there are differences, females are ahead of males on Kohlbergian tests of moral judgment, Duckett and Ryden (chap. 3) compared older students with younger students in nursing, and found the advantage going to the older students, Self and Baldwin described a study of applicants for medical school and reported that the DIT was related to admissions decisions—that is, applicants with higher DIT scores had a better chance of getting into medical school.[2] These, then, are some of the group comparisons that have been studied.

Effects of Professional Education Programs

The second kind of study contrasts beginning students in a multiyear professional program with graduating students from the same program. In the summary of literature in chapter 1, it was reported that years of schooling may be correlated with moral judgment development. McNeel (chap. 2) reported a meta-analysis of 22 studies of college freshmen and college seniors. The effect size for 4 years of college for moral judgment is about .80. This is an effect size that puts moral judgment among the largest of any effects of college (see Pascarella & Terenzini, 1991, for a review of hundreds of studies). McNeel estimated that first year students in college average 35.7 on the DIT, and seniors average 46.4. In previous reports, only a composite of students in college in all years was given (42.3 in chap. 1). Thus, McNeel's data give us more precision.

---

[2] Self and Baldwin speak against using moral judgment scores as admission criteria; it is the exit score that is important, not the entry score. Since professional school can significantly improve moral judgment scores and make up this deficit, they argue that it should not be used to block entry.

Previous research (chap. 1) suggested that formal education has its effect upon moral judgment by virtue of continued intellectual stimulation. McNeel added to this picture by showing how dogmatism and indoctrination in a college environment are inhibitors of moral judgment development, and that liberal arts (in the classical sense of questioning, inquiring, and openness to evidence and argument) are enhancing. McNeel suggested that college programs that are either too careerist (too narrow a focus on the technicalities of initial job preparation) or too dogmatic (in closing off questioning and inquiry) inhibit growth in moral judgment. Therefore, colleges that promote conservative religious beliefs might inhibit growth if they are dogmatic and indoctrinating. But McNeel pointed out that being religious does not inhibit growth. He showed that in the case of Bethel College, a liberal arts approach is compatible with strongly held religious convictions, and that both foster moral judgment development.[3]

McNeel also found that on his campus the programs that emphasize careerism are the programs that slow moral judgment development. The emphasis on careerism may be due to the curriculum, to student characteristics, or both. What do the other chapters report about the effects of professional education on moral judgment?

In short, some of the chapters do report gains in moral judgment scores, and some do not. Self, Baldwin, and Olivarez (chap. 9) did not typically find gains over the program for veterinary students ("The experience of veterinary medical education appears to inhibit the increase in moral reasoning"). Similarly, Self and Baldwin (chap. 8) did not usually find gains in the moral reasoning of medical students over the course of their program. Ponemon and Gabhart (chap. 6) did not consistently find gains in accounting students; however, students in an accounting program within a liberal arts curriculum do seem to gain more. On the other hand, some multiyear professional programs did report gains in their students' moral judgment. Bebeau (chap. 7) reported gains after the incorporation of ethics components into the curriculum. Similarly, Duckett and Ryden (chap. 3) reported significant gains of students in their nursing program. In summary, some professional programs that emphasize practical/technical training show gains and others do not. We come back later to consider what makes the difference.

Effects of Interventions

The third kind of study using standard instruments is the pre-post evaluation study of specific courses. Rest (1986, chap. 3) reviewed 56 such programs. Chapters in this volume by Sprinthall; McNeel; Duckett and Ryden; Self, Baldwin, and Olivarez; and Self and Baldwin also described evaluation studies. In these studies, generally the experimental or treatment groups statistically showed greater gains

---

[3] Dogmatism need not be limited to the *Right*. Dogmatism can also come from the *Left*, in the form that D'Souza (1991) called *political correctness*. It would be interesting to get data from some highly selective, high-priced liberal arts colleges in this country that have been swept with political correctness. Is it the case that they are actually inhibiting moral judgment development of their students?

than control or comparison groups. Let us now turn to characteristics of successful programs.

MORAL EDUCATION INTERVENTIONS

The major suggestions for interventions will be discussed as follows: (a) integrating direct experience with reflection; (b) using the Four Component Model for designing instruction; (c) using the Multi-Course Sequential Learning model; and (d) incorporating didactic teaching of fundamentals of logic and philosophy.

Direct Experience with Reflection

Sprinthall has been devising and developing educational interventions for over two decades (see chap. 5). He used pre–postevaluation data to tell him what educational interventions are working. His notion of *deliberate psychological education* fuses three elements: reading academic psychology, actively performing human service work, and a reflective seminar attempting to integrate the academic theory with the real-life experience. Sprinthall followed Dewey in asserting that immediate experience and active problem solving are crucial. A lecture course on theory does not tie down the concepts to something on the level of direct experience. In accord with reviews of the intervention literature (chap. 1), active practice in problem solving is important. But Dewey and Sprinthall went on to say that experience must be accompanied by creating a symbolic representation of the experience. The mere feeling that something significant happened at some time is not enough. In order to profit from the experience and have it as a resource to inform future encounters, a cognitive framework of understanding must be developed. Sprinthall, in his chapter, contended that experiential education without the opportunity for reflection (in the seminars) is not effective.

Using the Four Component Model

Bebeau (chap. 7) is most explicit about using the Four Component Model as a guide to planning instruction and for evaluation of the effectiveness of that instruction. One of the concerns of this approach is the integration of affect and cognition. She describes the viewpoint that moral development involves several component processes and that moral education must be concerned with all of the components. Also, Duckett and Ryden (chap. 3) used the distinctions among components in their instruction—and subdivide Component IV into *ego strength* and *social skill* components. Similarly, Sprinthall's emphasis on roletaking, and McNeel's point about including empathy underscored the importance in integrating various elements into educational programs.

Multi-Course Sequential Learning

Duckett and Ryden (chap. 3) described their approach to moral education in professional education in terms of Multi-Course Sequential Learning (MCSL). The basic idea here is that ethics is best not taught as a single-shot course, or as an incidental inclusion in courses (so integrated that you can't find it). Instead, the MCSL approach involves a series of units running throughout the program that address ethical issues as they naturally arise in the experience of the student. Their approach makes good curriculum sense, but requires an unusually high degree of deliberate curriculum explicitness and cooperation among faculty (in contrast to the more frequent Balkanization of the curriculum and hidden secrets of what goes on in different required courses). The approach described by Duckett and Ryden is a tribute to their faculty's cooperation and curriculum explicitness. The gains of their students attest to its effectiveness.

Direct Teaching of Fundamentals

Penn's contribution to moral education was discussed in McNeel's chapter. Penn (1990, 1992a, 1992b) argued that certain logical and philosophical concepts are critical to the formulation of a principled perspective, and that these basics can be directly, didactically taught. Penn did not argue against student activity in problem solving; rather he argued that students need not invent everything anew from scratch. For instance, in teaching chemistry, students are not merely pointed to the lab and told to mix up something. Their practical, direct experience is first informed by some basic knowledge and guidance through the experiments. In the same way, Penn argued, moral education ought not be totally free-form grappling with moral controversies, but student learning can benefit from didactically teaching some basic logical and philosophical elements first. Then students are challenged with cases of moral problem solving. The theoretical reasonableness of Penn's argument is strengthened by empirical results. Penn showed some of the highest gains in students' DIT scores of any moral intervention. McNeel's chapter described some of the teaching methods and materials developed by Penn.

Lack of Studies Demonstrating Consensus in Ethics

The four points just mentioned describe things that people are actually doing now to improve the effectiveness of educational interventions. But there is something else that needs mentioning, which is largely not being done. Recall from the preface that three assumptions about applied ethics were listed:

1. Assumption 1: Some ethical judgments are more justifiable than other judgments.
2. Assumption 2: There is some agreement among experts on moral judgments.
3. Assumption 3: Ethics courses affect students in some constructive ways.

13. SUMMARY: WHAT'S POSSIBLE?

Whereas attention has been given to Assumptions 1 and 3, too little attention has been given to Assumption 2. Ethics instructors throughout the country presumably evaluate students (in 10,000 courses annually, according to one estimate). In so doing, ethics instructors must be gathering some sample of student work or thinking, evaluating the work, and assigning grades or credits. What is lacking is demonstration that the evaluations by one instructor is comparable to the evaluation by other instructors—that there is such a thing as consensus among experts.

Bebeau (chap. 7) quotes students who state that ethical judgment is nothing more than idiosyncratic opinion, and describes the development of evaluation instruments that involve attaining consensus on criteria by experienced practitioners. For instance, setting the scoring criteria for her Dental Ethical Sensitivity Test (DEST) involves discussions and the consensus of practicing dentists, notably senior and highly respected practitioners, Fellows of the American College of Dentists. Hence, when scorers use these criteria and are checked for interjudge reliability, there is a basis for claiming that the evaluations represent more than just one person's idiosyncratic opinion. Further, use of the DEST by several schools around the country—sharing one set of consensually derived criteria—provides evidence that evaluation in ethics is not completely idiosyncratic. Moreover, it would be a good investment for ethics instructors at different institutions to exchange their evaluation tasks, criteria, and student sample work, and demonstrate that instructors can agree on the evaluation of student work. This would do much to document Assumption 2.

NEW INSTRUMENTS TO ASSESS MORALITY

The interest in new instruments for assessing morality comes from two directions. The first interest is in devising more relevant, updated, profession-specific tests of moral judgment, (than the standard tests). The second interest stems from the realization that there are more aspects to morality than moral judgment as assessed in terms of Kohlbergian stages.

Consider first the issue of devising new tests of moral judgment (Component II), as Chang (chap. 4) and Westbrook (chap. 11) described. They wanted to use dilemmas more relevant to their specific subjects with the hope of strengthening the links of judgment with behavior. Let us consider how Chang and Westbrook faced four key decisions in devising new tests: Decision 1: the choice of a data-collection technique; Decision 2: establishing a basis for claiming that some judgments are better than others; Decision 3: devising a strategy for validation; and Decision 4: devising an index.

Decision 1 concerns how data are to be collected. For instance, are data to be collected by interviews about moral dilemmas, yielding utterances that are matched with scoring criteria; by the dilemma-and-item format of the DIT, yielding ratings and rankings; by essays on current controversial topics; by responses to videotapes;

or by simulated role-playing situations? Both Chang and Westbrook followed the format of the DIT for their new instruments, but there is nothing magical about the DIT format. What is new about their instruments is that Chang used dilemmas specific to the teaching profession and Westbrook uses journalism dilemmas. Westbrook described the back-and-forth process with journalists that he used in writing and rewriting his dilemmas. Note that a critical feature of dilemma writing is that the dilemma needs to pit two conflicting ideals against each other (so that the solution is not merely finding an ideal, but involves resolving ideals that conflict).

It is often assumed that current controversial topics make the best dilemmas—the hotter and more talked-about, the better. Accordingly, old dilemmas—like the controversies about the Vietnam war—are worn-out dilemmas, distant from the subject's immediate experience, and hence are not good. To be sure, getting the subject's interest is important and interest is more likely with current, hot topics. However, the down side of using current, hot topics is that they are much talked-about, making it difficult to disentangle the subject's own structuring tendencies from verbalization coined by someone else. Remember, the assessment of moral judgment attempts to depict the natural ways that subjects make meaning of social events—their general default schemas—not a person's memory for verbalisms urged upon them by today's editorial, yesterday's TV show, or the required line of patter for the midterm in an ethics course. When topics are so current that slogans appear on bumper stickers, we are apt to get bumper sticker verbalizations for moral judgments.

Westbrook stated, "The challenge for the researcher in Journalism Ethics then, is differentiating between what is principled thinking concerning tough ethical dilemmas, and what are rotely acquired distillates, or worse, little-understood by-words." He talked about *formulaic shorthand phrases* that emerge from lengthy, complex legal decisions; about shorthand phrases becoming *distillates* of more extensive discussions; about bywords and catch phrases becoming learned by rote as *craft elements*, used to direct decisions reflexively. A major problem, then, in writing items or in interpreting interview material is that people may not mean the same thing with the same words.

There are several features designed into DIT items to minimize this problem:

1. Using short fragments as items rather than long speeches.
2. Using questions as items to raise issues instead of declarative propositions (in the hope that an issue raised as a question would be less apparent to those who don't have that issue in mind already).
3. Trying to equalize the items in length and complexity of syntax.
4. Introducing meaningless items (that have complex sentence syntax and specialized vocabulary) as an internal reliability check on the subject's test-taking set (for fuller discussion, see Rest, 1979, chap. 4).

Perhaps these devices will be useful in the new construction of instruments.

13. SUMMARY: WHAT'S POSSIBLE?   221

Decision 2 involves setting the criteria by which the researcher determines that some forms of moral judgment are better (or more developmentally advanced, more philosophically defensible) than others. The DIT uses Kohlberg's theory of six stages essentially (although there are some differences, see Rest, 1979, chap. 2). Westbrook's Journalism Instrument also drew on Kohlberg's descriptors and Kohlberg's rationale for claiming a certain developmental order. However, Chang's TTMR did not use Kohlberg Stages as criteria for describing forms of moral reasoning, nor did she use Kohlberg's stage theory to argue that some forms of moral reasoning are better than others. Rather, she used discussions with other professionals, thus arriving at "expert judgment" to classify responses as high, medium, or low in development. Chang's approach to setting criteria, in effect, focuses on a more intermediate level of conceptualization than the more general Kohlbergian analysis (as discussed in chap. 1). It is similar to the approach taken by Bebeau in setting criteria, in that it uses the consensus of expert judgment rather than Kohlbergian stages.

From a reading about what goes on in current applied ethics courses and from looking at their required reading selections, it seems that many ethics courses focus on the intermediate level of conceptualization. In these courses, the concepts used to drive professional decision making are intermediate-level concepts (e.g., notions such as *informed consent, paternalistic deception,* and *privileged confidentiality*). Therefore, we need to develop tests of moral judgment that key on these intermediate concepts. Using the approaches by Bebeau and Chang for identifying consensual expert judgment for setting criteria, it seems that we have a lot of work to do in developing profession-specific, intermediate-level tests of moral judgment. The topics and evaluation criteria of those who currently teach ethics courses can be a place to start collecting dilemmas and criteria. Ethics instructors can provide the key intermediate-level concepts for the development of standard assessment instruments.

Decision 3 involves having a strategy for building a case for the validity of a test. Building a case for validity means thinking about what studies can be done and what the findings have to show. In chapter 1, seven types of studies bearing on the validity of the DIT are listed. In effect, these can be viewed as validity criteria for the DIT. Other sets of validity criteria are, of course, possible. For instance, Chang (chap. 4) described the seven criteria she used for producing validity data for the Test of Teachers' Moral Reasoning (TTMR). The fundamental point here is that instrument development entails having a strategy to validate it and actually doing the studies.

Note that having criteria for validity enables us to know when our procedure is working. Otherwise, we devise instruments and have little basis for knowing if the instrument is really measuring what it purports to measure, or for knowing which part of the instrument is working better than another part. For instance, an instrument might contain two kinds of items: *High Items,* representing more defensible moral thinking; and *Low Items,* representing less defensible moral thinking. Then, if two groups of subjects are tested, one group being an *Expert* group, and the other, *Less Expert,* then there is a basis for determining if the instrument really generates different scores for the two groups. In addition, there is a basis for examining specific items of the instrument. The items that are not working need redesigning. Thus, by this bootstrap method, cycles of instrument creation and empirical testing can produce a useful instrument.

Decision 4 concerns the way a researcher combines information from many specific responses into an overall score or index. This procedure is *indexing*. For instance, Chang (chap. 4) in the TTMR produced four rankings from five stories for a total of 20 numbers. How she puts these 20 numbers together as a single, overall score that represents the subject's thinking is the issue of indexing.

A large part of Chang's chapter described experimenting with various ways of indexing. She doesn't just assume that the first idea that comes to mind for combining item responses is going to be the best index. Rather, she systematically uses her validity criteria to inform her which method of indexing consistently produces the most valid scores. She uses empirical research to shape instrument development.

Currently, Evens (Evens, in preparation) is conducting a dissertation that is looking into multidimensional scaling as a way of arriving at a better index for the DIT. A colleague, Mark Davison (Davison, 1977; Davison & Robbins, 1978), applied this methodology to DIT data. At that time, the database with which Davison had to work was limited, and, disappointingly, the index that came from Davison's work in the 1970s did not produce consistent improvement on the *P* score. Now, Evens is drawing upon the extensive database of over 58,000 DITs to retry this method. Her work is in progress, and it will take a little time before we know how this new index is working with the DIT. Nevertheless, other researchers may want to apply this scaling technique to their new measures (like the TTMR), especially if they use empirical data to determine the relative advancement of items.

Lastly—regarding new tests—recall that the Four Component Model indicated that other measures besides tests of moral judgment are necessary and relevant to a full assessment of moral development in the professions. Bebeau's work (chap. 7) on Component I: Moral Sensitivity, in the context of dentistry is the most sustained work on another component. Her chapter sketched out ideas for assessing other components as well. McNeel (chap. 2) also reported developing a measure of moral sensitivity for college students. Ideally, we would want to have measures of all four components customized for each profession—a big order for research in professional ethics.

LINKS TO BEHAVIOR

What good is all this assessment of all these components if it does not predict to behavior? What good are courses in moral education that bring about gains in these instruments if the gains are not related to real life?

Predicting real-life behavior has long been a concern of research. Chapters 1 and 12 refer to hundreds of studies and reviews of these studies. The short conclusion is that there is a consistent, statistically significant link of moral judgment with behavior, but the link is weak.

Chapters in this volume report significant links as well: Chang reports links of moral judgment with various aspects of school teaching; Bredemeier and Shields (chap. 10) report links with athletes' behavior; Self and Baldwin (chap. 8) report links with the behavior of medical doctors; Ponemon and Gabhart (chap. 6) report on the behavior of accountants; Sprinthall (chap. 5) reports on the behavior of high school studies; and Bebeau (chap. 7) reports on dentists who get into trouble with the ethics board.

Perhaps the most spectacular finding so far linking moral judgment to behavior is reported by Duckett and Ryden (chap. 3): First-year DIT scores of entering nursing students predicted an impressive correlation of .58 to clinical performance ratings of nurses in their later years. (This means that those students who had higher P scores in the first year were the students rated higher by their supervisors in their performance as nurses in a clinical setting.) A correlation of .58 is quite strong in social science research, and is all the more impressive considering that other variables do not predict this well.

In a different approach, Thoma's work (chap. 12) suggests that all these links might be strengthened by using the U score. The U score is derived from the DIT, requiring no additional subject time, but is computed from existing DIT data. Thoma reanalyzes five studies that previously linked the DIT's P score with behavior. He adds his U score to the P score, and substantially increases the link between the DIT (using both P and U) with behavior (see Fig. 12.1 showing increases in all five studies). In an appendix, Thoma specifies how to use the U score. There is no reason not to use Thoma's U score in all research linking the DIT with attitudes or behavior. It is quite likely that clearer, stronger results would result.

Ponemon and Gabhart (chap. 6) discuss a different approach to studying behavior:

1. Specify as the outcome variable one specific instance of professional decision making (e.g., fraud detection in reading financial documents, or underreporting of time actually spent on a project).
2. Write different pieces of information that might be used in decision making. Give different pieces of information to different treatment groups.
3. Measure different subject characteristics (e.g., extent of professional experience, DIT score).
4. Determine the interaction of information with subject characteristics in producing the outcome professional decision.

This kind of study simulates the microprocess of professional decision making. Ponemon and Gabhart describe studies finding a significant interaction of P score with information variables in producing the outcome decision. This type of study should be used much more in other professional fields.

Finally, we call attention to work that attempts to study all components of the Four Component Model simultaneously, with the hope of increasing prediction to behavior. Thoma discusses this approach. Bredemeier and Shields (chap. 10) propose organizing a program of research looking at four processes in three contexts for a matrix of 12 components.

CONCLUSION

These chapters have suggested many possibilities for a program of research in professional ethics. The authors hope that researchers will be inspired to check out some of the references provided and begin the studies that will more thoroughly investigate the ethical development of professionals.

REFERENCES

Davison, M. L. (1977). On a unidimensional, metric unfolding model for attitudinal and developmental data. *Psychometrika, 42,* 523–548.
Davison, M. L., & Robbins, S. (1978). The reliability and validity of objective indices of moral development. *Applied Psychological Measurement, 2*(3), 391–403.
D'Souza, D. (1991). *Illiberal education: The politics of race and sex on campus.* New York: The Free Press.
Duckett, L., Rowan-Boyer, M., Ryden, Crisham, P., M. B., Savik, K., & Rest, J. R. (1992). Challenging misperceptions about nurses' moral reasoning. *Nursing Research, 41*(6), 324–331.
Evens, J. (in preparation). *Indexing moral judgment using multidimensional scaling techniques.* Unpublished doctoral dissertation, University of Minnesota, Minneapolis.
Nokes, K. M. (1989). Rethinking moral reasoning theory. *Image: Journal of Nursing Scholarship, 21,* 172–175.
Pascarella, E. T., & Terenzini, P. T. (1991). *How college affects students.* San Francisco: Jossey-Bass.
Penn, W. Y., Jr. (1990). Teaching ethics—A direct approach. *Journal of Moral Education, 19*(2), 124–138.
Penn, W. Y., Jr. (1992a). *A logic primer: Skills for critical reasoning.* Unpublished manuscript, St. Edward's University, Austin, TX.
Penn, W. Y., Jr. (1992b). *Seeds of justice: A study of principled moral reasoning.* Unpublished manuscript, St. Edward's University, Austin, TX.
Rest, J. R. (1979). *Development in judging moral issues.* Minneapolis: University of Minnesota Press.
Rest, J. R. (1986). *Moral development: Advances in research and theory.* New York: Praeger.

Author Index

A

Adamson, E., 159, *160*
Aerts, E., 174, 181, 182, *186*
Ajzen, I., 201, *211*
Albee, G., 86, *97*
Allport, G., 86, *97*
American Institute of Certified Public Accountants, 112, *118*
American Society of Newspaper Editors Bulletin, 192, *197*
Arbuthnot, J., 151, *161*
Argyris, D., 157, *160,* 169, *170*
Armstrong, M., 108, 109, 110, 111, 114, 116, *118*
Arnold, D., 106, 108, 110, 112, 116, *118*
Arnold, M., 201, *211*
Aronson, E., 179, *184*
Aroskar, M. A., 53, 56, *67*
Attanucci, J., 157, *160*, 169, *170*

B

Baab, D. A., 127, 128, *145*
Bailey, D. A., 74, *82*
Bakan, D., 97, *97*
Baker, G. L., 150, *161*
Baldwin, D. C., Jr., 148, 153, 154, 155, 157, 159, *160, 161, 162,* 164, 165, 166, 167, 168, 169, *170, 171*
Bandura, A., ix, *xii*
Barber, B., xi, *xii*
Bargen, M., 40, *49,* 64, 65, *69,* 132, *146,* 150, *161, 162*
Barnard, D., 148, *160*

Barnett, M. A., 179, *184*
Barritt, E. R., 51, *67*
Bateson, G., 176, *184*
Baxter, G. D., 40, *47*
Bebeau, M. J., 12, *25,* 46, *47, 48,* 76, *82,* 122, 123, 127, 128, 129, 130, 131, 132, 134, 135, 137, *145, 146,* 157, *160*
Beckstrand, J., 59, *67*
Benner, P., 59, *67*
Benoliel, J. Q., 53, *67*
Benor, D. E., 152, *160*
Bergem, T., 75, *82*
Bergin, A., 85, *97*
Berkowitz, L., 179, *184*
Bernardi, R., 110, 112
Berndt, T. J., 179, *184*
Bernier, J., 94, 95, *99*
Bichard, S. L., 16, *26*
Bickel, J., 130, *146,* 160, *160*
Bindler, R., 53, *67*
Blasi, A., 21, *25,* 132, *146,* 160, *160,* 181, *184,* 199, 201, *211*
Blatt, M., 86, *97,* 159, *160,* 167, *170*
Blizek, W. L., 149, *160*
Bloom, R. B., 72, 73, *82,* 149, *160*
Bok, D., 28, *48*
Born, D. O., 122, 134, 135, *145*
Borzak, L., 36, *48*
Bowen, H. W., 31, *48*
Bowman, W. W., 189, *197*
Boyer, M., *48,* 56, 57, 58, 59, 62, *68*
Brabeck, M., 12, *25,* 157, *160*
Bredemeier, B. J., 174, 175, 176, 177, 178, 184, *185*

225

AUTHOR INDEX

Bridgeman, D. L., 179, *184*
Bridges, C., 33, *48*
Brown, L. M., 54, *68*, 157, *160*, 169, *170*
Bryan, J. H., 179, *184*, *185*
Buier, R. M., 33, *48*
Burwell, R., 32, 33, 38, 47, *48*
Butman, R., 32, 33, 38, 47, *48*

C

Califano, J. A., x, *xii*
Campbell, D., 88, *97*
Candee, D., 40, *49*, 64, 65, *69*, 132, *146*, 150, 151, 152, *160, 161, 162*
Caplan, A., 56, 57, 62, *68, 69*
Carper, B., 53, *67*
Cassel, C. K., 53, *68*, 130, *146*
Chang, F. Y., 77, 78, 80, *82*
Clouse, B., 31, *48*
Coakley, J. J., 180, *185*
Cognetta, P., 89, *97*
Cohen, P., 89, *98*
Cohen, S. P., 164, *171*
Colby, A., 1, 7, 11, 14, *25*, 156, *161*, 168, *170*, 203, *211*
Coleman, J., 93, *98*
Commons, M. L., 154, *161*, 168, *171*
Conroy, B. J., *82*
Cook, C. D., 40, *49*, 51, 64, 65, *67, 69*, 132, *146*, 150, 151, *160, 161, 162*
Cook, S. E., 51, *67*
Cooper, B. B., 174, 175, 181, 182, *185, 186*
Corsaro, W. A., 176, *185*
Cotton, J., 152, *162*
Crane, D., 150, *161*
Crisham, P., 56, 57, 59, 62, *68, 69*, 76, *82*

D

D'Souza, D., 216, *224*
Damon, W., 132, *146*, 181, *185*
Daniels, M. H., 150, *161*
Daugherty, S., 155, *160, 161*, 168, *170*
Davis, M. H., 40, *48*
Davison, M. L., 204, 205, 206, 210, *211*, 222, *224*
Deal, M. D., 73, *82*
Debellefeuille, B., 179, *185*
Deutsch, M., 179, *185*
deVries, B., 16, *26*, 167, *171*
Dewey, J., 88, *98*
Diessner, R., 72, *82*
Dison N., 53, *68*
Dobrin, A., 168, *170*
Dowell, R. C., 87, 89, *98*
Duckett, L., 215, *224*

Duckett, L., *48*, 56, 57, 58, 59, 62, 64, *68, 69*
Duda, J. L., 181, *185*

E

Earls, N., 176, *186*
Eitel, L., 43, *48*
Ellis, A., 94, *98*
Engholm, K., 44, *49*
Ernest, M., 123, 128, *146*
Etzioni, A., ix, *xii*
Evens, J., 222, *224*
Evers, S. L., 53, *68*
Exum, H., 88, 89, *98*
Eysenck, H., 85, *98*

F

Fauth, L., 43, *48*
Feinberg, J., 164, *170*
Felton, G. M., 58, *68*
Fennema, E., 90, *98*
Finkler, D., 149, *160*
Finn, D., 109, 110, 114, 116, *118*
Firth, R., 176, *185*
Fisher, R., 125, 136, *146*
Flavell, J., 86, *98*
Franks, R., 148, *161*
Frederickson, J., 46, *49*
Fry, S. T., 59, *68*
Furth, H., 94, *98*

G

Gaa, J., 115, *118*
Gabbin, A., 110, 114, *119*
Gabhart, D., 102, 103, 104, 108, 110, 111, 112, 113, 116, *119*
Gaff, J. G., 37, *48*
Gaff, S. S., 37, *48*
Galaz-Fontes, J. F., 154, *161*, 168, *171*
Gans, H., 190, *197*
Gaul, A. L., 58, *68*
Geer, S., 152, *162*
Geffner, R., 179, *184*
Gelfand, D. M., 179, *185*
Gerety, M. A., 74, 75, *82*
Gerler, E., 89, 91, 92, *99*
Gibbs, J. C., 1, 14, *25*, 149, 153, 155, *161*, 165, *171*
Giffin, H. L. N., 176, *185*
Gilligan, C., 2, 5, 11, 14, *25*, 59, *68*, 96, *98*, 149, 154, 156, 157, 158, *161*, 167, *171*, 209, *211*
Givner, N., 151, *161*
Glass, G., 85, *99*

AUTHOR INDEX

Glazer, A., 108, 110, 113, 114, 115, 116, 117, *119*
Goldman, S. A., 151, *161*
Goodlad, J., 29, *48*, 71, *82*, 87, *98*
Gortner, S. R., 58, *68*
Grief, E., 2, *25*
Gutheil, T. G., 154, *161*, 168, *171*

H

Haan, N., 174, 181, 182, 183, *185*, *186*
Habermas, J., 7, *25*
Hafferty, F. W., 148, *161*
Hahn, Imjoo G., 206, *211*
Hall, E. R., 175, *186*
Hall, J., 91, 92, *99*
Hall, R. H., 123, 136, *146*
Hart, L. A., 169, *171*
Hartman, D. P., 179, *185*
Harvan, R. A., 127, *146*
Hausen, M. J., 154, *161*, 168, *171*
Heath, D., 86, *98*
Hedin, D., 89, *98*
Henkel, S., 176, *186*
Hetherington, M., 92, *98*
Higgins, A., 1, *25*, 179, *186*
Hilton, J. B., 74, *82*
Hoffmann, J., 76, *82*
Holmes, A. F., 29, 46, *48*
Holt, L., 73, 75, *82*
Howe, K., 130, *146*
Huizinga, J., 176, *186*
Hunt, D. E., 86, *98*
Husted, S. D., 40, *49*, 64, 65, *69*, 149, 150, 151, 160, *161*, *162*
Hynes, K., 151, *161*

I, J

Icerman, R., 110, 114, 116, *118*
Jacobs, S. E., 35, *48*
Jecker, N. S., 157, *162*, 168, 169, *171*
Jeffrey, C., 110, 114, 116, *118*
Johnson, D. W., 180, *186*
Johnson, R. T., 180, *186*
Johnston, M., 73, 75, *82*
Johnstone, W. C., 189, *197*
Jones, S., 106, *118*
Jones, S. A., 54, *68*
Joyce, B., 96, *98*
Juarez, M., 39, *49*

K

Karcher, J., 110, 114, 116, *118*
Kauchak, D., 73, 75, *82*

Kay, W. J., 164, *171*
Kennelley, M., 110, 114, 116, *118*
Ketefian, S., 58, 59, *68*
Kimball, B., 71, *82*
Kitchen, H., 164, *171*
Kleiber, D. A., 179, *186*
Kohlberg, L., 1, 3, 7, 10, 11, 14, 15, 16, *25*, *26*, 28, *48*, 60, *68*, 73, 77, *82*, 85, 86, 94, *98*, 107, *118*, 149, 151, 156, 159, 160, *161*, 165, 167, 168, *170*, *171*, 179, 181, *186*, 200, 203, *211*
Kramer, R., 94, *98*
Krause, K., 152, *162*
Krichbaum, K., 64, *68*
Kulik, C., 89, *98*
Kulik, J., 89, *98*
Kurtines, W., 2, *25*

L

LaCrosse, J., 85, *98*
Lampe, J., 109, 110, 114, 116, *118*
Lane, L. W., 130, *146*
Lawrence, J. A., 204, *211*
Lawyer, J., 43, *48*
LeDuc, D. R., 189, *197*
Lee, L., 94, *98*
Leibowitz, A., 148, *162*
Leininger, M., 58, *68*
Lester, B., 46, *49*
Levitt, E., 85, *98*
Lickona, T., ix, *xii*
Lieberman, M., 1, 14, *25*
Light, R., 88, *98*
Loevinger J., 86, 87, *98*
Loxley, J. C., 32, *48*
Lubomudrov C., 75, *82*

M

MacCallum, J. A., 75, *83*
Malloy, D. C., 176, *186*
Marcia, J., 38, *48*
Margolis, C. Z., 150, 151, *161*
Martens, R., 180, *186*
Maruyama, G., 57, *68*
May, W. E., 133, 134, *146*
Mayberry, M. A., 58, *68*
McClelland, D.C., 86, *98*
McElhinney, T. K., 148, *161*
McGeorge, C., 17, *25*
McGuire, J. M., 176, *186*
McKibbon, M., 96, *98*
McNeel, S. P., 29, 30, 31, 32, 33, 34, 39, 41, 42, 43, 44, 46, *48*, *49*
McNergney, R., 75, *83*

Mead, G. H., 180, *186*
Mead, G. H., 87, *98*
Meetz, H. K., 123, *146*
Melese-d'Hospital, P., 169, *171*
Mentkowski, M., 32, 39, 43, *49*
Miles, S. H., 130, *146*
Miller, G. 85, *98*
Miller, H., 164, *171*
Modgil, C., 1, 16, *25*
Modgil, S., 1, 16, *25*
Morgan, E. J., 206, *211*
Mosher, R., 87, 89, *98*
Muyskens, J. L., 53, *68*

N

Nelson E., 110, 114, *119*
Nevins, K. J., 43, 44, *48*, *49*
Nicholls, J. G., 181, *186*
Nieburg, H. A., 164, *171*
Noddings, N., 59, *68*, 149, 157, *161*
Noerenberg, H., 179, *187*
Nokes, K. M., 215, *224*
Noreen, E., 117, *118*
Norman, G. R., 152, *160*
Notzer, N., 152, *160*
Novogrodsky, J., 73, 75, *83*
Nowicki, S., *99*
Nucci, L., 27, *49*

O

Oja, S., 95, *99*
Olivarez, M., 153, 155, 158, *162*, 164, 166, 168, *171*
Olson, L. K., 181, *185*
Ormond, I., 58, 59, *68*
Ozar, D. T., 122, 133, 134, 135, *145*, *146*

P

Pacheco-Sanchez, M. E., 154, *161*, 168, *171*
Parramore, B., 89, *99*
Parsons, M. A., 58, *68*
Pascarella, E., 20, *25*, 27, 28, 31, 32, 33, 34, 35, 40, *49*, 215, *224*
Peace, S., 96, *99*
Pederson, C., 57, *68*
Pedhazur, E. J., 211, *211*
Pedro, J., 90, *98*
Pellegrino, E. D., 148, *161*
Penn, W. Y., Jr., 41, 43, *49*, 218, *224*
Perry, W., 86, 94, *99*
Person, K., 73, 75, *82*
Pierce, A., 164, 167, *171*

Pillemer, D., 88, *98*
Plakans, B., 76, *83*
Ponemon, L., 102, 103, 104, 106, 108, 109, 110, 111, 112, 114, 115, 116, 117, *118*, *119*
Power, F. C., 1, *25*, 179, *186*
Priest, R., 33, *48*
Puka, B., 7, *25*
Purtillo, R. B., 53, *68*

R

Rarick, C. A., 40, *47*
Raush, H., 179, *186*
Rawls, J., 7, *25*
Regan, T., 164, *171*
Reiman, A., 89, 95, 96, *99*
Rest, J. R., 3, 7, 10, 11, 13, 15, 16, 19, 20, 21, 22, *25*, *26*, 28, 29, 34, 41, 42, 46, *48*, *49*, 53, 59, 60, 62, 63, *68*, *69*, 73, 75, 76, *83*, 88, 95, 96, *99*, 104, 108, 109, 114, 115, 116, 117, *119*, 123, 127, 131, *145*, *146*, 149, 151, 159, *161*, 166, *171*, 174, 177, *186*, 199, 201, 204, 205, 206, 208, 209, 210, *211*, 215, 216, 220, 221, *224*
Ricks, D., 85, *98*
Robbins, S., 222, *224*
Roberts, G. C., 179, *186*
Rogers, C., 89, 94, *99*
Rollin, B. E., 164, *171*
Root, S. K., 165, *171*
Rosen, B., 56, *69*
Rowan, M., 64, *68*
Rowan-Boyer, M., 215, *224*
Rowley, B. D., *161*
Rustad, K., 89, *99*
Ryden, M., *48*, 56, 57, 58, 59, 62, 64, *68*, *69*, 215, *224*

S

Safford, S. K., 168, *171*
Sandin, R. T., 27, *49*
Satterstrom, L., 75, *83*, 89, *99*
Savik, K., 59, 64, *68*, 215, *224*
Schaffer, M., 39, *49*
Schlaefli, A., 131, *146*, 159, *161*
Schmitz, K., *48*, 56, 57, 58, 62, *68*, *69*, 176, *187*
Schmutte, G., 88, *99*
Schrader, D. E., 154, *162*, 165, *171*
Schutz, W. C., 150, *161*
Scott, J., 89, 90, *99*
Scott, W. G., 29, 40, *49*
Self, D. J., 149, 152, 153, 154, 155, 157, 158, 159, *160*, *162*, 164, 165, 166, 167, 168, 169, *170*, *171*

AUTHOR INDEX

Selman, R., 87, 99, 180, *187*
Shadduck, J. A., 164, 165, 166, 167, 169, *171*
Shaub, M., 108, 109, 111, 114, 115, 116, *119*
Shaver, D. G., 29, 32, 33, *49*
Sheehan, D. V., 148, *162*
Sheehan, K. H., 148, *162*
Sheehan, T. J., 40, *49*, 64, 65, *69*, 132, *146*, 149, 150, 151, 152, 159, *160, 162*
Shelton, G. C., 168, *171*
Sherif, C., 179, *187*
Sherif, M., 179, *187*
Shields, D. L., 174, 175, 176, 177, 178, 184, *185*
Sierra-Morales, I., 154, *161*, 168, *171*
Sims, R. R., 29, 40, *49*
Sims, S. J., 29, 40, *49*
Singer, P., 169, *171*
Sirois, L., 88, *99*
Sirotnik, K. A., 29, *48*, 71, *83*
Skeel, J. D., 149, 157, 158, *162*, 168, *171*
Slawski, E. J., 189, *197*
Sloan, D., *49*
Smith, M., 85, *99*
Snarey, J., 94, *98*
Sockett, H., 71, *83*
Soder, R., 29, *48*
Soltis, J. F., 71, 72, *83*
Sprague, J., 76, *82*
Sprinthall, N. A., 18, *26*, 87, 88, 89, 90, 91, 92, 94, 95, 97, *98, 99*
St. Pierre, K., 110, 114, *119*
Stanley, J. C., 88, *97*
Staub, E., 179, *187*
Steinfels, M. O., 53, *69*
Stephens, D., 179, 181, *187*
Straight, M. J., 32, 39, 43, *49*
Strickland, B., *99*
Strike, K. A., 71, 72, *83*
Sullivan, P., 89, *98*
Sutton-Smith, B., 176, *187*
Swanson, K. M., *69*

T

Talbert, B., 46, *49*
Tannenbaum, J., 164, *171*
Tax, S., 35, *49*
Teeter, D. L., 189, *197*

Templin, T. J., 181, *185*
Terenzini, P., 20, *25*, 28, 31, 32, 33, 34, 35, 40, *49*, 215, *224*
Thal, S., 152, *162*
Thies-Sprinthall, L., 18, *26*, 94, 95, *99*
Thoma, S. J., 14, *26*, 71, 75, *83*, 130, 131, 132, *145, 146*, 159, *161*, 201, 202, 204, 205, 206, 208, 210, *211*
Thomas, B. R., 71, *83*
Thomas, M. H., 179, *186*
Tjosvold, D., 180, *187*
Trevethan, S., 167, *171*
Tucker, A., 89, *99*
Turiel, E., 16, *26*, 179, *187*, 204, 206, *211*

U, V

Ursone, D., 92, *99*
Ury, W., 125, 136, *146*
Van Wicklin, J., 32, 33, 38, 47, *48*
Veatch, R. M., 133, 134, *146*
Veterinary code of ethics, 163, *171*
Vygotsky, L., 93, *99*

W

Waithe, M. E., *48*, 56, 57, 58, 62, *68*, 132, *146*
Walker, L., 11, 14, 16, *26*, 167, *171*, 209, *211*
Walker, R. M., 130, *146*
Watson, J., 59, *69*
Weaver, D. H., 189, *197*
Weiss, M. R., 175, *185*
Wheaton, W. F., 75, *83*
White, K., 148, *162*
Whiteley, J. M., 32, *48*
Widaman, K. F., 149, 153, 155, *161*, 165, *171*
Wilhoit, G. C., 189, *197*
Williams, W. H., 164, *171*
Willms, J., 152, *162*
Wolinsky, F. D., 153, 154, 155, *162*, 165, 167, 168, *171*
Wolleat, P., 90, *98*
Wrubel, J., 59, *67*

Y

Yamoor, C. M., 46, *48*, 123, *145*

Subject Index

A

Accounting and auditing, 101–119
   illustrative ethics case, 104–106
Action research, 35–39
Action, *see* Behavior
Age/Education trends in moral judgment, 10, 13–15, *see also* Longitudinal/cross-sectional studies
   as validity criterion, 10
Assumptions of ethics courses, x, 218
Attribution of success/failure, 90–91

B

Behavior
   accountants and auditors, 112–118
   athlete's aggressive behavior, 174–178
   dentists' clinical performance, 132
   destructive, ix
   doctors' clinical performance and other behaviors, 150–159
   general discussion of the link between judgment and action, 10, 21–11, 199–203, 222–224
   nurses' clinical performance, 64–65
   as predicted by the Four Component Model, *see* Four Component Model
   school teachers, 75–76
   Twelve-component Model for moral behavior in sports, 177–184
   U-score as improving prediction, 223
Business, 40–41, *see also* Accounting and auditing
Business majors and DIT, 34

C

Care orientation as discussed by Gilligan and Noddings, 2, 11–12, 59–62, 96–97, 157–158, 167–168, 169–170, 209
Character, moral, (as Component IV) 24, 61, 136–137
Cognitive-developmental approach versus socialization view, 2–4, 28
College major and moral judgment, 34
College teachers, *see also* SPECTRUM
   DIT scores, 42
   intervention in faculty development, 43–45
Conservatism and moral judgment, 29
Conservative Christian colleges, 29–30
Contextual influences, 178–180
Correlations and distinctiveness of moral judgment, 21
Correlations of moral judgment with other psychological measures,
   DIT and Identity status of college students, 38–39
   with various measures relevant to accounting and auditing, 108–111
   with various measures relevant to medical doctors, 150–159
   with various measures relevant to school teachers, 73–75
   with various measures relevant to sports, 176–177
   with various measures relevant to veterinarians, 165, 168–169

SUBJECT INDEX

Counseling, 85–99
   crisis in the profession, 85–88
Cross cultural studies, 10, 18–20, *see also* Longitudinal/cross sectional studies

D

Default schema, 8
Defining Issues Test (DIT),
   in different professions, *see* Professions
   summary of validity, 10–22
   test described, 10–13
   what scores mean, 214
Dentistry, 121–146
Deontological versus teleological, 7
Divorce, counseling the children, 91–94

E

Education majors and DIT, 34
Educational interventions, 20–21
   assessing all Four Components, 123–137
   as validity criterion, 10
   characteristics of successful programs
      direct teaching of fundamentals, 218
      experience and reflection, 85–99, 217
      multi-course sequential learning, 55–58, 218
      using the Four Component Model, 62–64, 123–135, 217
   description of dentistry moral education program, 121–126
   description of moral education in veterinary schools, 164–165
   description of nursing moral education program, 55–58
   gains in DIT scores
      accountants and auditors, 113–115
      adults, 94–97
      college students, 41–42
      dentists, 127, 130–132
      doctors, 150–159
      high school students, 88–94
      nurses, 62–64
      veterinarians, 166–167
   meta-analysis of gains as promoted by role-taking, 88–90
   need for studies demonstrating consensus among experts, x, 218–219
   summary, 216
Effect size
   of DIT gains in college, 31–33
   of developmental measures in role-taking studies, 88–90

Ego-processing influences, 181–184
Empathy, 40
Ethical sensitivity, *see* Sensitivity
Experiential learning
   off-campus, 36–37

F, G

Four Component Model, 22–25
   in designing moral education, 60–62, 96, 123–138
   elaborated into Twelve Component model for sports, 177–184
   a fifth component, 61–62
   in predicting moral behavior, 203
GDEST, Geriatric Dental Ethical Sensitivity Test, 123–128

H

Haan's Interactional measure, 174, 175
Hard-stage model, 3
Hierarchy, 10, 16–18
Higher-is-better claim, see Hierarchy
Hunt's Conceptual Systems, 88–90, 95–96

I, J

Inhibiting factors of growth in moral reasoning, *see* Longitudinal/cross sectional studies, inhibiting factors
Intermediate level of analysis verses deeper "stage" analysis, 9, 221
   Teachers' Test of Moral Reasoning, 76–81
Interventions, *see* Educational interventions
Journalism, 189–198
Journalist's Instrument, 191–195
   dilemma construction, 191–194
   item construction, 194–195
   validity, 195

K, L

Knowing-the-right verses doing-the-right, x
Loevinger's Index of Ego Development, 87–90, 93
Longitudinal/cross sectional studies of moral judgment:
   accountants and auditors, 108–111, 116–118
   college students, 30–33, 215–216
   doctors, 149–159
   inhibiting factors in growth, 216, 108–111, 117–118, 154, 166
   nurses, 62–64
   school teachers, 72–73
   veterinarians, 165–167

SUBJECT INDEX

M

Medical doctors, 147–162
Meta-analysis of college effects on DIT, 31–33
Models of ethics education in the health professions, 54–58
Moral action, *see* Behavior
Moral behavior, *see* Behavior
Moral development as aim of higher education, 27
Moral Judgment Interview (Kohlberg's MJI), 11
Moral reasoning, *see* Defining Issues Test, Haan's Interactional measure, Journalist's Instrument, Moral Judgment Interview, Moral Reasoning-Orientation Interview, Socio-Moral Reflection Measure, Teachers' Test of Moral Reasoning
Moral reasoning orientation interview (MROI), 157
Motivation, moral, 24, 61, 132–135
Multi-Course Sequential Learning (MCSL), 55–58

N, P

New instruments
    DEST, see Sensitivity, moral
    GDEST, 123–128, 138–139
    Journalist's Instrument, 191–195
    key decisions in constructing new instruments, 219–222
    moral reasoning essays, 130–132, 140–144
    moral sensitivity for college students, 45–47
    MROI, 157–158
    Professional Role Orientation Inventory (PROI), 134–135, 144–145
    TTMR, 76–82
Nurses, 39–40, 51–69, *see also* Educational interventions, nurses
    clinical performance, 64–65
    moral judgment, 58–59, 62–64
Nursing, 51–70
Peer helping, *see* Role-taking
Penn's didactic approach to moral education, 41, 218
Personal competency influences, 180–181
Popularity of psychological theories, 1
Professions
    criteria of, xi, 133–134
    dangers of professionalism, 97
    DIT scores of different professional groups, 14, 214–215
    accountants and auditors, 108–112, 116
    athletes, 175–176
    business majors, 34
    college professors, 42
    dentists, 127, 130–132
    doctors, 149–159
    nurses, 39–40, 51–69
    teachers in school, 72–73
    veterinarians, 165–168
Professors
    DIT scores, 42
    student contact with and DIT gains, 37–38

R, S

Role-taking, 85–99
School teaching, 71–84
    as moral enterprise, 71
    moral judgment, 72–73
    TTMR (Test of Teachers' Moral Reasoning), 77–81
Sensitivity, moral, 23, 45–47, 60
    DEST, 123–128
    GDEST, 123–128, 138–139
Socialization view of morality, 2
Socio-moral Reflection Measure, 153, 166
SPECTRUM, 42–45
Stages of moral judgment,
    descriptions of Kohlbergian 6 stages, 4–9
Supervision of teachers, 94–96
Survey of nursing dilemmas, 53

T, U

TTMR, see School Teaching
Utilizer (U) score, 203–211, 223
    as increasing relation between DIT and behavior, 205–207
    details for using the U score, 210–211

V

Validity criteria for the DIT, 10
Veterinary medicine, 163–172
Vocationally oriented higher education, 29